BRAM STOKER

Bram Stoker

Carol A. Senf

UNIVERSITY OF WALES PRESS
CARDIFF
2010

www.uwp.co.uk

British Library CIP Data
A catalogue record for this book is available from the British Library.

ISBN 978-0-7083-2385-4 (hardback)
ISBN 978-0-7083-2306-9 (paperback)
e-ISBN 978-0-7083-2307-6

Printed by CPI Antony Rowe, Chippenham, Wiltshire

To Marlie Ann Senf (31 October 1916), my mother,
and
Andrew Joseph Senf (7 December 2008), my nephew,
the oldest and youngest members of my family

ACKNOWLEDGEMENTS

Although it has become something of a cliché to say that it 'takes a village to raise a child', the same thing is true of producing a book. Without the help and support of numerous people around the world, this book on Stoker would never have been born, let alone come to maturity.

One of the most important people is Professor Andrew Smith at the University of Glamorgan, and one of the editors of the series, Gothic Literary Studies, as well as a scholar whose work on the Gothic and on Stoker I have admired for a number of years. When Smith invited me to contribute a book on Bram Stoker and the Gothic to the series, Gothic Authors: Critical Revisions, I literally leapt at the opportunity. It was, in the words of Don Corleone, 'an offer I couldn't refuse'. After studying Stoker off and on for almost forty years, I was delighted to have an opportunity to pull together many of my thoughts on Stoker, in particular my ideas regarding his exploration of multiple genres.

While Smith provided the initial idea, the book would never have come together without the help of numerous colleagues and students at the Georgia Institute of Technology, with whom I have shared the occasional Stoker moment. Among the most important of those colleagues are Ken Knoespel, chair of my home unit, the School of Literature, Communication and Culture, and Jay Telotte, director of Undergraduate Studies, who allowed me a semester away from teaching to put the finishing touches on this book. Nor could I have pulled this book together without the help of the Georgia Tech Library who cheerfully located books that I needed.

Another supportive group is the members of the Canadian chapter of the Transylvanian Society of Dracula (TSD) who continue to remind me that *Dracula* and Stoker matter. In 2007 when I attended the TSD Symposium and Dracula Tour through Romania, I had the opportunity to meet people from all over the world who care about

Acknowledgements

Dracula and Stoker's other works. Among the most significant were Leslie Klinger, who was then preparing his annotated edition of *Dracula*, and the always inspiring Elizabeth Miller, author of a number of scholarly works on Dracula. Even though Stoker never went to Transylvania, the symposium and tour allowed me to meet people from all walks of life who care about *Dracula*.

Last but not least I must thank my family who have all learned to tolerate if not appreciate my interest in Stoker. My husband, Jay Farlow, even accompanied me on my 2007 trek to Transylvania. And my children, Jeremy and Andy, now all grown up, have learned not to roll their eyes and grimace whenever Stoker's name comes up.

Carol A. Senf
Atlanta

CONTENTS

Introduction: Tracing the Gothic through Stoker's Short Stories

ಸಂಖ

When Bram Stoker died in 1912, his obituary in *The Times* described him as 'the master of a particularly lurid and creepy kind of fiction' and, although he wrote eighteen books plus numerous articles and short stories, he is remembered today primarily for *Dracula*.[1]

This study explores Stoker as a Gothic writer, and this chapter introduces themes and ideas he develops in shorter works. While Stoker wrote most of his novels after 1902 when the Lyceum's collapse allowed him to write full time, Stoker began by writing short fiction and included some of these stories in three collections: *Under the Sunset* (1882), *Snowbound* (1908) and *Dracula's Guest* (1914).[2] Others remain as independent works. This chapter explores the short works in chronological order to demonstrate Stoker's development and to explore Gothic themes and ideas.

The Dublin years

After graduating from Trinity College in 1868, Stoker entered the Anglo-Irish civil service at Dublin Castle. References in *Personal Reminiscences of Henry Irving* reveal ambivalence about the work, financial worries and enthusiasm for writing: journalism, 'a dry-as-dust book on *The Duties of Clerks of Petty Sessions*' and short fiction.[3]

Four works which Stoker wrote while still in Dublin deserve attention for their Gothic elements: 'The Crystal Cup' (*London Society*,
22 September 1875), 'The Primrose Path. A Serial in Ten Chapters' (*The
Shamrock*, 6 February–6 March 1875), 'Buried Treasures. A Serial in
Four Chapters' (*The Shamrock*, 13 and 20 March 1875) and 'The Chain
of Destiny. A Serial in Ten Chapters' (*The Shamrock*, 1–22 May 1875).

'The Crystal Cup'

Stoker's first published story often appears in collections character-
ized as weird, mysterious or horror.[4] A story about the creative
process, it includes a medieval setting and a tyrannical ruler who
imprisons people at will. Although Death lurks in the background,
'The Crystal Cup' focuses on art and its power over human beings.[5]

Divided into three sections, it begins with the first-person account
of an imprisoned artist. The second section describes the Feast of
Beauty, established earlier by a mysterious 'royal master' (p. 150) who
controls the contest. An outsider who scales the walls to observe
the feast narrates section three. When the artist's beloved sings, one
of the king's retainers observes: 'Ah! I fear me some evil: the nearer
the music approaches to perfection the more rapt he becomes. I
dread lest a perfect note shall prove his death-call' (p. 157), and the
story concludes with death for monarch and singer. The deaths are
not terrifying, but the mystery surrounding them combines with its
medieval setting and tyrannical ruler to make the story Gothic.

'The Primrose Path'

Stoker's second published story, 'The Primrose Path', is decidedly more
Gothic.[6] Maunder describes it as 'a temperance novel' (p. 29) and an
example of 'Urban Gothic' or 'the intrusion of the monstrous ... closer
to home' (p. 30). Like Stoker's later fiction, it introduces Gothic elements into a realistic story and skillfully blends them, as Maunder observes:

> In this sense, the novel that points us towards the monstrous and the
> supernatural can also be described as 'realist' in ... that it gives detailed

attention both to individual characters and their environment; that we are presented with largely credible circumstances and events; and that Stoker deals with contemporary social problems. (p. 37)

Dalby's introduction also examines realistic elements, describing it as a 'moral tract on the degradation and evils of alcoholism'.[7] The protagonist, Jerry O'Sullivan, 'was a prosperous man in his line of life' (p. 17), and the three Dublin chapters are pleasant though they foreshadow the dark conclusion. Chapter I (subtitled 'A Happy Home') concludes: 'Jerry O'Sullivan had a sweet wife and a happy home. Prosperity seemed to be his lot in life' (p. 23). Offered an attractive job at a London theatre, he takes his wife Katey and children there against the advice of friends and the wishes of his wife and his mother. He immediately falls into bad company, becomes a drunkard and loses his job and his family's trust. Finally, in a drunken rage, he murders Katey before their horrified children and, immediately remorseful, cuts his own throat.

Although 'The Primrose Path' is a plausible story about alcoholism and domestic violence, it is hard not to notice the Gothic elements. Indeed, while the O'Sullivans have a support network in Ireland, they confront Gothic villains in London. Arriving at the theatre, Jerry discovers the company working on *Faust*.[8] Almost immediately Mons, the actor playing Mephistopheles, invites him to a tavern where he meets the work's most Gothic figure, Grinnell, the barkeeper whose repulsive face is 'so drawn and twisted, with nose and lips so eaten away with some strange canker, that it resembled more the ghastly front of a skull than the face of a living man' (p. 52). Although his face suggests evil, Grinnell does not force Jerry to drink but merely supplies alcohol and the place to imbibe it. It is almost as though Stoker splits the Gothic villain into two components, with Grinnell the devious planner and Jerry the physical executioner. As Jerry becomes little more than raging thirst and pummelling fists, Katey attempts to hold the family together. Hoping he will return to work, she avoids pawning his tools, choosing to pawn their furniture and, as a last resort, her wedding ring.

Five illustrations (Dalby's introduction attributes them to the Revd William Fitzgerald who illustrated *Under the Sunset*) reinforce the Gothic elements underlying this squalid though largely realistic tale. 'Death and Devil' pictures a skull-faced rider with a devilish figure behind him, and both death's head and devil appear in the second illustration, ironically titled 'Welcome to London' where Grinnell is the death's head behind the bar and Mons, the devil.[9] 'The Pleasures of Gambling' pictures a bar-room fight, but the hideous Grinnell at the bar is its only Gothic element. 'Down the Hill' pictures a group of wastrels, with Mons pouring alcohol into Jerry's glass and Grinnell supplying more bottles. The final illustration, 'The Murder of Katey', shows Jerry standing over his wife's body while their children huddle in the background.

Reminding readers that Jerry laughs 'the hard, cold laugh of a demon' (p. 68) before murdering Katey, Murray points to demonic elements in Jerry's character. Nonetheless, it is hard to see more than a glimmer of Stoker's great Gothic villains in these wooden images of evil. Most interesting is that Stoker already employs a strategy he will use successfully later, the synthesis of ordinary evil with mysterious Evil.

Similarly, although Katey resembles the persecuted woman of earlier Gothic fiction, she is a plausible working-class woman struggling to hold her family together:[10]

> She was up before daylight and into the market to buy vegetables which she then sold from house to house; she went charring; she tried needlework. Everything by which an honest penny could be turned she tried, and found no degradation in any employment no matter how lowly. (p. 77)

Although not dramatic, these qualities reveal her as stronger and more assertive than Maunder suggests:

> Katey is exactly the passive, childlike, open-hearted, innocent, self-sacrificing woman of the mid-Victorian domestic ideal. Yet it is the fact that she adheres so completely to this cultural ideal that makes her unfit for survival in the competitive, urban world.[11]

A passive or childlike character would not stand up to Jerry or Grinnell. That she cannot persuade them of the importance of her family only highlights the late nineteenth-century Gothic angst Bette B. Roberts identifies as 'the shifting anxieties of readers coping with the changes, uncertainties, and dangers of both Victorian and modern worlds'.[12] Stoker's genius is that he locates Gothic monsters in the world's most civilized city, not an exotic, faraway place.

'Buried Treasures'

The definition of Gothic in *The Harper Handbook to Literature* concludes by emphasizing mystery – 'Indeed, all mystery stories derive from the Gothic, and those that evoke terror . . . are frequently called Gothic' – but little else in 'Buried Treasures' would cause it to be labelled Gothic.[13] More love story and Christmas tale, it begins with a father telling Robert Hamilton that he cannot marry his daughter Ellen until he 'has sufficient means to keep her in comfort'.[14] Consequently, Robert takes his friend Tom to explore an old ship, their plans made more urgent by news of Ellen's wealthy suitor.

Robert, who shares Stoker's athleticism, dives into the wreck and finds a chest before the tide comes in. He asks Tom to return with him at Christmas, but Tom, unfortunately hospitalized, sends a letter to Ellen requesting her help. A storm sends her and her father to the coastguard station, but no one can locate Robert until Ellen hears his voice. Despite the title's emphasis on treasure, the story focuses on the lovers. Only the storm-swept night and mysterious voice reveal the Gothic notes of which Stoker is capable.

'The Chain of Destiny'

'The Chain of Destiny. A Serial in Ten Chapters' reveals Stoker's growing facility with Gothic elements.[15] Chris Morash describes it as Stoker's 'first foray into the vampire genre'.[16] Stoker's debt to his predecessors is evident in the setting, an ancestral 'house as would have delighted . . . Washington Irving or Nathaniel Hawthorne' (p. 159); Frank Stanford describes Scarp as 'a very stately edifice of seemingly great age, built of white stone' (p. 159). That the house is 'full of portraits' (p. 163) reinforces the influence of the past, and Frank is especially haunted by one portrait.

When Frank hears that the living replica of the portrait plans to visit, astute readers prepare for something mysterious. However, before Diana Fothering arrives, Stoker combines romance with Gothic horror when Frank dreams of 'three hags, decrepit and deformed, like typical witches' (p. 165), a shadow that becomes 'the phantom of the Fiend' (p. 165) and a small child. Like Jonathan Harker in the presence of Dracula's brides, Frank is literally paralysed by his nightmare.

Terror and curiosity lead him to explore the connection between Diana and Scarp's original owners. Morash comments on Stoker's debt to 'Carmilla' (LeFanu's novella explored the family relationship between Carmilla and the narrator), but Stoker never indicates whether the supernatural is involved.

Although the story remains ambiguous, Stoker uses Gothic elements to great effect. Exploring the library to find the link between Diana and Scarp's original owners, Frank discovers a curse on the Fotherings:

> From the text we learned that one of the daughters of Kirk ... married the brother of Fothering against the united wills of her father and brother, and ... the latter, then master of Scarp, had met the brother of Fothering in a duel and had killed him ... Fothering had sworn a great oath to revenge his brother. (p. 172)

The curse spells out the 'complete destruction, soul, mind, and body, of the first Fothering who should enter the gate of Scarp' (p. 172).

Frank is determined to protect Diana even though she does not fear the supernatural and tells him: 'I do not like doing anything from fear of supernatural things, or from a belief in them' (p. 182). Nonetheless, when she wakes screaming, Frank rushes to rescue her. Stoker never reveals whether anything is in the room, but Frank and Diana subsequently fall ill; his illness is cured only when she confesses her love. Although 'The Chain of Destiny' involves Gothic elements, including its setting, the emphasis on the past influencing the present, family secrets and a haunting portrait, Stoker never explains whether the mystery results from supernatural elements or a shared psychosis. Moreover, unlike 'Carmilla' and *Dracula*, it concludes by anticipating the future marriage of Diana and Frank and their inheriting Scarp from the childless Trevors.

'The Chain of Destiny', the last work Stoker published while still in Dublin (he published *The Duties of Clerks of Petty Sessions in Ireland* after moving to London), reveals him perfecting his craft but not yet using Gothic elements for more than creepy atmosphere. He certainly does not weave them into sustained social commentary.

Under the Sunset

Stoker dedicated *Under the Sunset*, a collection of children's stories, to his son Noel.[17] However, Maunder observes that it was also 'packaged for the 1882 Christmas market', evidence of Stoker's willingness to take advantage of popular literary trends.[18] Illustrated by W. V. Cockburn and William Fitzgerald, the collection reveals Stoker's range and demonstrates that, although he had not published much in seven years, he had somehow managed to hone his craft.

The stories reveal Stoker's continued use of Gothic themes and imagery. Indeed, Phyllis A. Roth reveals that the volume 'provides an appropriate introduction to the novels of horror' because it foreshadows 'their Gothic imagery and symbolism . . . their concern about the boundary between life and death' and 'Oedipal configurations and rivalries among their characters and Stoker's ambivalence toward his female characters'.[19] Of the stories, 'The Invisible Giant', 'The Shadow Builder' and 'The Castle of the King' are definitely Gothic while others have Gothic touches.

Douglas Menville concludes the introduction to the 1978 reissue by observing that none of Stoker's other books contains the 'eerie, poetic mixture of innocence and evil of *Under the Sunset*' (p. vii). Clive Leatherdale also emphasizes mysteriousness in *Dracula: The Novel and the Legend*:

> Although each of the . . . tales is self-contained, they all concern themselves with repeated motifs: familial love; the division of the world into Good and Evil; the horrendous punishments meted out to those who sin; the inevitable triumph of Good; and the mysterious boundary between life and death. The oppressive moralizing . . . was . . . common to . . . nineteenth-century fairy tales, and even the barbarous cruelty . . . was not out of keeping with the mainstream of the genre.[20]

More important, Leatherdale suggests that the stories foreshadow Gothic elements in later works. For example, Stoker continues to examine the issue of Good and Evil, and his novels, including *The Snake's Pass, The Mystery of the Sea* and *The Lady of the Shroud*, address evil that is human and realistic while *Dracula, The Jewel of Seven Stars* and *The Lair of the White Worm* feature larger and more inscrutable supernatural Evil.

Based on Charlotte Stoker's stories of the 1832 cholera outbreak in Sligo, 'The Invisible Giant' has strong Gothic elements. According to biographers, Stoker heard of this horrifying time while he was a small child, and the adult writer personified cholera as a haunting presence, 'a terrible thing . . . a vast shadowy Form with its arms raised' (p. 43), a fairy-tale ogre rather than realistic bacterial threat. Although based on an episode in Irish history – cholera claimed thousands of lives in Ireland – it focuses on mystery as seen through the eyes of the orphan Zaya, who warns her fellow citizens of the giant. Zaya offers herself as a sacrifice, but there seems no logical correlation between her behaviour and the giant's mysterious disappearance. The story emphasizes that human beings have no control over their lives and reinforces Roberts's notion that *fin de siècle* Gothic focuses on real uncertainties.[21]

'The Shadow Builder', a concrete representation of Death, also features horror and dread:

> Sometimes . . . the Shadow Builder sways resolute to his task, and round the world the shadows troop thick and fast . . . and even in the palaces of kings dark shadows pass and fly and glide over all things . . . for the Shadow Builder is then dread to look upon. (pp. 59–60)

The story also reveals the power of storms at sea: 'Quicker and quicker comes the dark cloud, sweeping faster and faster, and growing blacker and blacker and vaster and vaster as it comes' (pp. 63–4), the same naturalistic power described in 'Buried Treasure' and to which Stoker will return in *The Watter's Mou'*, *The Mystery of the Sea* and *The Man*.

'The Castle of the King' includes Gothic atmosphere and a plot that pits the living against the dead. It opens with a poet's learning his wife has died and details his quest to join her in the Land of Death. The rest of the story contrasts his love with terrifying obstacles:

'Then in this path along the trackless wilderness were strange and terrible things. Mandrakes – half plant, half man – shrieked at him with despairing cry, as . . . they stretched out their ghastly arms in vain' (p. 103). The end of his journey is the Castle of the King of Death, which anticipates Dracula's castle:

> Arose the tall turrets and the frowning keep. The gateway with its cavernous recesses and its beetling towers took shape as a skull. The distant battlements towered aloft into the silent air. From the very ground whereon the stricken Poet lay, grew, dim and dark, a vast causeway leading into the gloom of the Castle gate. (p. 112)

Because of his devotion, the poet is reunited with his beloved, who 'was standing in the ranks of those who wait . . . for their Beloved to follow them into the Land of Death' (p. 112). Dying, he destroys Death: 'Quicker then than the lightning's flash the whole Castle melted into nothingness; and the sun . . . shone calmly down upon the Eternal Solitudes' (p. 113). While love triumphs in this story, Stoker seems less confident about its power in *Dracula* and *The Jewel of Seven Stars*, though he returns to love in the romances, notably in *Lady Athlyne* and *The Man*, where real people experience plausible human problems, but find relief from suffering in their love of another flawed human being. Like other stories in *Under the Sunset*, 'The Castle of the King' depicts a magical world where a character battles a real situation, death, which Stoker presents metaphorically.

The final story, 'The Wondrous Child', depicts sibling rivalry. Two children seek their own baby and encounter terrifying animals who turn out not to be so terrifying after all – a tiger, 'an enormous Serpent, with small eyes that shone like sparks of fire, and two great open jaws' (p. 130), 'a mighty Bird of Prey' (p. 130), a shark and a crocodile. Consequently, while 'The Wondrous Child' is fantasy rather than Gothic, it includes moments that create apprehension and fear.

Stoker still had much to learn when he wrote *Under the Sunset*, but the stories stand on their own merits whether they are classified as Gothic, fantasy, 'Lewis-Carroll-style nonsense' tale, or fairy tale.[22] From a Gothic perspective, it is important to recognize that Stoker explores powerful mysteries: love, death and nightmares.

Short fiction in periodicals up to 1902

Over the next twenty years, Stoker arranged the Lyceum's national and international tours, handled Irving's correspondence, evaluated plays Irving received and socialized with everyone who was anyone. He turned to writing full time in 1902, but Dalby observes that his 'best short stories were written and published during the same seven-year period (1890–1897)'.[23] As one might suspect, many of them are Gothic, and almost all include Gothic elements.

'The Dualitists or, the Death-Doom of the Double-Born'

One of Stoker's darkest though not necessarily the most Gothic is 'The Dualitists' (published in *The Theatre Annual for 1887*).[24] This grim work features Ephraim and Sophonsiba Bubb, who, after ten childless years, are blessed with the birth of twins, Zerubbabel and Zacariah. They are happy until two hoodlums, Harry Merford and Tommy Santon, attack the children. Attempting a rescue, Ephraim accidentally kills the children instead of their attackers.

> But, alas! Love . . . shook the hand that never shook before. As the smoke cleared . . . he heard a . . . laugh of triumph and saw Harry and Tommy, all unhurt, waving in the air the trunks of the twins – the fond father had blown the heads completely off his own offspring. (p. 203)

Worse, the Bubbs are killed by the falling bodies of the twins and found 'guilty of . . . infanticide and suicide' (p. 209) while Harry and Tommy achieve great success. 'Fortune seemed to smile upon them . . . and they lived to a ripe old age . . . respected and beloved of all' (p. 209). Murray correctly describes it as 'an extraordinarily vicious story, devastating in its cynicism about human nature'.[25]

Its most Gothic element is its focus on mysterious human evil. By presenting Harry and Tommy as unrepentant monsters who move from vandalism to animal abuse to murder, the story emphasizes inherent evil:

When the supply of rabbits was exhausted . . . the war was continued with white mice, dormice, hedgehogs, guinea pigs, pigeons, lambs, canaries, parroqueets, linnets, squirrels, parrots, marmots, poodles, ravens, tortoises, terriers, and cats. Of these . . . the most difficult to manipulate were the terriers and the cats, and of these the two classes the proportion of the difficulties in the way of terrier-hacking was, when compared with those of cat-hacking, about that which the simple Lac of the *British Pharmacopoeia* bears to water in the compound which dairymen palm off upon a too confiding public as milk. (p. 205)

While 'The Dualitists' reveals individual human cruelty, the final line reinforces the problem of larger social evil.

'The Dualitists' is rarely reprinted, and practically no one discusses it except Valente, who concentrates on its Irishness and observes that Stoker adapted it from *The Corsican Brothers* by Dion Boucicault, a play the Lyceum first produced in 1880.[26]

'The Judge's House'

Often anthologized, 'The Judge's House', originally published in 1891 in *The Illustrated Sporting and Dramatic News*, is a particularly good example of the Gothic.[27] Like *The Turn of the Screw* and 'The Yellow Wallpaper', this story, which moves back and forth between mundane reality and supernatural mystery, is effective because it juxtaposes the Gothic with ordinary reality and makes it difficult to determine whether the protagonist is insane or haunted by something supernatural.

The story focuses on Malcolm Malcolmson, who seeks an isolated location to study for the Mathematical Tripos and rents a house 'so long empty that some kind of absurd prejudice has grown up about it' (p. 30), the first clue that the house may be haunted. A second clue lies in the noises he hears, though he agrees with his housekeeper's plausible explanations for them:

I'll tell you what it is, sir . . . bogies is all kinds and sorts of things – except bogies! Rats and mice, and beetles; and creaky doors, and loose slates, and broken panes, and stiff drawer handles, that stay out when you pull them and then fall down in the middle of the night ... Rats is bogies ... and bogies is rats; and don't you get to think anything else! (p. 32)

Malcolmson, immersed in mathematics, is even less interested in the supernatural:

A man who is reading for the Mathematical Tripos has too much to think of to be disturbed by any of these mysterious 'somethings', and his work is of too exact and prosaic a kind to allow ... for mysteries of any kind. Harmonical Progression, Permutations and Combinations, and Elliptic Functions have sufficient mysteries for me! (p. 31)

Eventually Stoker shifts from plausible explanations to focus on the supernatural. Unlike *The Turn of the Screw*, in which both supernatural explanations and naturalistic explanations are possible, or 'The Yellow Wallpaper', which explores postpartum depression, supernatural forces gradually gain power here. Malcolmson is not mad, for the physician describes him 'as sound and healthy a young man, mentally and bodily, as ever I saw' (p. 39), and the enormous rat who sits on the carved oak chair near the fireplace becomes the Judge: 'Slowly and deliberately the Judge rose ... and picked up the piece of the rope of the alarm bell ... drew it through his hands as if he enjoyed its touch, and then deliberately began to knot one end of it, fashioning it into a noose' (p. 43). Tying it around Malcolmson's neck, he then pulls away the chair. If readers question whether months of solitude cause Malcolmson to commit suicide, Stoker's conclusion reveals a distinct change on the Judge's portrait, which now wears 'a malignant smile' (p. 45).

Kate Hebblethwaite's introduction to *Dracula's Guest and Other Weird Stories with The Lair of the White Worm* observes that Stoker frequently uses plot devices that 'were longstanding staples of the Gothic tradition'.[28] Among the staples in 'The Judge's House' are rats, portraits and an old house. Both house and portrait reveal that a cruel past can haunt the rational and scientific present, and the rats remind readers that even ordinary things are mysterious. Indeed, 'The Judge's House' depicts a world overcome by vermin when Malcolmson sees that the 'rope of the great alarm bell was laden with rats. Every inch of it was covered with them' (p. 44), a scene demonstrating how Gothic writers reveal the natural world as beyond human control.[29]

'The Judge's House' is not just about the power of nature, however. One fascinating characteristic of Stoker's use of Gothic themes and imagery is his transcendence of heavy-handed Gothic. Readers may be terrified, horrified or simply revolted by rats, but the story also asks them to contemplate injustice. While the protagonist is a rational young man, the villain is the ghost of a cruel judge who uses the law to control others rather than achieve justice. Seeing him dressed in 'robes of scarlet and ermine', Malcolmson observes 'his baleful eyes glaring vindictively, and a smile of triumph on the resolute, cruel mouth' (p. 43). Stoker, himself a lawyer, will elsewhere use Gothic fiction to examine legitimate social power.

'The Secret of the Growing Gold'

Published the following year, 'The Secret of the Growing Gold' is another ghostly tale.[30] Maunder explores its Gothic elements, including 'familiar motifs of confinement, repression, regression and entrapment; the captive woman under threat and the brutish, sexually-threatening, aristocratic man'.[31] Especially interested in Stoker's treatment of women, Maunder observes that Stoker uses the persecuted heroine to examine 'the choices and restrictions imposed on women' while the Gothic villain allows him to reflect on problems inherent in patriarchy.[32] He describes Geoffrey Brent as 'a familiar Stoker type, the effete aristocrat, the vampire, the absentee landlord, an unequivocal brute who is irredeemably degenerate'.[33]

While noting Brent's similarity to the Gothic villain and his wife's resemblance to the persecuted heroine, Maunder overlooks another character, Margaret Delandre, the source of the ghostly hair that drives Geoffrey and his bride mad. Because Stoker carefully depicts the social distinctions between the Delandres and the Brents, the story rises above cliché: 'The Brents were accorded . . . a unique social dominance, and had ever held themselves as high above the yeoman class to which Margaret Delandre belonged' (p. 59). Moreover, the Delandres have fallen upon hard times: 'So, little by little, the family dropped lower and lower, the men brooding and dissatisfied, and drinking themselves into the grave, the women drudging at home, or marrying beneath them – or worse' (pp. 59–60). Because of this social difference, the community is surprised when Margaret and Geoffrey elope to Europe. Eventually, they hear she has died in an accident, but the reality is more horrifying and motivates her ghostly return.

Brent returns from Europe with an Italian wife and repairs Brent's Rock for her and their child. Geoffrey should be happy, but Stoker describes him as haunted, having 'a dark, anxious look on his face . . . he started at times as though at some noise that was unheard by others' (p. 63). His apprehension becomes clear when Margaret's ghost returns to tell her brother that Brent 'withdrew the lynch-pin and sent us over the precipice into the torrent' (p. 65).

Margaret's haunting takes a particularly chilling form when the golden hair for which she was known in life begins to fill the house: 'Before his horror-struck eyes the golden hair from the broken stone grew and grew; and as it increased, so his heart got colder and colder, till at last he had not power to stir, and sat with eyes full of terror watching his doom' (p. 69). Eventually, both Brent and his wife die:

> There by the deserted hearth Geoffrey Brent and his young wife sat cold and white and dead. Her face was peaceful . . . but his face . . . made all who saw it shudder, for there was on it a look of unutterable horror. The eyes were open and stared glassily at his feet, which were twined with tresses of golden hair, streaked with grey, which came through the broken hearth-stone. (p. 70)

As with 'The Judge's House', 'The Secret of the Growing Gold' demonstrates the past haunting the present as well as Stoker's use of Gothic imagery to illustrate social evils. However, instead of being tried for murder, Brent is punished by Margaret's returning spirit, and so is his totally innocent bride.

The Fate of Fenella

Stoker's next short work is a chapter in *The Fate of Fenella*, an experimental novel by twenty-four different authors and serialized in weekly instalments (*The Gentlewoman*, 1891 and 1892).[34] Maunder describes *Fenella* as a sensation novel, but Stoker's chapter is full of Gothic elements, including murder, hints of sexual excess, sleep-walking and madness.[35]

Stoker's chapter opens when Lord Francis Onslow meets his wife, Fenella, after a brief separation, and their conversation reveals the murder of which Fenella had been accused, tried and acquitted. Onslow apparently believes that she and the murdered man were having an affair 'because I saw him enter her room, and, God forgive me! I thought . . . that it was by her wish' (p. 74). The chapter introduces the possibility that perhaps Onslow, in a trance, killed De Murger, and Fenella is protecting him and concludes with Lord Castleton, who is baffled by the dark mysteries that he observes:

> Was it then wise to disturb existing relations between the husband and wife, sad though they were? Did they come together again, they might . . . arrive at a real knowledge of the facts, and . . . what would be the result? And besides, might there not be some danger in any suggestion made as to his suspicion of who struck the blow . . . Lady Francis had been acquitted . . . although she confessed to the killing; but her husband might still be tried . . . The problem was too much for Lord Castleton. His life had been too sunny and easy-going to allow of familiarity with great emotions, and such a problem as this was to him overwhelming. (pp. 77–8)

Once again, Stoker suggests that human institutions are ineffectual. As with 'The Secret of the Growing Gold', the legal structure is in-adequate, and Stoker's chapter questions where justice can be found.

'The Squaw'

Originally published in 1893, 'The Squaw', Stoker's second work to feature the United States, reveals primitive justice when a mother cat destroys the man who killed her kitten.[36] Like 'The Judge's House' and 'The Burial of the Rats', it also reveals the power of the natural world and demonstrates that human beings do not control their destiny.

Stoker also takes advantage of a Gothic setting, the medieval city of Nürnberg:

> A little to our right rose the towers . . . and nearer still . . . the Torture Tower . . . perhaps, the most interesting place in the city. For centuries the tradition of the Iron Virgin of Nürnberg has been handed down as an instance of the horrors of cruelty of which man is capable; we had long looked forward to seeing it. (p. 48)

Nürnberg is an odd destination for honeymooners, and the narrator/husband mentions that it is outside the general tourist circuit: 'Nürnberg at the time was not so much exploited as it has been since then. Irving had not been playing *Faust*, and the very name of the old town was hardly known to the great bulk of the travelling public' (p. 47).[37]

The newly-weds join another tourist, Elias P. Hutcheson. An American from Bleeding Gulch, Nebraska, Hutcheson initiates the story's violence when he accidentally kills a kitten playing with its mother near the city wall:

> Thus saying, he leaned over and . . . dropped the stone . . . [that] fell with a sickening thud . . . on the kitten's head and shattered out its little brains . . . The black cat cast a swift upward glance . . . and then her attention was given to the kitten, which lay still . . . whilst a thin red stream trickled from a gaping wound. (pp. 48–9)

Seeing her reminds Hutcheson of an Apache woman who tortured and killed a half-breed acquaintance, Splinters, for killing her child. Even more horrifying, though, Hutcheson casually mentions his part in this grisly story: not only does he kill her, but he carries with him a pocket-book made from Splinters's skin.

Hutcheson's familiarity with violence explains his fascination with the 'many implements of torture' (p. 53). He tells of fighting Native Americans and grizzly bears and being trapped in confined spaces, including a dead buffalo, a caved-in tunnel in a New Mexico gold mine and a caisson when he is setting the foundations of a bridge. Eager for more adventure, Hutcheson volunteers to experience the Virgin. What happens next connects the violence of the New World and the Old. Hutcheson is 'absolutely helpless and fixed in his voluntary prison' (p. 55) when the cat springs at the custodian holding the door open. Blood streaming down his face, he drops the rope that held the Virgin open:

> And then the spikes did their work ... when I wrenched open the door they had pierced so deep that they had locked in the bones of the skull through which they had crushed, and actually tore him – it – out of his iron prison till ... he fell at full length with a sickly thud upon the floor. (p. 57)

More horrifying, the cat pounces on him and licks the blood trickling down until the narrator seizes one of the executioner's swords and kills her.

There is no question that 'The Squaw' is Gothic, full of the violence and mystery that characterizes the least subtle forms of the genre, including the power of nature and the impact of the past over the present. Instead of rats, a mysterious black cat demonstrates superiority over the human characters before the narrator kills her. The medieval setting and the custodian's behaviour – the narrator comments that he 'must have had in him some of the blood of his predecessors in that ghastly tower' (p. 56) – remind readers of the power of the past. So does the fact that the narrator's first child is marked by the episode:

> The sight was too much for poor Amelia, and ... she fainted ... and I had to ... place her on a bench outside till she recovered. That she felt it ... was afterwards shown by the fact that my eldest son bears ... a rude birthmark on his breast, which has ... been accepted as representing the Nürnberg Virgin. (p. 54)

'The Squaw' reveals everything Stoker had learned from his predecessors about medieval settings, stock characters and violent behaviour.

By moving away from superficial aspects of the Gothic to explore its juxtaposition with scientific and rational life, 'The Squaw' transcends the crudest form of Gothic and enables Stoker to comment on contemporary issues: gender and the power of the United States, an interest also evident in *A Glimpse of America* (1886), *The Shoulder of Shasta* (1895), *Dracula*, *The Mystery of the Sea* (1902), *Snowbound* (1908) and *Lady Athlyne* (1908). Lillian Nayden's excellent article on Stoker's concern with America reveals that it explores the violence involved in settling the American West, especially the hostility between settlers and Native Americans.[38] Hopkins notes that it reveals Stoker's 'ambivalent ideas about America before writing *Dracula*'.[39] America's enormous potential and its violence fascinated Stoker, and Hutcheson epitomizes the violence associated with settling a new land. That the seemingly mild-mannered narrator quickly becomes violent reveals something more subtle and interesting, the violence lying beneath the civilized veneer.

If the title reveals Stoker's interest in Native Americans, it also reveals his interest in gender. Both Nayden and Maunder point to anxiety about powerful women.[40] Indeed, Amelia, who faints at seeing blood, is the only female character who resembles the persecuted maiden of earlier Gothic literature. Both the Native American woman and the mother cat retaliate when their offspring are killed even though their aggression results in their deaths.

Nayden's essay suggests that Amelia may also be threatening. Instead of openly challenging patriarchal power (and dying as a result), Amelia may be the unfaithful wife, her child the product of her clandestine relationship with Hutcheson. Maunder's discussion concludes by questioning her subtle usurpation of male power:

> Is she like the Iron Virgin then: the narrator's worst nightmare, precisely the kind of autopsying, illegitimating destabilizing mother that the entire narrative is about trying to keep in her place? The narrator, who tries to foreclose on these violent events and assert his masculine authority leaves the male reader ... to confront the ambivalent distinction between the idealized virtuous mother and the deadly new mother – who may be his own wife.[41]

One wonders why the newly-weds were quarrelling before Hutcheson's arrival and what happens to turn Amelia into the compliant wife and mother to which the narrator alludes at the conclusion.

More interesting is something else Maunder mentions, the narrator's resemblance to the Gothic villain:

The animalism of his own violence is hidden under the same civilized expressions of disgust, demonstrated by the men who excitedly join in the staking of Lucy ...and Margaret ...two young women who are transformed into a version of femininity vile enough to license their extermination ...What Stoker ...hints at is the existence of primal needs and drives in men, which call into question the smooth statements about England as a bastion of civilized values mouthed by the narrator.[42]

'The Squaw' thus illustrates Gothic darkness at the centre of civilization. Only surface polish separates the narrator (and by extension, the readers) from the Native American woman or the mother cat.

'The Man from Shorrox'

Stoker follows 'The Squaw' with 'The Man from Shorrox' (1894), a darkly humorous tale in which an Irish widow bests an impudent Manchester businessman by getting him drunk and putting him to bed in a room with a corpse.[43] On the surface an insubstantial tale, it includes one truly Gothic touch, the creepy sensation when the traveller wakes up touching the dead man. However, if the Gothic is meant to elicit fear, that fear is undermined by laughter at the traveller who gets what he deserves.

'A Dream of Red Hands'

'A Dream of Red Hands' ('A Novel in a Nutshell') appeared in *The Sketch* in 1894.[44] Although it includes Gothic elements (the seduction and death of a young woman, the murder of her aristocratic seducer and a protagonist haunted by guilt for that justifiable homicide), it is rarely discussed, perhaps because, as Murray notes in *From the Shadow of Dracula*, it 'is in essence a Christian morality tale' whose 'pietism seems risible today'.[45]

The narrator, a physician, treats an older man, Jacob Settle, for recurrent nightmares and learns of Jacob's past when, engaged to Mabel, he was working to earn money for them to marry. Before that happens,

Mabel is seduced by a wealthy man whom Jacob confronts and kills: 'God knows how it came about . . . but I found myself standing over his dead body, with my hands crimson with the blood that welled from his torn throat' (p. 121). Mabel dies giving birth to an illegitimate baby and, although Jacob avoids prosecution, he is haunted by the memory of killing his rival: 'I looked down, and was aghast, for the whole robe was smeared with blood. My hands were red; they glittered with the blood that dripped from them . . . Again, and again, and again, that awful dream comes to me' (p. 122).

Jacob moves away, and the narrator, visiting Glasgow, learns he has died saving another man from death:

> The hands were crossed on the purple breast . . . As I saw them my heart throbbed with a great exultation, for the memory of his harrowing dream rushed across my mind. There was no stain now on those poor, brave hands, for they were blanched white as snow. (p. 125)

While the story explores guilt, Stoker also comments on the treatment of working-class individuals:

> Oh, the usual thing! A rotten rope and men's lives of no account. Two men were working in a gasometer, when the rope that held their scaffolding broke . . . There was about seven feet of water in the gasometer . . . They swam together while their strength lasted . . . But one of them stood on the bottom and held up his comrade . . . and those few breaths made all the difference between life and death. They were a shocking sight when they were taken out, for that water is like a purple dye with the gas and the tar. The man upstairs looked as if he had been washed in blood. (p. 124)

One sees similar exploitation in *The Snake's Pass* and *Dracula* as well as owners' indifference in *The Mystery of the Sea*. Reinforcing that cruelty is Dr Munro's mention that such indifference to safety is 'the usual thing'.

Stoker's subtitle, 'A Novel in a Nutshell', emphasizes that during the 1890s he was working on longer fiction, publishing *The Snake's Pass* in 1890 and *The Watter's Mou'* in 1894. He was working on *Dracula* and *Miss Betty* when he published this story and would, over the next eight years, publish five novels, including *The Shoulder of Shasta* (1895), *Dracula* (1897) and *Miss Betty* (1898), establishing himself as a novelist as well as a writer of short stories.

'The Red Stockade'

While 'A Dream of Red Hands' is anomalous because of its religious message, 'The Red Stockade: A Story Told by the Old Coastguard' (October 1894) is unusual for its setting, the Straits of Malacca.[46] Knowing that good stories often include grisly details, Stoker has the narrator relate the danger facing mariners in a region known for piracy and also demonstrate how nature conspires against them:

> The slime shimmered in all kinds of colours ... and the whole place seemed alive with all that was horrible. The alligators kept off the boats and the banks close to us, but the thick water was full of eels and watersnakes, and the mud was alive with water-worms and leeches, and horrible, gaudy-coloured crabs. The very air was filled with pests – flies of all kinds, and a sort of big-striped insect ... which ... bites you like red-hot pinchers. (p. 216)

The description makes the rats in 'The Judge's House' look positively cute and cuddly, but worse things come when the sailors are ambushed and trapped here. Those who escape see their companions slaughtered, their heads impaled on spikes outside the stockade. The crew is bent on revenge, and the subsequent battle is bloody, though death is only part of the horror:

> The alligators had had a good day, and ... we could see them lie out lazily, as if they had been gorged. Aye! And here was enough left for the ground-sharks ... for the men on board told us that ... something would go along, bobbing up and down in the swell, till presently there would be a swift ripple of a fin, and then there was no more pirate. (p. 219)

Eventually, the sailors triumph. As with 'A Dream of Red Hands', 'The Red Stockade' reveals Stoker's mastery of Gothic details, though both focus on plausible human behaviour rather than supernatural mystery.

'Crooken Sands'

'Crooken Sands', also published in 1894, features plausible human behaviour, this time mixed with the Gothic figure of the doppelgänger and second sight, a mysterious ability to which Stoker returns in *The Mystery of the Sea* and *The Lady of the Shroud*.[47]

The story features a London merchant, Arthur Fernlee Markam, who, vacationing in Scotland, dresses as a Highland chieftain, to his family's embarrassment and the amusement of the locals. One, nicknamed Saft Tammie, reminds Markam of the danger of pretending to be something he is not and warns against vanity and quicksand. While Tammie is 'an odd sort of old man' (p. 132), the narrator hints at special talents: 'Whether it be that "second sight" which we Scotch people ... believe in, or some other occult form of knowledge' (p. 140). Prompted by Tammie's warnings, Markam concludes he has a doppelgänger, which he learns about by reading '*Die Döppleganger*, by Dr Heinrich von Aschenberg ... cases where men had led a double existence – each nature being quite apart from the other' (p. 140).

Seeing his other self engulfed in quicksand, he buries the clothing, noting that he hopes that his 'worser self is buried there along with it' (p. 144). Returning to London, he receives a letter from the company that sold him his Scottish clothing. It reveals that another man who shared his passion for highland costume had written while on holiday 'that he feared a judgment had come upon him for wishing to appear as a Scotchman on Scottish soil' (p. 144). That man is buried in quicksand while Markham comes to accept himself as a cockney businessman, acceptance that lets him reconcile with his family and regain 'something like his old peace of mind' (p. 143).[48] The primary Gothic touches in the story are the 'mystery and horror' (p. 141) Markam experiences when he believes he has two existences.

Short fiction after 1902

For the remainder of the nineteenth century, Stoker continues as Irving's business manager and writes in his spare time, becoming in 1902 a full-time writer. He published one collection of short stories,

Snowbound: The Record of a Theatrical Touring Party in 1908 and was working on several collections when he died in 1912.

Snowbound: The Record of a Theatrical Touring Party (1908)

Like *The Canterbury Tales* and the *Decameron*, *Snowbound* uses a framing narrative featuring a snowbound theatrical company whose members tell stories to amuse themselves until rescue. Although individual stories are occasionally reprinted, the collection was not reprinted until 2000.[49] Dalby's 'Bibliographical Note' explains its rarity by noting that it 'was issued as an ephemeral delicate paperback' (p. 7) and not intended to last. Bruce Wightman, who edited the reprinted edition, comments that it is not typical of Stoker: 'First, aside from references to . . . *Manfred*, with its witches and spirits, and the stage device known as the star trap, often employed for demon entrances, there is no supernatural catalyst within this collection' (p. 9). Indeed, Wightman's introduction focuses on *roman-à-clef* elements, emphasizes the truthfulness of the stories and notes that the storytellers are 'disguised portraits of those theatricals the author worked and toured with' (p. 9). Even the framing narrative is based on an event in January 1904, when the 'company's train became "snowbound" in the Adirondack Mountains' (p. 9). The stories also feature real situations, including trains crossing flooded bridges, a wake, an unfaithful wife, a young mother's death and various criminal activities.

Of fifteen stories, only 'A Star Trap' is truly Gothic, though others include Gothic details: 'A New Departure in Art' by the Low Comedian describes an Irish wake; 'A Deputy Waiter' focuses on the Singing Chambermaid's terror at being forced to sing for a lunatic, while 'A Moon-Light Effect' by the Scene Painter features a Gothic setting. Finally, the frame tale and 'Mick the Devil' reveal nature's overwhelming power.

Nature's power appears almost as another character in *Snowbound* as it does in other Stoker works. Indeed, all the characters in this collection are at the mercy of nature's power as 'The Occasion', which serves as the introduction, signifies: 'For a little while the train seemed to stumble along amongst the snowdrifts. Every now and again there would be a sudden access of speed as a drift was cleared . . .

Then would follow an ominous slowing down as the next snow-drift was encountered' (p. 13). Until the plough comes through, the company is in danger of dying 'like rats in a trap' (p. 15). 'Mick the Devil' reveals a different kind of natural power, flood:

> There's a spongy gap a couple of miles wide, with a trestle bridge across it . . . At the best of times I am anxious about that trestle . . . But now, with a fortnight's rain and the Mississippi up the levees and the bottoms flooded . . . that blessed place will be like an estuary of the sea. The bridge isn't built for weather like this, and the flood is sure to be well over it. A train running on it will have to take chance whether it is there at all; and if any of it is gone . . . God help the train! (p. 64)

Stoker's emphasis on nature reminds readers of the Gothic's connection to English Romanticism – in this case the sublime – a power also evident in *The Shoulder of Shasta*, *Dracula* and *Lady Athlyne*.[50] In 'A Moon-Light Effect', the Scene Painter relates being commissioned to create scenes for *Manfred*, Byron's poetic drama, and expresses hope that the 'scene of the Thunderstorm in the Alps' will establish his reputation. What happens, however, is comic, not Gothic. Instead of exploring nature's beauty, 'A Moon-Light Effect' concludes with a 'Moonlight Flit', which Wightman defines as leaving 'without paying one's debts. A traditional piece of roguery with tour theatricals in bad lodgings' (p. 159).

Related by the Low Comedian, 'A New Departure in Art' tells of an Irish wake, where he realizes he is in the presence of something larger than himself. Generally known for the broadest kind of physical humour, this low comedian comes to see something grander in his calling.

Readers would not associate the Singing Chambermaid with the Gothic, but 'A Deputy Waiter' relates her terror when a gun-wielding man forces her to sing:

> Well, I sang, and sang, and sang . . . As I grew fainter he levelled his pistol at me and forced me to go on from very fear of death . . . He made me go faster and faster still, beating time with the revolver . . . I held on in mortal fear till even sheer terror could no longer uphold me. The last thing I saw as I fell senseless . . . was his scowling face and

the bobbing muzzle of the revolver as he called, 'Faster! Faster!'
(p. 103)

Although the police inspector reveals that she had been victimized
by a clever criminal who diverted her attention so another thief could
steal valuables, the terror is real while it lasts, and readers experience
it with her.

The stories in *Snowbound* cover a range of genres, but 'A Star Trap',
the only thoroughly Gothic story, is the story most frequently anthologized.[51] The Master Machinist who tells it was an apprentice when his
boss Jack Haliday married a younger woman who later falls for the
Harlequin, Henry Mortimer.

Remembering that other company members gossip about Mortimer
and Loo Haliday, the narrator observes a change in Haliday as well:
'He looked worried and had a devil of a temper . . . He was always a
hard worker, and the panto season was a terror with him . . . As the
week went on he got more and more pale; and I began to think he was
in for some sickness' (p. 137). Because of the danger involved, Haliday
insists on checking the trap but looked so 'very white and ill – that
the stage manager . . . said to him that if he liked to go home and rest
he would see that all his work would be attended to' (pp. 138–9).

Instead of leaving, however, Haliday watches the performance with
his wife. When the trap fails to open, Mortimer is killed, and the
narrator later picks up pieces of the broken trap as well as a 'queer-
looking piece of flat steel . . . that didn't belong to the trap' (p. 141).
Concluding that Haliday sabotaged it, he throws the piece away, not
revealing the truth until he tells the snowbound company:

> I was not called at the inquest . . . So nothing was known; and all went
> on as usual. Except that after that Mrs Haliday didn't stand in the wings
> during the harlequinade, and she was as loving to her old husband as
> a woman can be. It was him she used to watch now; and always with a
> sort of respectful adoration. She knew; though no one else did, except
> her husband – and me. (p. 144)

The tale transports several Gothic staples – violence, hidden sexuality,
a villain and an imprisoned maiden – into the realm of ordinary life.
This strategy has the effect of closing the gap between Gothic mystery

and ordinary life. Rather than displacing it to a distant time or place, Stoker suggests here, as he does in his more famous works, that mystery and awe are part of everyday life.

Stoker's later short fiction

Stoker devoted more time to novels after 1902 but continued writing and publishing short fiction. He published two stories about the same time as *Snowbound*: 'The Eros of the Thames: The Story of a Frustrated Advertisement' (October 1908) and 'The Way of Peace' (December 1909).[52] 'Eros' is not Gothic aside from the fact that Peter Jimpson, a professional swimmer, risks his son's life to advertise his skill. His desire for fame is thwarted when, after he has thrown his son from London Bridge, another man dives into the river to rescue him, and Peter is subsequently arrested for attempted murder.

'The Way of Peace' initially appears even less Gothic. Introducing it as a tale of 'quiet Irish humour and tenderness, about the happiest couple in the country, and the secret of it' (p. 34), the narrator reveals its dark underside, including the famine when 'min an' weemin' – an' worse still, the poor childhers – was dyin' be shcores' (p. 39) as well as abusive behaviour, for Michael Hennessey beats his wife Katty for trying to thwart him and tells the narrator, who is engaged to be married, what he told her: 'But always remimber that I'm a man an' used to a man's ways; an' a man doesn't like bein' ordered about be any wan – even be a wife that he loves an' that loves him' (p. 42). Although presented as friendly advice to a younger man, the story reveals underlying cruelty in a man who feels justified in using corporal punishment on his wife and children.

Dracula's Guest

Some of Stoker's most Gothic works appear in *Dracula's Guest*, the collection he was preparing when he died.[53] Richard Dalby and William Hughes's bibliography notes that the volume, which Stoker's widow published in 1914, 'contains work written or published during the peak of Stoker's popularity as a writer of popular and Gothic fictions'.[54] Other stories ('The Gypsy Prophecy', 'The Coming of Abel Behena' and 'The Burial of the Rats') were, according to Hebblethwaite's Introduction to *Dracula's Guest and Other Weird Stories with The Lair of the White Worm*, 'published for the first time in 1914'.[55] It's impossible to say whether 'Dracula's Guest' is a draft of an early chapter, an independently written story, or material excised to make *Dracula* a more printable length. Murray observes in *From the Shadow of Dracula*, 'None of the competing theories can be definitely proved or disproved . . . The possibility that it was edited after Stoker's death further muddies the waters.'[56]

Four stories from *Dracula's Guest* that have not been discussed so far are 'The Gypsy Prophecy', 'The Coming of Abel Behena', 'The Burial of the Rats' and 'Dracula's Guest'. 'The Gypsy Prophecy' involves newly-weds, Joshua and Mary Considine, Joshua's friend, Dr Gerald Burleigh and a mysterious gypsy who predicts John will murder Mary.[57] The superstitious Mary blunts the household knives, but Mary is injured when she falls on a knife Joshua's brother has sent him from India. Indeed, 'The Gypsy Prophecy' reveals a mysterious truth: while Joshua confesses he prefers certainty to mystery, the Gypsy and Mary see something the rational men do not. The story never mentions second sight, but here as elsewhere, Stoker suggests forces more powerful than science and brings that mystery into the heart of the modern world.

'The Coming of Abel Behena' also introduces mystery into ordinary events.[58] In *The Shadow of Dracula*, Murray notes that it is set in a real place, a small fishing village 'on the west coast of Cornwall, which he discovered . . . on a long walking tour of the area'.[59] Maunder suggests that Stoker's stories 'test some of the themes, situations and characters and techniques that recur in his full-length novels',[60] noting that 'the narrative is driven by the demands made by the heroine, Sarah Trefusis' whose greed anticipates 'the monstrous appetite for men, blood and money, demonstrated by Lucy . . . or Arabella March'.[61]

While Sarah is a greedy woman, not a supernatural monster, this story of a love triangle has definite Gothic overtones. When Sarah cannot decide between Abel and Eric, her mother proposes that the men pool their money and toss a coin for the money and Sarah. Abel wins and, promising to take the money to Bristol and ship on a voyage to trade with it, agrees to return on Sarah's birthday to marry her. Rage and jealousy transform Eric, and Stoker reinforces demonic elements in this ordinary man, noting that sunset 'intensified the natural ruddiness of his complexion … as though he were steeped in blood' (p. 85). Stoker furthermore suggests that Eric sells his soul. When Abel observes he won the coin toss with God's help, Eric responds, 'Take the money and go. I stay. God for you! The Devil for me!' (p. 86).

The successful Abel is returning when his ship is caught in a storm and everyone jumps overboard. Eric rushes to help and throws a rope to someone struggling in the water but, recognizing Abel, lets him slip back into the sea. Although he marries Sarah, their happiness is marred when Abel's body washes ashore, its hand seemingly outstretched towards them. There is no suggestion of supernatural intervention, and the story is interesting primarily because the Gothic elements emphasize ordinary human flaws.

'The Burial of the Rats' reveals a different strategy.[62] While there is no question it takes place in the real world, it includes definite Gothic elements, including a mysterious landscape, powerful representatives of the past and the power of the natural world. Murray notes perceptibly that Stoker 'compares a squalid area of Paris with rural Ireland' and reminds readers that Stoker often uses Gothic imagery to comment on a familiar world.[63]

The narrator sets the scene by describing a mysterious landscape. Piling detail on detail, he observes a 'wild and not at all savoury district' (p. 95) that is '*terra incognita*, in so far as the guide book was concerned' and 'a country as little known as that round the source of the White Nile' (p. 97). The descriptions hint at something as mysterious as Transylvania (*Dracula*) or Styria ('Dracula's Guest'). Carefully locating the story in the not-so-distant past, Paris in 1850, Stoker introduces individuals who have lived through a dark and violent period of French history, including an old woman who 'had been one of the *tricoteuses* who sat daily before the guillotine and had taken an active part among the women who signalized themselves by their violence in the revolution' (p. 99). Her friend Pierre 'was in everything, from the Bastille to Waterloo' (p. 99).

Past violence impacts the present when the narrator realizes the rag pickers plan to murder him for his valuables. In a reversal of the traditional Gothic plot in which a villain pursues a young woman through an underground labyrinth, he escapes from 'a regular murder-trap' (p. 105) and is chased by representatives of the blood-thirsty past: 'I was in momentary peril of my life: my safety depended on my action . . . yet I could not but think of the strange dogged persistency of these old men . . . What must they have been in the vigour of their youth' (p. 109). Like other Gothic works, this tale evokes terror that the past will overwhelm the present.

Before being rescued, the narrator experiences the power of the natural world when he falls 'headlong into a reeking, stagnant pool . . . filthy and nauseous beyond description' (pp. 108–9) and takes the soldiers back to the hut, where they discover the rats are more powerful than they:

> It was a gruesome sight. There lay a skeleton . . . Between the ribs rose a long spike-like dagger . . . The rats are many here – see their eyes glistening among that heap of bones – and you will also notice . . . that but little time was lost by them, for the bones are scarcely cold! (pp. 114–15)

Although the story concludes happily with the narrator married to his beloved, the final sentence reminds readers that the past is never entirely eradicated: 'But when I look back . . . one of the most vivid incidents that memory recalls is that associated with my visit to the City of Dust' (p. 116). No matter how civilized humans become, they cannot escape the awesome power of nature or the terrors of the past.

One of Stoker's most Gothic stories is the title story, 'Dracula's Guest', which includes a setting in a deserted village in Styria, an area often associated with the Gothic, the tomb of a vampire countess and an unexpected May snowstorm.[64] The first-person narrator, like Jonathan Harker, is travelling to Dracula's castle and begins with 'all the joyousness of early summer' (p. 17) but quickly experiences terror when the coachman drops him in a deserted area on Walpurgis night, when 'according to the belief of millions of people, the devil was abroad – when the graves were opened and the dead came forth and walked' (p. 22). Furthermore, although the narrator brags that 'Walpurgis-Nacht doesn't concern Englishmen' (p. 19), he becomes terrified when the spring weather turns to snow and then to hail, at which point he confesses, 'I was alone – unmanned, shivering with cold in a shroud of snow' (p. 22), weather so awful that the 'shelter of even a tomb was welcome' (p. 23). When lightning illuminates the darkened tomb, he is immediately confronted with the supernatural, 'a beautiful woman . . . seemingly sleeping on a bier' (p. 23). What happens next is even more horrifying:

> The dead woman rose for a moment of agony, while she was lapped in the flame, and her bitter scream of pain was drowned in the thunder-crash. The last thing I heard was this mingling of dreadful sound, as again I was seized . . . and dragged away . . . and the air around seemed reverberant with the howling of wolves. The last sight that I remembered was a vague, white, moving mass, as if all the graves around me had sent out the phantoms of their sheeted-dead. (p. 23)

Horror builds on horror when he awakens with a large animal lying on him and 'licking my throat . . . I saw above me the two great flaming eyes of a gigantic wolf. Its sharp white teeth gleamed in the gaping red mouth, and I could feel its hot breath fierce and acrid upon me' (p. 24). The soldiers who rescue him confirm that it is no ordinary wolf, and any doubts readers have are answered when the narrator reads Dracula's telegram telling the soldiers to protect his guest from harm.

Although Stoker's fiction often reveals his use of Gothic elements to comment on troubling aspects in his world, 'Dracula's Guest' is almost pure Gothic. Terror is the appropriate response at being caught by uncanny powers that no human being can control. It is thus a fitting conclusion to Stoker's life as well as an appropriate introduction to him as a Gothic writer. The remaining chapters reveal Stoker as an extraordinarily versatile writer who experimented with the major genres of his day, including the romance, the historical novel and the Gothic tale of terror. That he weaves Gothic elements into practically everything he wrote is proof that he deserves to be studied as a Gothic writer, indeed, one of the greatest Gothic writers of all times.

1

Gothic Material in The Snake's Pass, The Watter's Mou' *and* The Shoulder of Shasta

ഇൽരു

Dracula is unquestionably a Gothic masterpiece because Stoker perfected his craft while he worked as business manager for the Lyceum and wrote in his spare time. William Hughes notes in *Beyond Dracula* that eight novels were 'thus completed effectively on a part-time basis, the research and writing often effected on tour or in breaks between productions or rehearsals': *The Snake's Pass* (1891), *The Watter's Mou'* (1894), *The Shoulder of Shasta* (1895), *Dracula* (1897), *Miss Betty* (1898), *The Mystery of the Sea* (1902), *The Jewel of Seven Stars* (1903) and *The Man* (1905).[1]

Even though Stoker had little time to polish them, these novels demonstrate growing skill with narration, establishing both setting and mood and weaving together elements from different genres, including romance, invasion narrative, science fiction, Westerns, adventure tales, travel literature, temperance literature and the Gothic. This chapter explores the three novels that lead up to *Dracula*.

The Snake's Pass

His only novel set in Ireland, Stoker's first novel was serialized in *The People* (20 July–30 November 1890) and later published by Sampson Low, Marston and Co. Revealing his interest in using Gothic materials to comment on social and political problems faced by people back home, *The Snake's Pass* is a first-person narrative by a young Englishman, Arthur Severn, who travels to Western Ireland on a holiday and falls in love with the land and Norah Joyce.[2] Before they can marry, however, he and a college friend, Dick Sutherland, must rescue her and her father from the Irish usurer, Black Murdock, who has gained control over her father's property. This novel, which Phyllis A. Roth characterizes as a romance in *Bram Stoker*, 'uses a conventional romance pattern' but also 'foreshadows the tales of mystery and horror to come'.[3] It also adapts Gothic elements to explore complex social issues, including the relationship between England and Ireland and the need to improve Ireland's economy in the decades following the Great Famine and the subsequent emigration of much of its remaining population.

Joseph Valente, Nicholas Daly and David Glover comment on Stoker's interest in Ireland in *The Snake's Pass*.[4] Although Valente explores Stoker's treatment of Ireland, he spends relatively little time on *The Snake's Pass*, objecting to its adherence to the 'generic conventions of the "metropolitan marriage"'.[5] Daly and Glover compare it to its predecessors, Glover here revealing Daly's influence:

> Indeed, as Nicholas Daly has suggested, one of the novel's precursors may have been Dion Boucicault's comic melodrama, *The Shaughraun* (1874), a play which also unites an English hero and an Irish heroine against a rapacious local moneylender–although ... the gombeenman was already a well-developed fictional type by this date.[6]

Of particular interest to this study is Glover's observation that *The Snake's Pass* 'detaches the Gothic component ... and domesticates it', a strategy Stoker uses again in *Dracula*, which is also set in a modern world, where trains run on time, grisly stories appear in newspapers and characters use telephones and telegrams to share information.[7] Stoker prepares for this juxtaposition of the mysterious and the ordinary in *The Snake's Pass*, and Black Murdock, the Gombeen Man (a usurious moneylender), is a more or less realistic predecessor for Dracula.

More important than the moving of the Gothic component from the medieval past to the industrial present and from a distant land to his own country is Carol Margaret Davison's observation in 'The ghost of genres past' that Stoker moves into uncharted ground when he uses the Gothic to explore social concerns:

> What has received precious little attention, to date, is the corollary of the unusual pairing of social realism and the Gothic: raising the ghost of the Gothic within the realist tradition haunts the certainties – both aesthetic and ideological – of that nascent form.[8]

Indeed, this blurring of Gothic excess with contemporary social concerns distinguishes Victorian Gothic from its predecessors.

Paul Murray observes in *From the Shadow of Dracula* that Stoker was thinking about social problems as he wrote, so much so that he sent a copy to the prime minister, William E. Gladstone, an acquaintance and frequenter of Irving's Beefsteak Room.[9] Not only was Gladstone interested in Home Rule for Ireland during the 1880s and 1890s, he was also interested in the 'oppressive role of the "gombeen man", or moneylender, in Irish rural life'.[10] Moreover, Murray comments on Stoker's hope that science and technology might solve the social issues he depicts:

> Dick Sutherland, an engineer . . . hopes for government measures to reclaim the Bog of Allen, the kind of developmental idea which characterized Stoker's thinking about Ireland and derived from the thinking of mid-nineteenth-century Irish nationalists such as Thomas Davis.[11]

Such interest in science and technology is woven skillfully with a number of Gothic elements and results in a novel that uses Gothic excess to highlight social issues. Stoker's increasing skill is evident in the extent to which he has moved beyond Gothic conventions and stereotypes.

Among the most striking Gothic elements are the emphasis on nature's mysterious power, the looming presence of the past, a persecuted maiden, a villain and supernatural powers that threaten to dwarf human characters. Unlike Gothic novels that use fragmented narratives to increase readers' awareness of mystery (*Frankenstein, Dr Jekyll and Mr Hyde, Wuthering Heights* and *Dracula*, to name a few), *The Snake's Pass* uses a straightforward chronological narrative. Indeed, the primary mystery is that Arthur, the first-person narrator, is an English tourist who is unfamiliar with the landscape, the people and their customs.

The novel opens with Severn's description of a location that might have come straight from Burke's *Philosophical Inquiry into the Origin of Our Ideas of the Sublime and the Beautiful* (1757).[12] Severn observes the steep precipices and 'almost primal desolation' (p. 9) of the landscape, commenting on its eerie quietness:

> Earth, sea and air all evidenced the triumph of nature, and told of her wild majesty and beauty. The air was still – ominously still. So still was all, that through the silence, that seemed to hedge us in with a sense of oppression, came the booming of the distant sea, as the great Atlantic swell broke in surf on the rocks or stormed the hollow caverns of the shore. (p. 10)

While nature's power is a standard component of Gothic literature, Severn has more reason than most to acknowledge its power, having lost his parents at sea: 'I was only a very small boy when they were lost in a fog when crossing the Channel' (p. 11).

Arthur and his Irish driver Andy Sullivan confront a powerful storm that forces them to seek shelter in Mrs Keligan's sheebeen:

> The storm seemed to sweep through the valley in a single instant – the stillness changed to a roar, the air became dark with the clouds of drifting rain. It was like the bursting of a waterspout ... and came so quickly that I was drenched ... before I could throw my mackintosh round me. (p. 14)

The equally mysterious shebeen is a place that, according to Roth, 'captures both local color and country customs' and introduces Severn and Stoker's English readers to the strangeness of Irish life.[13]

Although Severn's difficulty in understanding the conversation he overhears is another reminder that Ireland was strange and uncanny to most English readers, the primary indicator of strangeness is the bog. Both setting and symbol, as well as a place often associated with the Irish, the bog is evidence of Ireland's impoverished state because it is unsuitable for agriculture (though the peat can be cut and used for fuel). It would have been hard for Stoker to choose anything more indicative of Ireland for, as Hughes observes in *Beyond Dracula*, the bog represented Ireland in the minds of English people:

> The bog . . . is, in English prejudice, an overt signifier of Irish topography, and the source of derogatory racial stereotypes – the bog dweller, the 'bog trotter'. In *The Snake's Pass* it is an especially rich symbol, one which encodes a reading of Irish problems and British solutions into the fabric of a supposedly local issue. As Arthur is informed when he takes shelter in the . . . shebeen, the shifting bog has become closely identified with Murdock and his activities through the myth of its creation – a version of the expulsion of the snakes from Ireland by St Patrick in which the King of the Snakes transforms himself into the shifting bog.[14]

Furthermore, because bogs are inherently unstable, they evoke danger. They are also dark places where mystery might lurk beneath the surface, and Stoker links several Irish characters (notably Norah and Murdock) with the uncanny geographical region.

Sutherland, whom Murdock has hired to study the bog, initially describes it as 'more treacherous than either [quagmire or quicksand]. You may call it, if you are poetically inclined, a "carpet of death!"' (p. 59). Indeed, several people face death in the bog, and the novel culminates in its sweeping Murdock out to sea:

> For a while the superior size and buoyancy of the roof sustained it, but then it too began slowly to sink . . . And then came a mighty roar and a gathering rush. The side of the hill . . . seemed to burst. Murdock threw up his arms . . . Then came the end of the terrible convulsion. With a rushing sound, and the noise of a thousand waters falling, the whole bog swept . . . down the mountain-side – to the entrance of the Shleenanaher – struck the portals with a sound like thunder, and piled up to a vast height. And then the millions of tons of slime and ooze, and bog and earth, and broken rock swept through the Pass into the sea. (p. 230)

This passage fulfills Sutherland's intimation that the bog is a looming and overwhelming presence. Reinforcing its mysterious nature, Andrew Maunder explains in *Bram Stoker* that it encapsulates the 'uncanny and

Gothic elements of the landscape' and that Arthur 'comes back to it as a central reference point, a symbolic representation of the monstrous and the "unfathomable"'.[15] Nevertheless, while Hughes and Maunder see it as a Gothic symbol, Murray reminds readers that Stoker would have seen it as literal though nonetheless horrifying: 'Much of the background to the novel was real enough. Bog-slides were well documented in Irish records as far back as the eighteenth century: rare and unexpected occurrences, they were mysterious and terrifying to the local people.'[16] Emphasizing the bog as a real place, chapter V, 'On Knockanacar', includes several scientific explanations for geological phenomena, evidence that Stoker often contemplated real problems even when he employed Gothic details.

In addition, Stoker links Norah and Murdock with the bog. While there is nothing especially Gothic in the fact that Andy Sullivan frequently compares Norah to the bog, it reinforces her identification with Ireland, both mysteries to Severn at the beginning of the novel. On the other hand, Stoker reinforces the Gothic power of the bog and Murdock by linking them together. Indeed, Murdock is connected both to the bog and to the powerful King of the Snakes, his rapacious appetite resembling that of the uncanny being who demanded the yearly sacrifice of a baby. Commenting on his oppression, the peasants speculate that the bog is the form the King of the Snakes took when St Patrick ordered the snakes out of Ireland, and Maunder describes him as a reincarnation of the King of the Snakes. The conflation of past and present, legend and history, human and geography reminds readers that Stoker builds up elements to produce an overwhelming sense of Gothic power.

Murdock's character reveals that Stoker may have been thinking of the Gothic villain when he created him. For example, Arthur's first glimpse of him peeking in the shebeen window marks him as dark and Other: 'Pressed against the empty lattice where the glass had once been, I saw the face of a man – a dark, forbidding face it seemed in the slight glimpse I caught of it' (p. 30). Not only is Murdock introduced as he is looking in at a group of comrades, he is also, like other Gothic villains, more animal than human. Sutherland refers to him as 'that human-shaped wolf' (p. 87), others refer to him as the King of the Snakes reincarnated. Furthermore, while he is not an aristocrat living in a ruined castle, he is presented as above the law.

Allison Millbank observes in '"Powers old and new": Stoker's alliances with Anglo-Irish Gothic' that he 'is the classic Gothic villain with omnivorous desires for power and represents also the Gothic usurper'.[17] And Stoker demonstrates that Murdock uses the law to his own advantage.[18] He also anticipates Dracula, being briefly presented as thirsting for blood: 'An' so ye think to baffle me! Do ye? Well! I'll have that money out – if I have to wade in yer blood' (p. 212).

Commenting that Murdock sometimes appears as a sexual predator, in *Beyond Dracula* Hughes quotes a contemporary review that 'coyly suggests that Murdock entices Norah out onto the bog "for the purpose of possessing himself of her person"'.[19] In general, however, Murdock is among the least sexual of Gothic villains, being more interested in Phelim Joyce's land than Norah's body.

Although Murdock may remind readers of other Gothic villains (Varney, Manfred or Uncle Silas, to name a few), Stoker's genius is that he uses Gothic excess to point to social ills. Murray observes:

If Black Murdock's roots lie partly in the symbolism of the snake, they also derive from the social conditions of nineteenth-century Ireland. Eviction was a fact of life in the landlord-tenant conflict that had convulsed the country in the years before *The Snake's Pass* was written. There were those who had over-extended themselves by borrowing money at high interest to buy the land of evicted tenants and, in most cases, found themselves without sufficient means to continue farming. Moneylending at exorbitant rates flourished and Black Murdock was representative of a very real social problem that existed in the Irish countryside of that time. The moneylender was an established fictional type in Irish novels of the nineteenth century.[20]

Thus Murdock is not simply a Gothic type but also an example of a problem that existed when Stoker wrote *The Snake's Pass*:

He's a man that linds you a few shillin's or a few pounds whin ye want it bad, and then niver laves ye till he has tuk all ye've got – yer land an' yer shanty an' yer holdin' an' yer money an' yer craps; an' he would take the blood out of her body if he could sell it or use it anyhow! (p. 26)

As Sutherland observes of the bog, 'Legends have always a base in fact' (p. 65), and the excesses of the Gothic have a base in fact as well. Certainly, Irish writers are known for their expertise in the Gothic, possibly the result of being overwhelmed by powers beyond their control.[21]

In addition to the uncanny landscape and the predatory villain, *The Snake's Pass* incorporates other conventions frequently associated with the Gothic. Among the most obvious are the looming presence of the past and the existence of forces that threaten to overpower human characters. Indeed, the novel begins with Arthur's learning about the King of the Snakes who supposedly created the Snake's Pass when St Patrick drove the snakes out of Ireland and about French soldiers who hid a treasure chest in the vicinity. These stories are woven through Severn's narration of present day events, and the novel concludes when the lost golden crown and the treasure are discovered. Finding the treasure allows Joyce to invest in his native land, and finding the crown provides a connection to an ancient and respected past:

> Here and there, were inscriptions in strange character . . . 'Ogham! – one of the oldest and least known of writings,' said Dick, when the light fell on them as he raised the lantern.
>
> At the far end of the cave was a sort of slab or bracket . . . Norah went towards it, and called us to her with a loud cry . . . In her hand she held an ancient crown of strange form. (p. 241)

The crown thus underscores Norah's Irishness and reinforces that she is no persecuted Gothic heroine. In a reversal of conventional gender roles, she saves Arthur from the bog: 'But Norah bent forward . . . and grasped my coat collar in her strong hands. Love and despair lent her additional strength, and with one last great effort she pulled me upward – and in an instant more I lay on the rock safe and in her arms' (p. 228). The reference to Norah's strength seems anomalous, but Stoker repeats it at the conclusion when Dick erects a memorial on that spot:

> Round its base were sculptured the history of the mountain from its legend of the King of Snakes down to the lost treasure and the rescue of myself . . . The legend on the stone was:

Norah Joyce
A Brave Woman
On this spot
By her Courage and Devotion
Saved a man's life. (p. 246)

The emphasis on female strength signifies that Norah is no persecuted Gothic maiden. Like Mina in *Dracula* and Diana in 'The Chain of Destiny', Stoker's young women often defy the Gothic conventions of women as persecuted maidens or predators.

While Stoker distinguishes Norah from the conventional Gothic heroine, he also reminds readers that she is uncanny, primarily because she is Irish. Before Severn and Norah can marry, she must be educated like other women and, therefore, less strange. Indeed, Arthur's and Norah's correspondence must pass the scrutiny of the schoolmistress:

> It was hard not to be able to tell her . . . I loved her, but it had been expressly arranged . . . that I should only write in such a manner as would pass . . . the censorship of the schoolmistress. 'I must be,' said Norah . . . 'exactly as the other girls are – and, of course, I must be subject to the same rules'. (p. 245)

When she returns, Arthur sees 'a peerless beauty . . . Every natural grace and quality seemed developed to the full. Every single grace of womanhood . . . every subtle manifestation of high breeding – every stamp of the highest culture' (p. 247). The wild peasant girl who had rescued him from the bog, though, seems gone forever.

In 'The Curious Case of the Miltonic Vampire' Maggie Kilgour comments that Gothic focuses on the unfamiliar:[22]

> As Ian Duncan has argued, the Gothic . . . reflects a national culture in which 'The distinction between what is foreign and what is native in history seems hard to maintain . . . the alien and the familiar, the natural and the unnatural or supernatural, are richly confused . . .' It seems striking that so many British Gothic writers are not 'English': Stoker, Wilde, Maturin, Le Fanu, Polidori, Stevenson.[23]

Norah's education is one more way Stoker uses conventions he had inherited to focus on other issues entirely.

The Watter's Mou'

The Watter's Mou is a slighter story if only because it is so much shorter.[24] Hughes, in the *Bibliography*, notices 'sporadic outbursts' of Gothic elements.[25] However, this chapter demonstrates that Stoker continues his movement away from conventional Gothic. Like *The Snake's Pass*, it modifies Gothic conventions to focus on plausible human characters and reveals that greed and the normal events of the natural world can be as horrifying as supernatural forces.

Among the Gothic elements that Stoker adapts in this work are the villain, terrifying and overwhelming weather conditions that threaten to overpower human characters, a dark and mysterious woman and violent and emotional responses to everyday events. As with *The Snake's Pass*, these Gothic elements encourage readers to see evil in their own world rather than focus on something supernatural.

The villain, Solomon Mendoza, resembles Murdock. Not only does he have the 'hard, cruel, white face' (p. 180) that often characterizes the Gothic villain but he also shares the villain's desire to take advantage of people who are down on their luck, in this case the heroine's father. A fisherman 'who had seen days more prosperous', MacWhirter borrowed against his fishing boat until it 'was so heavily mortgaged that at any moment he might lose his entire possession' (p. 169). Indeed, the loss seems inevitable because Mendoza has 'the reputation of being as remorseless as he was rich' (p. 169). To save his boat and his livelihood, MacWhirter is persuaded to smuggle goods for Mendoza, as Maggie explains to Willy Barrow, who is both her fiancé and, as chief boatman in the preventive service, someone pledged to uphold the law against smuggling:

> 'Indeed, I'm thinkin' that it's just because that he is respeckit that Mendoza wants him to help him. He kens weel that nane would suspeck father' . . . here she clipped her lover close in her arms . . . and her breath came hot in his face till it made him half drunk with a

voluptuous intoxication . . . 'he kens that father, my father, would never be harmt by my lover!' (p. 182)

Unlike the intrusive and seemingly omnipresent Murdock, however, Mendoza remains in the shadows, sending his minions to do his dirty work. When Maggie urges her father and brother to throw the smuggled goods overboard and return home, one of these underlings cautions: 'Nothing overboard shall be thrown. These belongs . . . to Mendoza. If they be touched he closes on your boat and ruin it is for you' (p. 200). Lacking the supernatural abilities of Dracula or Tera, Mendoza nonetheless causes the deaths of the lovers and the increasing impoverishment of a marginalized group.

In addition to featuring a character whose greed resembles the power of the Gothic villain, *The Watter's Mou'* also takes place in a place where nature threatens its inhabitants. Commentary on Stoker often explores the presence of the sea in his fiction. Indeed, in *From the Shadow of Dracula*, Paul Murray cites one of Stoker's contemporaries who suggests that Stoker has two subjects, the sea and the supernatural:

> The anonymous author of a profile of Stoker in the *Literary World* in 1905 divided his fiction into two categories, the supernatural and the marine, with *The Watter's Mou'* (1895), *The Mystery of the Sea* and *The Man* specimens of the latter, 'for they all possess a paramount attraction in their sea-scapes and sea-scenes'.[26]

In *The Un-Dead: The Legend of Bram Stoker and Dracula*, Peter Haining and Peter Tremayne demonstrate that *The Watter's Mou'* is an 'authentic portrait of the coast and its people' as well as the first Stoker book to 'reveal his very real interest in . . . strange geographical formations: the selfsame kind of grotesque rock formations that are depicted around Castle Dracula in the Transylvanian mountains'.[27] Stoker had revealed his interest in landscape in *The Snake's Pass*, but Haining and Tremayne demonstrate the unique power of his marine landscapes. The story opens by describing nature at its most powerful:

> It threatened to be a wild night. All day banks of sea-fog had come and gone, sweeping on shore with the south-east wind, which is so fatal at Cruden Bay . . . From the . . . sea came a ceaseless muffled roar, which

seemed . . . most full of dangerous import when it came through the mystery of the driving fog. Whenever the fog-belts would lift or disperse, or disappear inland before the gusts of wind, the sea would look as though swept with growing anger; for though there were neither big waves as during a storm, nor a great swell as after one, all the surface of the water as far as the eye could reach was covered with little waves tipped with white. Closer together grew these waves as the day wore on, the angrier ever the curl of the white water where they broke. In the North Sea it does not take long for the waves to rise; and . . . it was taken for granted that there would be wild work on the coast before the night was over. (p. 166)

If the opening speaks of danger, a second passage focuses on nature as a death dealer:

'The Watter's Mou'? To try to get in there in this wind would be to court sudden death. Why, lass, it would take a man all he knew to get out from there, let alone get in, in this weather! And then the chances would be ten to one that he'd be dashed to pieces on the rocks beyond,' and he pointed to where a line of sharp rocks rose between the billows on the south side of the inlet. Truly it was a fearful-looking place . . . for the great waves broke on the rocks with a loud roaring, and . . . they could see the white lines as the waters poured down to leeward in the wake of the heaving wave. The white cluster of rocks looked like a ghostly mouth opened to swallow whatever might come in touch. (p. 183)

A third passage reveals that Nature dominates human beings: 'In such a mystery of darkness as lay before, above, and around her, her own personality seemed as nought. Truly there is an instinct of one's own littleness which becomes consciously manifest in the times when Nature puts forth her might' (p. 191). Danger, magnitude, mystery, darkness and the presence of something awe-inspiring. It is almost as though Stoker were checking off Gothic connections with the natural world. Nonetheless, he never tips the balance towards any-thing supernatural or implausible. Having grown up by the sea and travelled widely, Stoker knew how powerful nature could be.[28]

Stoker has a surprisingly good eye for nature, a characteristic that has received surprisingly little critical commentary. His female characters, on the other hand, often attract critical attention, and Maggie MacWhirter shares some traits with Gothic villainesses. Murray, for example, comments on her doubleness, observing that she 'seems to herself to be two people and is capable of behaviour that is predatory as well as sweetly feminine'. Her Berserker blood connects her to Dracula: 'The historical Berserkers, savage warrior gangs of Norse and Germanic history, had contributed to ... the werewolf legend ... In *Dracula*, the Count proudly identifies his Szekely ancestry with them and personally shares many of the attributes of a werewolf.'[29] Maggie, however, seems less a predator, so her Berserker background reinforces primarily her determination.

What links Maggie to various Gothic villainesses including Mathilde and Carmilla is a voluptuousness uncommon in Stoker's heroines. Murray comments that her dark side 'expresses itself in sexual advances which sometimes anticipate those of the female vampires towards Jonathan Harker in Castle Dracula, as well as an attempt to lure Willie into wrong doing for her father's sake'.[30] The following passage reveals her voluptuousness:

> She drew Willy close to her ... and whispered to him in a low sweet voice, that thrilled with emotion:
> 'Willy, Willy, darlin'; ye wouldna see harm come to my father' ... and in a wave of tumultuous, voluptuous passion she kissed him full in the mouth. Willy felt ... half dazed. Love has its opiates that soothe and stun even in the midst of their activity. He clasped Maggie close ... and for a moment their hearts beat together and their mouths breathed the same air. (p. 180)

One might argue that Maggie seduces Willy into following her to his death:

> Then he looked down and saw ... tossed high upon the summit of the wave, a mass that ... looked like a tangle of wreckage ... twirling in the rushing water round a dead woman, whose white face was set in an aureole of floating hair. Without a word ... Willy Barrow sprang out on the projecting point of rock, and plunged down into the rushing wave whence he could meet that precious wreckage and grasp it tight. (p. 222)

Unlike the vampire-women in Dracula's castle, however, she wants to save her father's good name. She is thus a protector rather than a predator. Indeed, although *The Watter's Mou'* concludes with the deaths of its hero and heroine, it is more romance than Gothic in its focus on the power of love:

> There, on the very spot whence the boat had set sail on its warning errand, lay its wreckage, and tangled in it the body of the noble girl who had steered it – her brown hair floating wide and twined round the neck of Sailor Willy, who held her tight in his dead arms.
>
> The requiem of the twain was the roar of the breaking waves and the screams of the white birds that circled round the Watter's Mou'. (pp. 223–4)

A true romance would conclude with the marriage of the young couple, not their deaths.

The Shoulder of Shasta

The Shoulder of Shasta, published by Constable in 1895, is another romance.[31] Roth, who divides Stoker's fiction into romances and tales of horror, does not mention it in her discussion, but there is no question that *Shasta*, with its failed and successful love affairs, falls under her general definition of romance:

> All of Stoker's novels are romances in the sense that all depict the forming of couples, the conflicts and misunderstandings between partners (or, in the cases of the horror tales, problems occasioned by the forces of evil), and the overcoming of difficulties in resolutions of happy marriages ... Heroines require rescue from compromising situations, or from the sea, a bog, or a vampire; heroes learn to understand the true nature of Woman. On the whole ... the pure romances are far less interesting than the tales of horror, those novels which include mystery and the preternatural and which employ the Gothic components of horror and the uncanny.[32]

Roth adds that the horror tales often include romance plots, adding that 'their major and characteristic effects and achievements result from the subordination and incorporation of the romance plots into the suspense and general uncanniness of the Gothic genre'.[33]

Although *Shasta* immediately precedes *Dracula*, Stoker's biographers and scholars generally ignore it. Harry Ludlam observes only that Stoker glimpsed Mount Shasta while on tour and jotted down another story idea before the tour was over.[34] Murray also points to the significance of the setting, observing that Stoker would have 'known the scenery around San Francisco . . . from his travels in the United States', but adds that the setting 'was inspired to some extent by E. Marston's 1886 book, with which Stoker was familiar, *Frank's Ranche or My Holiday in the Rockies*'.[35] Most interested in similarities between Stoker and his heroine, Murray notes that both were invalids and adds that Stoker invests Esse with his enthusiasm for the theatre as well as his youthful study of Swedenborg, who 'posited that God is the life within all creation. There is an absolute unity of God in both essence (*essentia*) and being (*esse*). Stoker's use of Esse as the name for his Swedenborgian character can be seen as a conscious echo of this philosophical strand.'[36]

Hughes, Louis S. Warren, Hopkins and Alan Johnson, who annotated and introduced the recent reprint of Stoker's most American work, have more to say.[37] Hughes, in *Beyond Dracula*, explores Grizzly Dick as an example of masculinity and American uncouthness, noting that he is 'socially presumptuous, but there is no doubt . . . that his intentions are honourable. It is the relationship between his intentions and the context in which he has been placed that is faulty.'[38] Interested in exploring the connection between Dick and Buffalo Bill Cody, Warren comments on Stoker's thoughts on imperialism, racial issues and the growing power of the United States. Of the scholars who have written about it, Hopkins is the most interesting though she lumps it with *Miss Betty* and *The Primrose Path* as 'the weakest and most disregarded of Stoker's . . . fictions', noting primarily that these works are useful for what they reveal about *Dracula*.[39] In particular, she points out similarities between Esse and Lucy, concluding that both suffer from 'disturbed nights' and comments on Stoker's interest in American characters: 'From 1883, the Lyceum company, and Stoker with it, toured America almost annually, and this is reflected in novels like *The Shoulder of Shasta* and *Lady Athlyne*, as well as in the important role played by the Texan Quincey Morris in *Dracula*.'[40] In his introduction, Johnson underlines the fact that Stoker wrote *Dracula* and *Shasta* at the same time:

> *The Shoulder of Shasta* is essentially a romance. The novel has a purport-
> edly realistic Californian setting, considerable ... humour, an exciting
> interlude of high adventure, and a rather close, careful study of the
> developing thoughts and feelings of the heroine ... It was published by
> Constable as light reading ... and ... it is an intriguing and informative
> resource for readers who aim to understand Bram Stoker and ... *Dracula*,
> which he had outlined as early as 1890 and published in 1897. (p. 10)

Furthermore, Hopkins and Johnson comment that this insubstantial romance reveals Stoker's interest in international politics, suggesting meat beneath the fluff. No one else has commented on its admittedly rare Gothic elements, but what especially interests me is that Stoker adapts Gothic elements to focus on contemporary issues: changing roles for women; the relationship between the United States, then emerging as a major political power, and England; the mysteries of nature; and the threatening qualities of primitive people. There is no reason to summon supernatural monsters or human villains when the real world poses its own threats.

Shasta, to return to Roth's definition, is definitely a romance that involves the forming of couples and concludes with the anticipated marriage of its youthful heroine. Esse has come to California for her health, and she and her former governess Miss Gimp believe them-selves to be in love with Grizzly Dick. Both eventually come to their senses, however, discovering that this crude child of nature is best left in the wild, and the novel concludes with Esse's discovering her soul-mate, the English painter Reginald Hampden.

Moreover, Stoker manipulates standard Gothic convention by having the heroine rescued from an overwhelming predicament, this time a mother bear and two cubs which Esse encounters while sketching in the forest. Even though a protective bear is nothing like a Gothic villain, Esse reacts like the persecuted maiden as she lies waiting for something to happen: 'But the suspense was awful. Her temples began to throb, and she felt an almost irresistible desire to scream out. Each instant the monster seemed to be coming closer, closer, till its great paw was stretched to tear her heart out' (p. 68).

At that moment Dick, conveniently in the forest, shoots the bear though not until she has broken his leg or before her maddened mate has come to her aid.

What is interesting about this scene is that Stoker changes the conventions of the hero and threatened maiden and thus points out that the world is changing for women. Instead of waiting passively for rescue, Esse becomes the rescuer:

> With a bound she . . . seized her revolver, and as the bear . . . hurled his vast body towards her, she fired once, twice, at random . . . The good fortune which now and again waits on novices seemed to have guided her aim, for one of the baleful eyes seemed . . . to become obliterated, and then to spout out blood. The grizzly quivered, and . . . fell over . . . in a heap. (p. 71)

Although Stoker attributes the second grizzly's death to beginner's luck, the fact that Esse half carries the seriously wounded Dick back to receive medical help is nothing short of heroic. Esse at this instance is clearly as much the hero of her own life as she is the persecuted maiden.

Stoker surrounds Esse and her entourage with physical dangers typical of a remote region populated primarily by wild animals and potentially hostile Native Americans and occasionally demonstrates how real these dangers are. For example, one Native American servant threatens Esse's mother as she lies in her hammock:

> The seconds seemed to be years, and in the agonizing suspense she could hear . . . the blood running through the veins of her neck. Then slowly and cautiously a pair of coppercoloured hands stole gently down the netting of the hammock, and with deft moment the fingers began inserting themselves under her head. (p. 50)

Mrs Elstree has every reason to feel apprehensive, having seen 'a chest full of scalps' that included 'a scalp of a woman's golden hair' (p. 50), and Dick has confessed that this same Indian had approached him to kill her for her gold.

While Stoker does not ignore the dangers associated with the wilderness, he seems less interested in the physical dangers faced by

the traditional Gothic heroine than in the potentially compromising social situations that threaten Esse and Miss Gimp. It seems that modern women are more capable of managing physical dangers than they are social entanglements.

There are parallels between the romantic confusions that Esse and her former governess face although Miss Gimp's situation is comic relief because it is so exaggerated and because she is an unlikely romantic heroine:

> Her hair was tightly screwed up over her rather bald forehead, and in her appearance seemed to be concentrated all that was hard in Nature, heightened by the resources of art ... Miss Gimp woke with a snort ... and, after scowling at Esse, turned over ... with a vicious dig at her pillow and an aggressive grunt. (pp. 41–2)

Despite her lack of experience with romance, Miss Gimp assumes Dick is courting her when she discovers gifts of game outside her window. While Esse slips away to laugh at 'the brain-sick, love-sick fancies of an old woman whose whole being seemed a mockery of the possibilities of love' (p. 57), the reality is more sinister. As Dick explains, the offerings were left for Miss Gimp's parrot: 'The old lady takes the Indians like she was a queen, an' all the while it ain't her they're after at all. There ain't one of them that wouldn't take and put a tomahawk through her skull or skelp her ... It's the parrot!' (p. 53). Mistaking both the lover and the love object and treating Native Americans with contempt, Miss Gimp risks losing her life rather than finding love.

Esse, on the other hand, risks social suicide when she mistakes gratitude to Dick for love and asks her guardian Peter Blyth to invite him to San Francisco to meet her friends. Even before he shows up, she realizes that a long-term relationship is impossible:

> Then again, Dick might not see his way to come to live in cities, and Esse had already begun to appreciate the refinements of life sufficiently well to make it impossible for her to even contemplate an isolated life in the woods or on the mountains. Picnicing, and especially in a honeymoon form, might be delightful, fascinating, of unspeakable joy; but such life, without relief, would never suit her as an unvarying constancy. (p. 108)

Furthermore, Dick embarrasses her, first by his inappropriate dress and behaviour and, subsequently, by threatening Blyth with a knife when he realizes that people are laughing at him. Because no one is hurt, this episode is comic, but it reinforces that true love can be found only between compatible people.

Although Dick's violent behaviour is untypical, Stoker may have modelled it on the violence of the Gothic villain, which Massimiliano Demata describes:

> The two protagonists of the novels, the Caliph Vathek and the Faustian wanderer John Melmoth, share the physical and psychological nature of the Gothic villain in that both are over-reaching, satanic characters in pursuit of a forbidden knowledge which will also be the cause of their tragic end.[41]

A heroic figure in the wilderness, Dick resembles the overreachers that Demata describes when he visits San Francisco, where Esse's house is 'the very centre of the most pleasant circle':

> Every stranger who arrived was . . . introduced to her, and not a few found an excuse for prolonging their stay . . . to share again her charming hospitality . . . There was a constant succession of luncheons, dinners, balls, picnics, and all those harmless gatherings . . . which have a charm . . . in their freedom and the relaxing of the bonds of conventionality. (p. 109)

After visiting Esse's home, Dick is content to return to his mountains:

> Let me get back to the b'ars an' the Injuns. I'm more to home with them than I am here. Be easy, Little Missy, an' ye too, all ye ladies and gentlemen; it'll be no pleasant thinkin' for me . . . away among the mountings, that when I kem down to 'Frisco, meanin' to do honour to a young lady . . . I couldn't keep my blasted hands off my weppins in the midst of a crowd of women! Durn the thing! I ain't fit to go heeled inter decent kempany! (p. 124)

Leaving Esse in Reginald's care, Dick returns to Shasta. He may not fit into Esse's crowd, but they quickly accept him as a natural gentleman rather than an overreacher and predator, and the novel concludes with a reference to him: 'There was about him something so fresh, and wild, and free – so noble a simplicity and manhood, that more than one woman present did not wonder that Esse had asked him to come down to 'Frisco' (p. 128).

Even though Dick returns quietly to his mountain, it is important to see him, along with Quincey Morris and Elias P. Hutcheson ('The Squaw'), as representative Americans. Dick is unthreatening because he is content to remain in his place, but Morris and Hutcheson are punished for taking frontier behaviour to Europe and, in Quincey's case, attempting to integrate into that society, a response that may reveal Stoker's apprehension at the rising power of the United States.

So far it is obvious that Stoker adapts typical Gothic elements, including the overreaching villain and the persecuted maiden, to focus on contemporary issues. He is closer to traditional Gothic when he describes the sublime landscape surrounding Shasta and depicts other aspects of the natural world that threaten to overwhelm his human characters. The wilderness around Shasta corresponds to Burke's descriptions of the sublime, with the narrator initially focusing on vastness:

> Beyond, in the distance, rose the mighty splendour of Shasta Mountain, its snow-covered head standing clear and stark into the sapphire sky, with its foothills a mass of billowy green, and its giant shoulders seemingly close at hand ... but of infinite distance when compared with the foreground, or the snowy summit.
>
> There is something in great mountains which seems now and then to set at defiance all the laws of perspective. The magnitude of the quantities, the transparency of cloudless skies, the lack of regulating sense of the spectator's eye in dealing with vast dimensions, all tend to make optical science like a child's fancy. Up at the present height, nearly three thousand feet, the bracing air began to tell on their spirits. (pp. 25–6)

This passage might have come directly from Edmund Burke, who noted that greatness of 'dimension, is a powerful cause of the sublime' and also that magnificence 'is likewise a source of the sublime'.[42] While Burke explores the aesthetic response to the sublime, he and Stoker are more interested in the impact of such overwhelming settings on human emotion. For example, the awestruck Esse observes 'the great ghostly dome of Shasta seemed to gleam out with a new, silent power' (p. 33):

> And then her eye lit on the mighty curve of the mountain top, whose edges, as the high sun took them, were fringed with dazzling light. She turned to her mother, and with a sort of hysterical cry fell over against her, clasping her in her arms and hiding her tears on her bosom. (p. 46)

Such scenes threaten to overwhelm her with emotion while she and her entourage remain in the wilderness around Mount Shasta.

Stoker's vision of the natural world resembles Ann Radcliffe's awe-inspiring vistas and also includes suggestions of horror and the uncanny that are characteristic of the post-Darwinian world. No longer does nature appear the creation of a beneficent deity or a friend when someone is in danger of being killed by bears or scalped by the human residents of this strange and alien world. Clive Bloom, who edited *Gothic Horror: A Guide for Students and Readers*, comments that the Gothic presents the world as diabolic, 'a landscape in which a demonized nature and a malevolent human nature could be plotted within the artifice of a new aesthetic outlook and a new literary genre', and Stoker's California is both breathtaking and diabolic.[43] Lurking in the beautiful landscape are wild beasts and wild people, both of whom threaten the human characters.

Joseph Grixti, in *Terrors of Uncertainty: The Cultural Contexts of Horror Fiction*, and Linda Dryden, in '"The coming terror": Wells's outcast London and the modern Gothic', explore the Gothic emphasis on exotic places and things.[44] Grixti comments on 'their implicit distinction from everyday reality – their exotic settings, stereotypical or larger-than-life characters, unusual or anachronistic situations'.[45] Dryden looks at social commentary in *fin de siècle* Gothic:

> Gothic fiction is often a fiction of transformations where identity is unstable and sanity a debatable state of being. The Gothic of the fin de siècle itself underwent something of a transformation. Located in the historically remote past or in isolated, wild locations, amid the suggestive relics of an ancient past, the traditional Gothic was a fiction about history, and about geography. Yet, at the end of the nineteenth

century, a new Gothic mode emerged, a modern Gothic, whose narratives focused on the urban present, refracting contemporary concerns through the lens of a literature of terror.[46]

Even though *Shasta* is set in an isolated, wild location, it is not so remote that readers will not consider England's relationship with its former colony and the wild inhabitants of that relatively new land.

In addition to the terror of being stalked by bears and Native Americans, there is also the horror associated with Miss Gimp's store of rotting meat. In fact, Stoker's narrator spares no disgusting detail:

> When they went into Miss Gimp's room there was no possibility of mistaking the odour. Even a properly arranged larder is not always the most pleasant of places, but a lady's bedroom is in no way adapted for the storage of dead flesh. Esse for a moment felt qualmish ... Miss Gimp pulled out the lowest drawer of all and disclosed to Esse's gaze a horrible looking leg of deer meat all blue, damp and sodden; and which had been rudely hacked from the carcase. The look and the smell almost turned Esse faint. (pp. 58–9)

Such attention to disgusting sights and odours is common in contemporary horror fiction, so much so that Stephen King, in *Bare Bones: Conversations on Terror with Stephen King*, observes that his own work operates on three levels:

> There's terror on top, the finest emotion any writer can induce; then horror; and, on the very lowest level of all, the gag instinct of revulsion. Naturally, I'll try to terrify you first, and if that doesn't work, I'll try to horrify you, and if I can't make it there, I'll try to gross you out. I'm not proud.[47]

Robert Mighall's study of Victorian Gothic observes that early Gothic novels, including *Castle of Otranto*, *A Sicilian Romance* or *Melmoth* never mention smell while Stoker's novels include numerous references to bad odours, including Dracula's breath and the stench of the white worm's underground lair. He suggests that this change stems from modern attitudes to hygiene:

In Stoker, the narrator gropes for analogies gleaned from 'clinical' or sanitary situations and experiences to evoke that which cannot quite be described ... The new Gothic landscape of the slum thus demands an appropriate language to evoke its horrors, and employs the familiar Gothic trope of the unspeakable.[48]

Native American attitudes to uncooked meat are one way Stoker identifies them as primitive and Other, closer to animals than to civilized human beings.

The novels that precede *Dracula* demonstrate Stoker gaining experience as a writer as well as developing as a master of the Gothic. Judging from the novels explored in this chapter, however, most readers find it difficult to anticipate the Gothic masterpiece Stoker produced a mere two years after *The Shoulder of Shasta*.

2

Dracula: *Stoker's Gothic Masterpiece*

&⊃)&⊄&

Despite my enthusiasm for Stoker's fiction and agreement with Andrew Maunder that readers cannot see him as the author of only one novel, the typical reader of this study will be interested primarily in *Dracula*, Stoker's acknowledged masterpiece and a work generally identified as Gothic.[1] Furthermore, while Stoker's other works are sometimes difficult to locate, *Dracula* has never been out of print, has been translated into numerous foreign languages, is available in a number of inexpensive paperback editions, many of them annotated by scholars, and has inspired more movies, television shows and other popular culture than any other Gothic work.[2]

Attempting to explain its popularity, Barbara Belford notes in her biography of Stoker, that Stoker spent more than seven years on it, a degree of care unusual for him:

> His first notes were made on March 8, 1890, on the completion of *The Snake's Pass* ... the last date recorded was March 17, 1896, after publication of *The Watter's Mou* and *The Shoulder of Shasta*. By February of 1892 he had sketched out a plot, placing events in the next calendar year.[3]

Dracula was published in 1897, and scholars, studying his notes, the typescript of the novel and other sources, comment on the numerous changes he made.[4] Thanks to careful work by Elizabeth Miller and Robert Eighteen-Bisang, readers can study his notes in *Bram Stoker's*

Notes for Dracula: A Facsimile Edition.[5] The notes and accompanying commentary provide fascinating insights into Stoker's research and how he transformed the vampire myth and other Gothic conventions into a work that haunts readers more than a century later. Readers can also access parts of the manuscript through *The New Annotated Dracula*, edited by Leslie S. Klinger, 'the first annotated version ... to make use of the manuscript ... Prior to 2005, only a few pages ... had been examined by scholars.'[6]

Even as I worked on this study, new scholarship appeared to supplement the already extensive scholarship on *Dracula*. Commenting on the extent of this scholarship, Klinger observes, 'Miller's *Bram Stoker's Dracula: A Documentary Volume* (2005) lists in its "Checklist for Reference and Further Reading" over "250 works of *Dracula* criticism and dozens of bibliographical references and annotated editions"' (p. 540).[7] Equally interesting are the numerous methodologies scholars use. Klinger's chapter, 'Sex, lies, and blood: *Dracula* in academia', provides an overview of scholarly treatments.[8] J. P. Riquelme, whose edition is designed to introduce students to scholarly approaches, revised and updated his introduction for the *Documentary Volume* and provides the following overview:

> Beginning in the 1950s and increasingly since the 1970s, it has drawn responses from academic critics interested in a wide range of topics and perspectives, including historical and literary sources, narrative technique, psychoanalysis, gender roles, anthropology, Victorian culture, capitalism, the history of Gothic writing, poststructuralism, imperialism, postcolonialism, and Irish studies.[9]

Many of these approaches touch on the Gothic, to which Murray notes *Dracula* was linked from the beginning:

> The *Daily Mail* ranked Stoker's powers above those of Mary Shelley and Edgar Allan Poe, as well as ... *Wuthering Heights*. The *Spectator* too related Stoker to his predecessors ... feeling that he had set out 'to eclipse all previous efforts in the domain of the horrible', including those of Wilkie Collins and Sheridan Le Fanu.[10]

Stoker's mother, according to biographers the source of some frightening stories and legends that he transformed into literature, was one of the first to comment on the Gothic connection: 'no book since ... *Frankenstein* or indeed any other at all has come near yours in originality, or terror ... I have read much but I have never met a book like it at all in its terrible excitement.'[11]

Among recent scholars, Scott Vander Ploeg argues that *Dracula* is not Gothic, but he is the exception that proves the rule.[12] More typical of contemporary scholarship are Scott Brewster and Clive Bloom; Scott Brewster describes *Dracula* as 'the paradigmatic Gothic text'.[13] Clive Bloom's Introduction to *Gothic Horror: A Guide for Students and Readers* observes, '*Dracula* is both a synthesis and a nostalgic revival of gothic themes'.[14] Jerrold E. Hogle, in 'Theorizing the Gothic', describes *Dracula* as 'the text most revived and reinterpreted by the theorizing of the Gothic over the last four decades'.[15] Robert Mighall goes further in *A Geography of Victorian Gothic Fiction: Mapping History's Nightmares*, characterizing *Dracula* as 'perhaps the most discussed of all Gothic novels. No other novel has been called on so often and with such urgency.'[16]

Furthermore, much of this commentary continues to note that, despite our familiarity and the fact that its eponymous character has been transformed into Count Chocula and The Count from *Sesame Street*, *Dracula* (the novel) remains Gothic rather than camp because it touches on mysterious forces that continue to frighten readers.[17] Roth devotes an entire section of her *Dracula* chapter to '*Dracula* as Gothic Fiction' and observes: '*Dracula* exerts a complex fascination owing both to Stoker's skill and to the enduring appeal of the Gothic genre of which it is a superb and instructive example.'[18]

Because so much commentary explores the desires and fears that *Dracula* addresses, this chapter addresses major Gothic issues in turn. Beginning with Stoker's narration, it explores what frightened Stoker and his contemporaries. Their enthusiasm for conquering new lands and people was undermined by the fear that conquered people might retaliate. Aware that women sought economic, political and sexual equality resulted in fear that equality would transform women into monsters, and Stoker's contemporaries also feared other changes in gender roles, a concern made more obvious during the trials of Stoker's friend Oscar Wilde. These fears of other races and classes as well as concerns about women and other marginalized peoples are generally classified as fear of the Other. Additionally, as western Europeans became more secular and committed to science and technology, they sometimes imagined potential dangers associated with these discoveries and the fear that science might supplant ethical and religious values. Simultaneously, as individuals celebrated a world in which traditional relationships disappeared, they also looked backward, sometimes nostalgically, more often apprehensively. All these concerns are coupled with the fact that characters in *Dracula*, confronting matters outside their comfort zone, question their sanity. The chapter concludes by examining how Stoker builds on and adapts Gothic conventions: a setting that embodies the past, nature as an awe-inspiring presence, a persecuted maiden, a villainous aristocrat who attempts to shape the world to his particular vision and doubles that cause readers to wonder exactly who and what produces fear.

Narrative strategy

One of *Dracula's* most interesting characteristics is Stoker's narration.[19] With the exception of the Dutch professor Abraham Van Helsing, the American Quincey Morris, Dracula and his three brides, Stoker's characters are English and, with the exception of Dracula and Arthur Holmwood, later Lord Godalming, middle class (physicians, lawyers and a teacher and aspiring journalist) and advocates of science, rationalism and modernity. While they occasionally mention religion, their journals, diaries, memos and letters merge with newspaper accounts to relate an unbelievable tale of their confrontation with a supernatural adversary and relic of a medieval past.

The first chapter has Jonathan Harker remark that trains in eastern Europe are rarely on time and that customs are strange and unpredictable, and the next chapters take him deeper and deeper into a mysterious landscape from which he barely escapes. Commenting on Stoker's narrative in 'The Narrative Method of *Dracula*', Seed examines *Dracula's* Gothic landscape and characters:

> The first four chapters . . . present a miniature pastiche-Gothic novel.
> In place of the Apennnes, as in . . . *The Mysteries of Udolpho*, we now

have the mountains of Transylvania. Although Dracula claims that his descendants stretch back to Attila . . . his literary pedigree is . . . more obvious. Like Montoni and Heathcliff, he is defined by his strength, pride, and recurring association with darkness.[20]

Exploring Stoker's narration, Maunder comments that what Stoker's contemporaries saw as fearful is 'packaged together in a fragmented narrative and sometimes confusing narrative structure'.[21] In *Dracula*, readers suspect something supernatural even before Harker watches Dracula 'crawl down the castle wall . . . *face down*, with his cloak spreading out around him like great wings' (p. 75, Stoker's italics), but the real horror begins when the narrators realize that this medieval monster is stalking them and their loved ones through London, which Maunder calls 'a stronghold of civilization but also a place that is extremely vulnerable to attack and can be a place of danger'.[22] It is one thing to encounter an uncanny being in an uncanny place, more frightening to encounter that same being in one's own back yard. The narrators are slow to realize the nature of the problem, however, for their trust in science and rationalism gets in the way, as Van Helsing reminds his former student:

> You are clever man, friend John; you reason well . . . but you are too prejudiced. You do not let your eyes see nor your ears hear, and that which is outside your daily life is not of account to you . . . there are things which you cannot understand, and yet which are. (p. 279)

Readers can identify with their unwillingness to believe what is essentially unbelievable, and the narrative structure constantly asks readers to reflect on what the narrators see. Jean Marigny argues that the narrative is deliberately confusing and fragmented because Stoker wants readers to confront mystery:

> It appears that the narrative framework of *Dracula* is meant to confuse and puzzle . . . In keeping with the tradition of Gothic masterpieces like *The Monk* . . . Stoker makes use of many different narrative voices . . . the only linear narrative is Jonathan Harker's journal at the very beginning.[23]

Because, with the exception of those first chapters, *Dracula* consists of fragments by numerous individuals, many of them with different perspectives, readers must assemble matters for themselves to make sense of *Dracula's* world.

Stoker confronts readers with questions of mystery and truth at the beginning, which opens with an unnamed editor who points to the difficulty in discerning truth: 'all needless matters have been eliminated, so that a history almost at variance with the possibilities of later-day belief may stand forth as simple fact' (p. 26). Jonathan Harker concludes the narration by commenting on its near impossibility:

> It was almost impossible to believe that the things which we had seen with our own eyes and heard with our own ears were living truths. Every trace of all that had been was blotted out. The castle stood as before, reared high above a waste of desolation. (p. 512)

He reinforces its implausibility by referring to their story as 'a mass of type-writing' and 'hardly one authentic document' (p. 512).

Because of Stoker's narration, readers question the truth even though numerous accounts swear to its veracity, agreeing that the impossible is possible. Indeed, in the second half, the narrators essentially collaborate on a single story without Stoker losing sight of each narrator's uniqueness.

Immersed in mystery, readers must solve it on their own terms at least in the beginning when the narrators do not understand what they encounter. For example, shortly before he escapes, the normally rational Harker responds violently at finding Dracula in his chapel:

> There was a mocking smile on the bloated face which seemed *to drive me mad*. This was the being I was helping to transfer to London, where, perhaps for centuries to come he might . . . satiate his lust for blood, and create a new and ever-widening circle of semi-demons to batten on the helpless. The very thought *drove me mad*. A terrible desire came upon me to rid the world of such a monster. (p. 100, my italics)

The references to madness underline the fact that Harker's behaviour is far from rational. A prisoner in Dracula's castle, Harker fears for his life and sanity, escaping shortly after the scene above. Readers next hear of him through a letter that reinforces madness, observing that he has been 'suffering from a violent brain fever' (p. 166) for six weeks. The letter cautions Mina: 'Be careful with him always that there may be nothing to excite him . . . for a long time to come; the traces of such an illness . . . do not lightly die away' (p. 167). Learning of literal madness, readers may question what Harker revealed earlier. Indeed, much in the text reminds readers to question what they read.

Even more dramatic is Seward's reaction to Lucy, to whom he had proposed earlier. Watching her throw down a child that 'she had clutched strenuously to her breast', he confesses he could kill her 'with savage delight' (p. 304). Such violence is unexpected and out of character for someone who describes himself as civilized and modern but who also questions his sanity: 'What does it all mean? I am beginning to wonder if my long habit of life amongst the insane is beginning to tell upon my own brain' (p. 212).

The emphasis on madness might cause readers to distrust the narrators, especially Harker or Van Helsing who falls into a fit of hysteria that troubles Seward. Nonetheless, these individuals, all of whom question their sanity, construct a narrative that pits them against individuals they characterize as monstrous and Other: Seward quotes Harker who says that 'by dinner-time they will be able to show a whole connected narrative. He thinks that in the meantime I should see Renfield . . . a sort of index to the coming and going of the Count' (p. 320). By this point, the narrators are collaborating on a crusade against Dracula and his minions which they defend among themselves: 'A year ago which of us would have received such a possibility, in the midst of our scientific, skeptical, matter-of-fact nineteenth century?' (p. 334).

Stoker's narration is masterful because it emphasizes that life is mysterious and also demonstrates the power of group thinking. Perhaps the most important questions readers should ask are the following. How do we respond to the narrative? And what causes rational and civilized narrators to respond with such violence? Stoker's Preface to the Icelandic edition of Dracula (published in 1901 as *Makt Myrkkanna, Powers of Darkness*) treats Gothic mystery differently and suggests he had changed his mind on the topic.[24] In the translation, Stoker identifies himself as the editor.[25] And in the Preface to the Icelandic edition he indicates 'no doubt whatever that the events here described really took place' though he continues to emphasize the mysteriousness of what had happened: 'And I am further convinced that they [the events here described] must always remain to some extent incomprehensible, although continuing research in psychology and natural science may ... give logical explanations of such strange happenings which, at present, neither scientists nor the secret police can understand.'[26] The Icelandic edition thus privileges science though it concludes with an allusion to *Hamlet*, act I, scene iv, that emphasizes mystery: 'there are more things in heaven and earth / than are dreamt of in your philosophy'.[27] Klinger's edition follows the same line of thinking, arguing that the events in *Dracula* actually occurred.

While readers can appreciate Klinger's careful piecing together of details and pointing out of contradictions, I believe that Stoker deliberately emphasizes what is mysterious and frightening, not what can be explained. That strategy, which worked in 1897, is equally effective today as Dracula and his female minions become the incarnations of what was mysterious and frightening to his narrators and his readers. Even though neither Stoker's contemporaries nor readers today believe supernatural monsters would suck their blood, the circumstances these monsters evoke are frightening. Nonetheless, judging from his letter to Gladstone, which states that the 'horrors and terrors ... are calculated to "cleanse the mind by pity & terror"', Stoker believed *Dracula* was cathartic and hoped that dramatizing fears would help readers work through them.[28]

Fear of the Other: race, class and the British Empire

A number of scholars comment on fear of the Other in Gothic literature. Judith Halberstam, in 'Technologies of Monstrosity,' describes *Dracula* as 'a composite of otherness'.[29] Glennis Byron explores a globalized fear of the Other during the 1890s:

> While the specific nature of the threatening other varies among different *fin-de-siècle* Gothic texts, the 'norm' that is threatened ... is located

firmly within late Victorian Britain. While earlier Gothic fictions are usually distanced in both time and space, late nineteenth-century Gothic tends to insist ... on 'the modernity of the setting'.[30]

Byron emphasizes that these texts frighten because of their immediacy, a tendency that continues with contemporary writers like Stephen King and Dean Koontz or even makers of video games that confront players with monstrous opponents.[31]

If Byron focuses on immediacy, Avril Horner and Sue Zlosnik, in 'Comic Gothic', comment on what we fear:

> The effect ... is to generate fear: the serious Gothic work challenges the reader with the question 'What are you afraid of?' and, in so doing, evokes feelings of horror, terror and revulsion. Internal fears are frequently embodied in external threats ... While concerned, at the level of plot, to reestablish 'good', the serious Gothic text is marked by an obsession with darkness, death and 'evil' as a supernatural force. Thus, serious Gothic writing is frequently religious in the broadest sense of the term.[32]

While neither Byron nor the Horner and Zlosnik discussion uses the term Other, familiarity with Gothic texts suggests that people fear what they perceive as different from themselves, often labelling it not as exotic or interesting but as evil.

Harker's diary introduces fears that Stoker develops as the novel progresses. At the beginning Harker is off on his first independent professional adventure. Even before he starts to fear for his life, however, he comments on how different eastern Europe is: 'The impression I had was that we were leaving the West and entering the East' (p. 28). Later he comments that the area where he is travelling is 'one of the wildest and least known portions of Europe' (p. 29), a place where 'every known superstition in the world is gathered' (p. 30). Apprehensive about the racial and cultural Other before he encounters Dracula, Harker becomes more anxious when Dracula echoes what he had been thinking: 'We are in Transylvania; and Transylvania is not England. Our ways are not your ways, and there shall be to you many strange things' (p. 56).

Dracula brings Harker to Transylvania to learn English law, customs and language. Outside Transylvania, however, he is inevitably recognized as foreign, 'a stranger in a strange land' (p. 55).[33] He travels on Russian ships, is welcomed at Whitby by a band playing a French air (p. 135) and identifies himself as 'a foreign nobleman, Count de Ville' (p. 375). Indeed, Leatherdale, Halberstam, Malchow and Davison see him as not merely foreign, but Jewish.[34] Davison refers to the birth of Jewish nationalism in the 1880s and 1890s, noting that it occurred during 'the period of right-wing nationalism' and was a 'cause for concern for some Britons'.[35] Leatherdale detects anti-Semitism in the following passage: 'We found Hildesheim in his office, a Hebrew of rather the Adelphi Theatre type, with a nose like a sheep, and a fez' and underscores racial characteristics:[36]

> Racial issues punctuate this chapter. Having had Russian vessels transport Dracula to and from England, we now find his return to the East administered by a stereotypical Jew. Being in cahoots with Jews made Dracula yet more despicable to the average 1890s reader. Stoker was typical of his time when it came to anti-Semitism.[37]

Stoker's emphasis on Dracula's foreignness causes *Dracula* to be identified as a particular kind of *fin de siècle* Gothic literature, Imperial Gothic, by scholars who comment on Dracula's racial and cultural otherness. The best and most influential are Hughes, Stephen Arata and Patrick Brantlinger.[38] The latter attributes Imperial Gothic to 'an increasing emphasis on and anxiety about the British Empire'.[39]

Jimmie Cain and Athena Vrettos see Dracula as representing particular locations.[40] Cain argues that, worried by Russia's increasing power, Stoker creates Imperial Gothic fantasies about Russia and the Balkans in *Dracula* and *The Lady of the Shroud* and that 'English tourism and spiritualism mask a colonial agenda in a corner of the real world outside the empire's grasp'.[41] Vrettos calls Transylvania 'a substitute for the Dark Continent' and 'Europe's unconscious'.[42]

Furthermore, Harker sees Dracula not only as racially and culturally other but as representing a different way of life, an embodiment of the past. Not only does he live in a castle, he identifies himself as a hunter and a warrior: 'The warlike days are over. Blood is too precious a thing in these days of dishonourable peace; and the glories of the great races are as a tale that is told' (p. 69). Those differences allow Dracula's opponents to crusade against him and anyone else they perceive as threatening.

Dracula, Renfield and the women vampires are also perceived as Other because the narrators see them as animals. Their pointed canine teeth immediately link them to the animal world as Harker notes:

> There was a deliberate voluptuousness which was both thrilling and repulsive, and . . . she actually licked her lips *like an animal*, till I could see in the moonlight the moisture shining on the scarlet lips and on the red tongue as it lapped the *white sharp teeth*. (p. 81, my italics)

Similarly, Mina, seeing Dracula for the first time, is struck by his animal nature: 'His face was not a good face; it was hard, and cruel, and sensual, and his *big white teeth*, that looked all the whiter because his lips were so red, were pointed *like an animal's*' (p. 258, my italics). Having tracked Dracula to his home in Piccadilly, the narrators connect him to the animal realm: 'There was something so *panther-like* in the movement – something *so unhuman* that it seemed to sober us all from the shock of his coming' (p. 418, my italics). Finally, as Dracula escapes, Seward observes: 'As the Count saw us, a horrible sort of *snarl* passed over his face, showing the *eye-teeth long and pointed*. But the evil smile as quickly passed into a cold stare of *lion-like* disdain' (p. 419, my italics). Planning to track him to Transylvania, the narrators use Dracula's animal nature as an excuse to destroy him. Seward writes: 'I care for nothing . . . except to wipe out *this brute* from the face of creation. I would sell my soul to do it!' (p. 416, my italics). Seward sees similar behaviour in Lucy when she drops the child '*growling* over it *as a dog growls* over a bone' (p. 304, my italics). Work by naturalists such as Darwin and Huxley revealed the close relationship between humans and animals, but many preferred the older paradigm that imagined humans as entirely different from animals. Indeed, Stoker's narrators use imagery that suggests their fear of being connected to animals.

While vampires can be considered members of an entirely different species, Renfield appears surprisingly human when he identifies himself as a friend of Arthur's father or sacrifices himself to save Mina. Generally, however, animal traits dominate. Like Dracula who has power over lesser animals and even, at certain times, can become a wolf, a bat or a dog, Renfield controls animals. He has an uncanny ability to catch flies, spiders and sparrows, and he reveals his animal nature when cornered: 'When we closed in on him he fought *like a tiger*. He is immensely strong, and he was more like *a wild beast* than a man. I never saw a lunatic in such a paroxysm of rage before; and I hope I shall not again' (pp. 171–2, my italics). Later, Seward describes him 'lying on his belly on the floor licking up, *like a dog*, the blood which had fallen from my wounded wrist' (p. 220, my italics).

What connects these characters is that they are perceived as Other and, therefore, as something to be hated or feared. Renfield's madness links him temporarily with other characters who question their sanity, but his habit of eating flies, spiders and sparrows offsets that humanity. Identified as Other, Dracula and his Transylvanian brides, Lucy and Renfield are figures of fear and horror and can thus be eradicated.

Monstrous women and other gender concerns

The previous section emphasized that Stoker's narrators fear the racial, ethnic or species Other. While it is tempting to argue that Stoker shared those fears of eastern European Jews arriving in London, of Africans rising up against their conquerors, or of Germany or the United States gaining ascendancy, those arguments are more difficult to make.

It is equally difficult to argue that Stoker shared his characters' hostility towards assertive women because he created male characters who become anxious when women step outside traditional gender roles and revere women who adhere to them. Even Mina, in many ways the smartest of Dracula's opponents as well as someone who resembles the liberated New Woman, is appalled at her response to Dracula. Caught in her bedroom sucking blood from his breast, she confesses: 'I was bewildered, and strangely enough, I did not want to hinder him. I suppose it is a part of the horrible curse that such is, when his touch is on his victim' (p. 396). As the narrators race to Transylvania, she becomes more and more marginalized, and by the end of the novel totally silent. Seven years after their victory, the woman who assembled the documents that allowed them to destroy Dracula is no longer writing or typing or following train schedules. Instead, her male colleagues celebrate her maternal skills. 'This boy will some day know what a brave and gallant woman his mother is' (p. 512). It is as though she can no longer speak for herself.

Scholarly explorations of Stoker's women characters are so contradictory that a synthesis is difficult. While some scholars call him an out-and-out misogynist, others believe he supported the New Woman.[43] His treatment of women was what initially drew me to the novel. Horrified by the attack on Lucy, which I read as a kind of gang rape, I was equally appalled by Van Helsing's treatment of Dracula's brides. That Stoker has Mina criticize the New Woman also raised intriguing questions about the novel's social and historical context. My initial response was that Stoker's 'treatment of women . . . does not stem from his hatred of women in general but . . . from his ambivalent reaction to a topical phenomenon – the New Woman', and I still believe Stoker was thinking of the New Woman when he wrote *Dracula*.[44] Whatever he thought himself, he knew readers would react, and Mina is an educated woman with definite opinions on that movement.[45] She notes after a walk that she and Lucy had a hearty 'severe tea' and would 'have shocked the "New Woman" with our appetites' (p. 151), a phrase that suggests they are as athletic as the bicycle-riding New Women. Later she hints at the New Woman's desire for equality and possibly at her promiscuity:

> She has more colour in her cheeks . . . If Mr. Holmwood fell in love with her seeing her only in the drawing-room, I wonder what he would say if he saw her now. Some of the 'New Woman' writers will . . . start an idea that men and women should be allowed to see each other asleep before proposing or accepting. But I suppose the New Woman won't condescend . . . to accept; she will do the proposing herself. (p. 152)

The reference to 'do the proposing herself' echoes Sarah Grand's 1893 best-seller *The Heavenly Twins* (Grand is credited for coining the phrase 'New Woman') in which one of the eponymous twins proposes to her future husband. Mina shares certain characteristics with the New Woman, but she invests them with an assertiveness that makes her uncomfortable.

More uncomfortable with assertive behaviour, her male colleagues fear women who step outside traditional roles. Jonathan responds, for example, that Dracula's brides are not women at all: 'I am alone in the castle with those awful women. Faugh! Mina is a woman, and there is nought in common. They are devils of the Pit!' (p. 102).

Almost three decades after writing about Stoker and the New Woman, I still believe he was thinking about women who questioned their traditional roles, but I am less confident he shares his narrators' prejudices. Reading research done since 1982 (especially the *Notes* and the Belford and Murray biographies), as well as *The Man, Lady Athlyne* and *The Lady of the Shroud*, provides a broader context for *Dracula*. What is not in question, however, is that his narrators respond with horror to overt sexuality and violence.

The previous section demonstrates that Harker fears Dracula's brides because he sees them as more animal than human. Initially perceiving them as a respite from Dracula, 'three young women, ladies by their dress and manner' (p. 79), he becomes apprehensive about their sexual aggression: 'There was something about them that made me uneasy, some longing and at the same time some deadly fear. I felt in my heart a wicked, burning desire that they would kiss me with those red lips' (p. 80). Returning to Dracula's castle to purge it of evil, Van Helsing reinforces this sexuality when he locates the first bride: 'She lay in her Vampire sleep, so full of life and voluptuous beauty that I shudder as though I have come to do murder' (pp. 499–500). Just as Harker briefly forgot his commitment to Mina, Van Helsing is so entranced by the beautiful vampire that he forgets his objective until Mina's cry brings him back to reality: 'Certain it was that I was lapsing into sleep, the open-eyed sleep of one who yields to a sweet fascination, when there came through the snow-stilled air a long, low wail, so full of woe and pity that it woke me like the sound of a clarion' (p. 500).

It is difficult not to read the scene in which Van Helsing destroys Dracula's brides as hostile towards women, especially when he describes it as 'butcher work' (p. 502) or read the graphic description of Lucy's destruction. Roth observes that 'the portrait of Woman is increasingly negative ... Indeed, the horror and fascination of Stoker's later novels derive from their visions of Woman', and Arata argues that Tera, Teuta and Arabella represent archaic forces returning to disrupt modern life and notes that 'fear of women is never far from the surface of these novels'.[46]

Because Dracula's brides appear in fewer than a dozen pages, readers should avoid reading too much into them. Moreover, because the narrators also see them as either foreign or animal, one might argue that their depiction ought not be read as disparaging of women at all. Removing them from the picture, readers are left to wrestle with Stoker's portrayal of two major characters, Lucy and Mina.

Stoker introduces Lucy in letters to Mina, which reveal her as more shallow and frivolous than her serious and hard-working friend. The only child of wealthy parents, she has recently left school, and her letters refer to 'picture-galleries and for walks and rides in the park' (p. 105).[47] She apparently has little to do except wait for the right man to propose so she can settle down to traditional married life. Moreover, her letters provide no evidence of introspection or thoughts about her future, and that vapidity is reinforced by her mother's treatment of her. Not only has Lucy not been told that her mother is dying, she does not know that Mrs Westenra has arranged, despite her solicitor's protest, for Arthur to inherit her property. Commenting on this decision, Leatherdale notes how damaging it would be: 'Had Lucy opted against marrying Arthur, and survived, she would now be destitute.'[48] There is little evidence she would have understood the consequences of her mother's decision, and Brennan, writing about the New Woman in *Dracula* and *Nosferatu*, observes that she 'lacks the maturity typical New Woman characters exhibit'.[49]

Lacking maturity and self-awareness, Lucy nonetheless shares the New Woman's desire for sexual equality. Telling Mina about receiving three proposals, she wonders: 'Why can't they let a girl marry three men, or as many as want her, and save all this trouble?' (p. 110). Ironically, Lucy's wish for multiple husbands is granted when, after Dracula drains her blood, she receives transfusions from the men who had proposed to her and from Van Helsing. Arthur is comforted that the transfusion has made her his bride, but Van Helsing reinforces the sexual connection by telling Seward: 'Then this so sweet maid is a polyandrist' (p. 263), a word Miller argues was a euphemism for 'prostitute' in Stoker's time, citing as evidence the *Pall Mall Gazette*, 14 July 1887, asking to 'make the regulation of the movements of female polyandrists a police function'.[50]

Stoker makes Lucy less responsible for what happens by having her succumb to Dracula while sleepwalking, and she has only vague recollections of these encounters, which she welcomes when she is unconscious and rejects when she is conscious, a change that Seward observes without understanding its significance:

> It struck me as curious that the moment she became conscious she pressed the garlic flowers close . . . It was certainly odd that whenever she got into that lethargic state, with the stertorous breathing, she put the flowers from her; but that when she waked she clutched them close. (p. 243)

Similarly in a trance she attempts to seduce Arthur but, later, becoming conscious, thanks Van Helsing for rescuing Arthur.

After death transforms her, Lucy becomes more frightening to the male narrators when, in addition to aggressive sexuality, she reveals the same lack of maternal skills as Dracula's brides. Mina, on the other hand, is decidedly maternal. Meeting Arthur, she comforts him:

> I felt an infinite pity for him, and opened my arms unthinkingly. With a sob he laid his head on my shoulder, and cried like a wearied child . . . We women have something of the mother in us . . . I felt this big, sorrowing man's head resting on me, as though it were that of the baby that . . . may lie on my bosom, and I stroked his hair as though he were my own child. (p. 325)

She eventually mothers all the men with whom she comes in contact, and they celebrate her motherhood at the conclusion.

In addition, Van Helsing records Mina's response to the aggression of Dracula's brides: "'Come, sister. Come to us. Come! Come'" . . . I turned to . . . Mina, and my heart with gladness leapt . . . The terror in her sweet eyes, the repulsion, the horror, told a story . . . that was all of hope. God be thanked she was not, yet, of them' (p. 497). Mina's reticence may stem from having internalized the conventions of her culture, including reluctance to display emotion:

> Jonathan was holding me by the arm, the way he used to . . . I felt it very improper, for you can't go on . . . teaching etiquette and decorum

to other girls without the pedantry of it biting into yourself a bit; but
... he was my husband, and we didn't know anybody who saw us – and
we didn't care if they did – so on we walked. (p. 257)

While most scholars see Mina as asexual, the word 'pedantry' is
interesting. One wonders whether she controls her emotions and
sexuality because she is rational or whether, as an orphan and depend-
ant, she has learned circumspection. She recognizes, for example, that
she is not equal to her male companions, and she knows what happens
to women who violate convention.

Mina keeps her own counsel, and Stoker's male characters praise
her intellect but do not altogether trust her. Roth, in 'Suddenly
sexual women in Bram Stoker's *Dracula*', observes that intellect allows
Mina to fit in with the predominantly male group of vampire hunters:
'This view of the incompatibility of intelligence and sexual fertility
in women is a standard Victorian conviction and is ... demonstrated
vividly in ... Mina Harker who has a "male mind" and no female
sexuality.'[51] She is 'one of the boys' except when she becomes a
mother.

Mina is interesting because she is a new kind of Gothic heroine.
Indeed, Stoker replaces the weak and passive maiden of traditional
Gothic literature with a more interesting woman character/narrator.
While women in New Woman literature often work in fields recently
opened to them, primarily medicine and law, Mina combines desire
for marriage and motherhood with facility for skills needed in the
modern world: shorthand, typing and knowledge of train schedules.
She confesses feeling oppressed by uncongenial responsibilities: 'I have
been simply overwhelmed with work. The life of an assistant schoolmistress is sometimes trying' (p. 103). She welcomes motherhood and
the opportunity to help Jonathan with his work.

The same letter indicates that she and Jonathan are keeping journals,
he to record his travels, she to hone her memory: 'I shall try to do
what ... lady journalists do: interviewing and writing descriptions
and trying to remember conversations ... one can remember all that
goes on or that one hears said during a day' (p. 104). Thus the diary
she keeps to practise shorthand reveals introspection and the mental
acuity needed to combat Dracula. After telling Van Helsing that
Jonathan has gone to Whitby to see what he can learn about Dracula,

she offers to search newspapers for information about Dracula's movements. Unlike Van Helsing, who depends on folklore, Mina seeks accurate information.

While the male characters praise Mina's intelligence, they are trapped in a view that William Patrick Day describes as 'genteel and benign paternalism':

> The men attempt to place Mina Harker in this category, and had they succeeded, their community would have been a . . . version of traditional male hegemony over the feminine. But in fact, Mina becomes the most powerful figure in the group . . . By initially excluding her from the witch hunt for Dracula, the men . . . make her more vulnerable . . . When they recognize this, they must take her into the circle as an equal, and Mina . . . really plans the pursuit . . . her courage far outstrips that of her male comrades', for she is in danger of losing her soul as well as her life.[52]

Hoping to protect her, the men leave her alone while they battle Dracula, a decision against which she rebels:

> All the men . . . seemed relieved; but it did not seem . . . good that they should brave danger and, perhaps, lessen their safety − through care of me; but their minds were made up, and, though it was a bitter pill . . . to swallow, I could say nothing, save to accept their chivalrous care of me. (p. 339)

Her diary reveals that Mina shares one trait with Lucy and Dracula's brides, their rebelliousness. Dracula's brides resent his authority and talk back whenever they can while Lucy, dreaming of marrying three men, slips out to enjoy the night's forbidden pleasures. The biggest difference between Mina and the others is that she is aware of her rebellion against male authority, and subsequent events prove her right.

Everything about Mina suggests that she is a new kind of heroine. While unlike the woman depicted in New Woman literature, she is not the old Gothic passive heroine either, and Milbank reinforces her newness by analogy to Irish history: 'If Lucy Westenra represents the Anglo-Irish gentry of the past, Mina Murray represents "Young

Ireland" and its bourgeois future – a new "Ascendancy". Murray is one of the commonest Irish . . . names from the Norman period onwards.'[53]

Before leaving this discussion of gender, readers should note that Dracula's threatening sexuality, though apparently heterosexual, is more complex. One of the first twentieth-century examinations, 'The psychoanalysis of ghost stories' by Maurice Richardson, explores sexuality, referring to *Dracula* as an 'incestuous, necrophilious, oral-anal-sadistic all-in-wrestling match' and analyses various sexual fears.[54] More recent discussions of gender and sexuality, on the other hand, interpret him as decidedly homosexual. Describing the novel as 'a compendium of fin-de-siècle phobias', Nina Auerbach nonetheless focuses on homosexuality.[55] She, Hopkins and Talia Schaffer link *Dracula* to the Wilde trials.[56] Auerbach explains that Wilde was being tried while Stoker wrote the novel, and Hopkins confirms that many dates in *Dracula* 'correspond directly with those of the Wilde trial, allowing the novel to be read as a covert examination of the plight of the homosexual in society'.[57] Schaffer points to parallels between *Dracula* and the trial, adding that Dracula should not be confused with the real Wilde since he 'represents the ghoulishly inflated vision . . . produced by Wilde's prosecutors; the corrupting, evil, secretive, manipulative, magnetic devourer of innocent boys'.[58] She also links the trial to the novel's narration, noting that its 'composition, with its newspaper clippings and emphasis on journalistic techniques . . . obliquely acknowledges its debt to the Wilde-saturated newspapers of April, May, and June, 1895'.[59]

Examining sexuality, readers discern that Stoker's characters are as conservative in their attitudes towards sexuality as they are modern in their reliance on technology. Describing themselves as modern – in Harker's words, 'nineteenth century up-to-date with a vengeance' (p. 77) – they nonetheless fear what is new, different and strange. Whether Stoker shared their prejudices remains a question that may never be answered. His characters, however, revert to traditional values, seeing anything else as aberrant, Gothic and frightening.

Stoker's Gothic Masterpiece

Dracula and Victorian science and technology

It seems incongruous that works that focus on contemporary fears are also concerned with the past, but the Gothic was haunted by the past from its earliest beginnings. Furthermore, while *Dracula* is Stoker's acknowledged Gothic masterpiece, his other works reveal his concern with the impact of the past on the present. Mummies, vampires, enormous serpents or dragons, legends and buried treasure. Stoker's incarnations of the ancient or the medieval past refuse to die and, more horrifyingly, destroy the living in their quest to remain powerful.

While the Gothic was always haunted by the past, Julian Wolfreys and Linda Dryden argue that Victorian Gothic had an especially problematic relationship with the past because of scientific and technological progress during the nineteenth century, and fear of the past continues in the twentieth and twenty-first centuries.[60] A man of his time, Stoker is ambivalent about the past, sometimes appearing confident that the future would be brighter, at others seeming to believe that forces of the past could never be overcome. That twenty-first-century readers share his ambivalence explains why *Dracula* – indeed, the Gothic in general – continues to speak to us. Almost from the first page, Stoker confronts readers with incarnations of the past, and Harker, a modern resident of urban England proud of scientific and technological developments, is horrified by Dracula's pride in his military prowess: 'The warlike days are over. Blood is too precious . . . in these days of dishonourable peace; and the glories of the great races are as a tale that is told' (p. 69). He becomes more frightened when he realizes that this anachronism is moving to his own modern England. Even more frightening is the realization that everything he has come to trust may be ineffectual against this evil.

Dracula is also full of references to modern conveniences, such as trains, typewriters and transfusions, and scholars and reviewers comment on its science and technology, often pointing to the conflict between modern forces and superstition, and occasionally to the fact that forces of modernity collaborate with traditional powers. A review in the *Spectator* points to that combination:

Mr. Stoker has shown considerable ability in the use . . . of all the available traditions of vampirology, but we think his story would have

73

been all the more effective if he had chosen an earlier period. The up-to-dateness of the book – the phonograph diaries, typewriters, and so on – hardly fits in with the mediaeval methods which ultimately secure the victory for Count Dracula's foes.[61]

Twentieth- and twenty-first-century reviewers are more enthusiastic about Stoker's emphasis on contemporary matters.[62] Jenna Harris observes that *Dracula* would have felt modern to Stoker's contemporaries because of the topical allusions:

> Stoker sets *Dracula* in ...Victorian England, at a time when both science and technology were rapidly advancing. A book review from the *Spectator*, published on 31 July 1897 ... mentions the 'up-to-dateness of the book' . . . shown through . . . Jonathan's shorthand, Mina's typewriter, and Seward's phonograph; as well as Van Helsing's blood transfusions and . . . hypnotism. The musical allusions are also contemporary. Mina and Lucy ... listen to Spohr and Mackenzie ... the night after the count's first attack ...Victorian readers would have seen . . . their own world in . . . the text.[63]

She observes that these topical references make *Dracula* feel dated to later readers, an assessment with which I disagree. Stoker raises philosophical issues about the relationship between past and present, issues not linked to specifics but to the fact that human beings are haunted by forces that threaten to overwhelm them. Indeed, one reason for the emergence of the Gothic at the end of the eighteenth century and its continuation in subsequent centuries is that new ways of thinking – indeed, of being – replaced traditional views and conflicted with them.

Manuel Aguirre and Clare Simmons demonstrate that Dracula's opponents fear him as an embodiment of the past. Best known for *Reversing the Conquest: History and Myth in Nineteenth Century British Literature*, Simmons explains, in 'Fables of continuity: Bram Stoker and medievalism', that the 'medieval and the modern work in tandem in Dracula's final defeat'. She prioritizes medieval wisdom, noting that technology 'is not in itself enough to defeat his powers'.[64] Aguirre assesses the strengths of Dracula's opponents:

Dracula can only be defeated by a group . . . whose skills include science (Seward) and spiritualism (Van Helsing), whose members are both British and foreign (Dutch, American), and whose strength resides in . . . the bringing together of disparate data by . . . Mina Harker, whose victimization . . . makes her an intermediary between human and vampire, so that she alone, through . . . rapport with Dracula's mind . . . can lead the way for her group.[65]

He thus reinforces Van Helsing's assessment that human beings 'have on our side power of combination – a power denied to the vampire kind; we have resources of science' (p. 334).

Although Van Helsing uses religion and folklore against Dracula, he also embodies modern thought, as signified by his credentials: 'Abraham Van Helsing, M.D., D.PH., D. Lit., ETC.' (p. 185). That Dracula's opponents fear and distrust the past and trust modern instruments – Winchester rifles, steam launches and telegraphs – signifies their modernity. This chapter demonstrates, however, that the narrators are not entirely reliable and, furthermore, that Stoker may not share their views. Indeed Byron's essay, 'Gothic in the 1890s', argues that readers should be suspicious of modern science and technology:

If the city is now the primary Gothic landscape, the primary figure at the heart of most Victorian *fin de siècle* texts is the scientist . . . But science did not just offer reassuring ways of categorizing and ordering, of locating and fixing lines of difference; it was also a transgressive and disruptive force.[66]

Greenway's article on normal science observes that Seward's character comments on the science of his day and the way it was practised. While Seward sees himself as a scientist who uses modern technology and experimentation, Stoker questions his faith. In fact, Greenway's essay concludes by questioning modern wisdom:

At first glance, the Victorian view of history as a conquest of barbarity and superstition seems affirmed in the happy ending. The men . . . as scientist, solicitor, and aristocrat, have become husbands and providers while Mina, who has the best mind of the lot, has become Jonathan's secretary . . . The irony in this tableau, however, suggests that these conventions . . . are merely forms of structured ignorance.[67]

Looking at the conclusion, I concur with Greenway that what is so frightening and so modern about *Dracula* is that, because Stoker provides no certainties, readers question everything they have come to believe. Hoping for answers, readers find only ambiguities. Even Dracula's destruction may be a lie, his opponents' science inadequate. At the end his castle remains, dwarfing his opponents. No wonder that screenwriters and directors keep bringing Dracula back. Stoker's brilliance is to suggest that he is more powerful than everything that attempts to replace him.

Madness, religion and confusion about boundaries

If *Dracula* is frightening because it reinforces readers' suspicions that the authorities (including people, institutions and disciplines) they trust are ineffectual, it is more frightening because its emphasis on insanity implies readers can no longer trust themselves. Bloom, in 'Epilogue: further thoughts on the Gothic', comments on the importance of insanity to the Gothic:

> The two poles of gothic horror are insanity and Hell, the ruling image is of death, the central symbolism cosmic annihilation and the invasion of supernatural otherness beyond rational consciousness; the underlying theme: the withdrawal of God and the long night of the soul beyond salvation. Gothic horror is about that which should not be, whose comprehension is the end of sanity and the opening of the abyss, in which cursed state of knowledge the forbidden becomes manifest, the veil is withdrawn and the fabric of the material universe falls to dust. For that which "should not be" to manifest itself to consciousness, making visible the otherness of cosmic indifference, is profoundly disturbing.[68]

Following the emphasis of traditional Gothic, Stoker features insanity by setting entire scenes in Seward's lunatic asylum and by having characters (Seward himself, Van Helsing, Renfield and Harker) question their own or another's sanity. Indeed, Eighteen-Bisang and Miller indicate that the characters who eventually became Renfield and Seward were part of Stoker's original plan and that they 'form a dyad from the beginning' their commentary suggesting Stoker thought about madness from the moment the vampire novel began to gel in his mind.[69]

Revising *Dracula* to begin with Harker's trip, Stoker introduced insanity not in a medical setting but in the horrifying encounter with three monstrous women that causes him to question his sanity: 'God preserve my sanity . . . Whilst I live on here there is but one thing to hope for: that I may not go mad, if, indeed, I be not mad already' (p. 78). While Harker questions his personal sanity, Seward leads readers to question what distinguishes sane behaviour from madness. The director of a lunatic asylum, Seward has a number of patients under his care but concentrates on R. M. Renfield, his 'pet lunatic' (p. 329) whom he classifies as 'a zoophagous (life-eating) maniac' (p. 126), a designation that connects him with Dracula. As Seward observes Renfield eating flies, spiders and eventually sparrows – behaviour that is unconventional, if not mad – he also considers that Renfield is sometimes surprisingly lucid. Meeting Mina, Renfield seems as sane as supposedly normal characters:

> Dr Seward is loved . . . even by his patients, who, being some of them hardly in mental equilibrium, are apt to distort causes and effects. Since I myself have been an inmate of a lunatic asylum, I cannot but notice that the sophistic tendencies of some of its inmates lean towards the errors of *non causae* and *ingoratio elenchi*. (p. 328)

Stoker never mentions Renfield's background, but his Latin reveals him as educated; the notebook in which he records his experiments suggests scientific training; and his familiarity with Van Helsing shows him to be well read. In fact, almost everything about him re-inforces his resemblance to the central professional characters.

If Renfield's alternations between lucidity and insanity cause readers to contemplate their own sanity, Seward's commentary re-inforces human mental fragility. Before realizing he faces a super-natural power, Seward questions his sanity: 'What does it all mean? I am beginning to wonder if my long habit of life amongst the insane is beginning to tell upon my own brain' (p. 212). Later, when Van Helsing tells them about vampires, Seward questions the group's sanity: 'I sometimes think we must be all mad and that we shall wake to sanity in strait-waistcoats' (p. 377). The most dramatic illustration of the fragile barrier between sanity and insanity is a scene often described as the King Laugh passage, which occurs shortly after Lucy's destruction. When Van Helsing bursts out laughing, Seward questions whether 'the strain . . . has broken down even his iron strength' (p. 260). Denying hysteria, Van Helsing attributes his response to his sense of humour, but sensitive readers may question that analysis: 'He laughed till he cried, and I had to draw down the blinds lest any one should see us and misjudge; and then he cried till he laughed again; and laughed and cried together, just as a woman does' (pp. 260–1). The scene undermines readers' confidence in him even as it reinforces the fragile division between sanity and insanity.

If *Dracula* is unsettling because it reminds readers that what they accept as sane may be mad, it is also frightening to realize that characters with whom readers identify resemble the monsters they are pledged to destroy.[70] For example, when Dracula leaves the castle wearing Harker's clothes, he expects people to assume that he is Harker, as indeed happens when the woman seeking her child sees Harker at the window and cries out, 'Monster, give me my child' (p. 92). Escaping Dracula's castle, Harker grabs handfuls of gold just as Dracula will do in London, another parallel. There are also numerous examples of blood and bloodletting. If Dracula is a monster, a foul thing 'of the night . . . without heart or conscience, preying on the bodies and the souls of those we love best' (p. 333) because he is a bloodsucker, he is not alone. Renfield attacks Seward and cuts his wrist so badly that it 'bled freely, and quite a little pool trickled on to the carpet' (p. 220). Appalled by Renfield's subsequent behaviour – 'He was lying on his belly on the floor licking up, like a dog, the blood which had fallen from my wounded wrist' (p. 220) – Seward forgets that he too is a bloodletter and a bloodsucker. While proposing to Lucy, he plays with a lancet, an instrument for drawing blood and bloodletting, a popular therapy; later, when Arthur invites him to examine her, Seward tests the 'quality of her blood' (p. 183) after she cuts her hand. Seward also sucks blood, once when a scalpel wounds Van Helsing (p. 185), once from his own finger, incidents that reinforce similarities between the heroes and individuals they characterize as monsters. Because the threats are imprecise, *Dracula* continues to frighten. Wiser than the overly confident heroes who see themselves as Good and their opponents as Evil, readers see similarities between monsters and heroes. Realizing that the monster is us, readers recoil in horror.

J. P. Riquelme prepared an annotated edition of *Dracula*.[71] And, in 'Toward a history of Gothic and Modernism: dark modernity from Bram Stoker to Samuel Beckett', he observes that threats come from inside:

> Although Gothic narratives regularly focus on marriage or on social and sexual relations . . . often those relations are threatened or abrogated, as in . . . *The Castle of Otranto* . . . and . . . *Frankenstein* . . . Gothic sexuality may also take a bizarre form, as in . . . *Dracula* . . . Some of those issues were already present . . . in the earliest Gothic narratives, because the threat to marriage, family, and home amounts to a threat to the stability and the future of culture. That dark threat comes from inside.[72]

By focusing on the relationship between the Gothic and Modernism, Riquelme suggests a change from early Gothic and what follows, a change that moves threats to the self from the outside to the inside.

Observing that *Dracula* reveals a 'prevalent xenophobia', the ultimate external threat, Belford adds that, though presented as 'a sinister foreign seducer', Dracula 'elevates the desire and fear . . . to be violated by a dark outsider', and Stoker reinforces that victims must desire whatever vampires represent and invite them in for them to have power.[73]

At one point, Leatherdale criticizes Stoker for being imprecise about the source of Dracula's evil:

> Throughout, Dracula's evil has been sponsored by the devil . . . Then Stoker shifted his ground, stating that Transylvania was a mysterious land . . . where monsters might breed. Now he suggests Dracula/crime/insanity/child-brain are linked. Dracula is now a composite, motivated partly by the devil, partly by geology, and partly by . . . notions of

crime. Rather than making Dracula a more-rounded complex figure, Stoker serves only to compromise his essential evil.[74]

But is that not the point? Evil is mysterious and uncanny because people generally believe people like them are incapable of it. It is also familiar because in moments of deepest insight individuals recognize it is caused by people exactly like them. If geology were responsible, people could easily avoid it. Stoker wisely concentrates on characteristics – sexuality and mental ability – to which normal readers can relate.

The monster at our service

Contemplating why *Dracula* still frightens, readers can also consider that Stoker thought about class as well. Most of *Dracula*'s central characters are middle-class professionals while Dracula is a nobleman who lives with three 'ladies' in a castle and brags of his lineage: 'Here I am noble; I am *boyar*; the common people know me, and I am master' (p. 55). In England, he presents himself as a count and the emphasis on lineage reminds readers that Gothic villains were often aristocrats. Indeed, Punter characterizes Dracula as 'the final aristocrat' in *The Literature of Terror*.[75] The aristocracy is a locus of fear in Gothic literature because by the eighteenth century it had outlived its usefulness. No longer a protective force during wars and other periods of crisis, the aristocracy was perceived in the nineteenth century as moribund and predatory. (For example, Matthew Arnold's *Culture and Anarchy* describes the aristocracy as Barbarians.) In making his villain an aristocrat, Stoker follows Radcliffe, Polidori and the author of *Varney the Vampire*.

Dracula is also connected to the working/servant classes. Not only can he function as coachman, chef and valet in Transylvania, but he also blends with the English working class. Able to transport his boxes of earth and converse with the keeper at the zoological gardens, he shares with them a penchant for drink. While prudent middle-class characters rarely drink beer, wine or spirits, labourers often characterize themselves as thirsty. Even the Westenra female servants are easily rendered incapable by drinking sherry that Dracula has laced with laudanum. One can understand why Stoker's readers, like Van Helsing who refuses to use the maids' blood in transfusions, might fear intemperate labourers and servants in their midst.

Stoker's adaptation of Gothic conventions

Even though Stoker transformed traditional Gothic, he understood it as a mode of presenting the world. In 'Bram Stoker and Irish Gothic', Raymond T. McNally summarizes these conventions, beginning with Walpole's fiction that his story 'came from an old manuscript' and was 'based on real people and actual places'.[76] McNally adds that Walpole also emphasized 'arcane or antique documents' which 'became a staple in many subsequent Gothic tales'. Although Stoker shifts from antique documents to newspaper accounts and diaries, he retains the Gothic emphasis on mystery. McNally lists common Gothic elements: the ancient castle, the tyrannical nobleman, a naive heroine threatened by that nobleman, the hero, foreign names that add 'an exotic, alien atmosphere' and 'miraculous occurrences'.[77] Because many of these conventions were examined earlier, the remaining discussion focuses on the castle and the triad of villain, heroine and hero. Finally, although McNally does not mention nature, readers cannot ignore a force so important to Stoker.

Dracula is consistently associated with his dwellings, and the frightened Harker sees 'a vast *ruined* castle, from whose tall black windows came no ray of light, and whose *broken battlements* showed a jagged line against the moonlit sky' (p. 46, my italics). Everything about this residence suggests that it embodies a violent past, and Harker imagines it was designed to protect women during sieges:

> The castle was built on . . . a great rock, so that on three sides it was . . . impregnable, and great windows were placed . . . where sling, or bow, or culverin could not reach, and consequently light and comfort, impossible to a position which had to be guarded, were secured. (pp. 76–7)

Readers, imagining Dracula's castle, may be surprised that Stoker's notes include no specific details, as Miller and Eighteen-Bisang note:

Although Stoker reminds himself to 'describe' the castle, there is no such description in the Notes. Castles are a staple of Gothic fiction ... usually located in remote mountainous regions, and have towering battlements, hidden rooms, secret passages, gloomy dungeons and creaking doors.[78]

Lack of specificity helps readers understand that Stoker imagined an embodiment of the past, an idea rather than a specific castle. Indeed, Dracula reinforces his connection to the past. Learning that Carfax dates 'to mediaeval times' (p. 59), he replies: 'I am glad that it is old and big. I myself am of an old family, and to live in a new house would kill me' (p. 60).

In contrast, Stoker's English scenes signify modernity. Brightly lit with gas lamps and connected by electrical and telephone wires, they reinforce that Stoker's narrators are oriented to the present. Mina's description, though brief, emphasizes oldness: 'The Castle ... now stood out against the red sky, and every stone of its broken battlements was articulated against the light of the setting sun' (p. 510). While the castle remains at the end, Stoker apparently planned to destroy it. Belford notes 'a startling change from manuscript to novel'.[79] In the manuscript, the castle is destroyed after Dracula's death, but because someone 'deleted 195 words' describing its destruction, Belford questions whether the conclusion was 'too evocative of Poe's *The Fall of the House of Usher*' or whether Stoker or his publisher had a sequel in mind.[80] Vander Ploeg offers another explanation:

> No records explain why Stoker chose to delete this material, but ... it too strongly indicates a supernatural link between Dracula and his castle ... It is worth considering that not only did Stoker conceive of the more mystical ending, but that he consciously rejected it ... this suggests how much the author wanted to distance his story from Gothic romanticism.[81]

Because readers may never know the truth unless someone finds Stoker's diary or a message to the printer, there is room for another plausible explanation: The castle remains to demonstrate that 'the old centuries had, and have, powers ... which mere "modernity" cannot kill' (p. 77). That reading undermines the confident conclusion generally attributed to *Dracula* and reinforces the mystery associated with the Gothic.

Readers of Gothic literature do it a disservice to ignore the extent to which the best Gothic is haunted by the past. Simmons, for example, contrasts that Gothic relationship with a nostalgic relationship:

> From the reader's perspective, while both the Gothic and medievalism involve the . . . juxtaposition of the reader's present with the narrator's past, the emotions prompted may be different: the reader of the Gothic can enjoy temporary terror . . . but find relief in the knowledge that present-day England is not Gothic, at least on a literal level.[82]

While Simmons rightly distinguishes medievalism from the Gothic, she minimizes the power of the past in Gothic literature. In the best Gothic literature, the fear of being overwhelmed by the past is all too real. Indeed, Glover's reading of the first chapters reinforces that power. He comments on a 'young Englishman's sense of shock at slipping into a premodern world . . . that is all too vivid'.[83] Powerful and overwhelming, the past threatens to cause modern characters to 'slide back down the evolutionary chain'.[84] Readers fear that pull as well.

Gothic literature reinforces the power of the past by making its villains members of old families, its heroines and heroes representatives of either professional classes or younger branches of the family. Eighteen-Bisang and Miller explore Stoker's adaptation of aristocratic power:

> Stoker followed the literary convention of making his anti-hero a member of the aristocracy. A cursory survey of Gothic literature yields a plethora of nasty Counts: Morano in . . . *The Mysteries of Udolpho*, de Bruno in . . . *The Italian*, Doni in . . . *Ernestus Berchtold*, Cenci in . . . *The Cenci*, Montonio in . . . *The Fatal Response* . . . Manfred and . . . Count Fosco. Gothic fiction often links the temporal power of aristocrats . . . with supernatural powers.[85]

Stoker's villainous nobleman falls in line with these 'nasty' counts, but his heroine is less naive than her predecessors, whom Kate Ferguson

Ellis describes in 'Can you forgive her? The Gothic heroine and her critics':

> The task of the classic Gothic heroine is to escape from the castle that has become her prison, to preside over its demystification a process that usually requires its violent destruction, and to claim the fortune and lineage that the villain has sought to make his own.[86]

The conclusion demonstrates that, even if one accepts Dracula's destruction, the future may not be rosy, for the heroine is still in prison. Indeed, Lucy is destroyed by men who love her, and Mina is silent. Reading *Dracula*, I am struck with the thought expressed by Jean-Baptiste Alphonse Karr's epigram: 'plus ça change, plus c'est la meme chose. The more things change, the more they remain the same.'

Because nature is so powerful in Stoker's fiction, it is important to explore its presence in *Dracula*, which tends to substitute supernatural power for nature's power. That he contemplated nature's power over human beings is evident in the notes, which record conversations with Whitby fishermen about a whaler that was lost in a storm (p. 151) and with Coast Guard Wm Pethereick about 'various wrecks' (p. 155). The storm that wrecks the *Demeter* results from supernatural power, but Stoker based it on storms he experienced personally or knew of. That he continued to mull over the question of natural power versus supernatural power is evident as late as the typescript, according to Miller and Eighteen-Bisang who point to another change in the final chapter. After Van Helsing destroys Dracula's brides, Stoker deletes this passage from the typescript: 'storm bursts on castle. Wild whirling figures of women on tower – obliterated by lightning.'[87] Other passages suggest Stoker imagined Dracula as a force of nature:

> The very place, where he have been . . . for all these centuries, is full of strangeness of the geologic and chemical world . . . There have been volcanoes, some of whose openings . . . send out waters of strange properties, and gases that kill or make to vivify. Doubtless, there is something magnetic or electric in . . . these . . . forces which work for physical life. (p. 436)

Furthermore, Van Helsing indicates that natural forces, including garlic and wooden stakes, have power over Dracula. Because vampires are connected to the moon and the tides, 'he can only change himself at noon or at exact sunrise or sunset' (p. 336); 'he can only pass running water at the slack or the flood of the tide' (p. 336); and 'a branch of the wild rose on his coffin will prevent him from leaving it' (p. 336). Vander Ploeg argues that such references demonstrate 'that Dracula is more of an accident of nature than a supernatural entity' and offers a scientific explanation:

> In referring to the magnetic and electric and chemical and gaseous agents at work in producing him, Stoker puts in Van Helsing's empirical paradigm scientific beliefs . . . current in the Victorian period. In effect, these . . . explain away the residual tatters of the supernaturalism that begin the novel.[88]

However, because supernatural explanations dominate plausible scientific explanations, mystery remains. No science can explain Dracula to readers.

After reading *Dracula* for the first or the twenty-first time, readers contemplate the haunting power of *Dracula* and Dracula. Ultimately *Dracula* remains one of the greatest Gothic novels because it is mysterious, and human beings are terrified of what they can neither understand nor control. Hopkins concludes her study with Stoker's 'darkly Gothic obsession with the double which . . . has lost none of its power to disturb'.[89] Neither has his obsession with everything humans cannot understand or control. Just when I think I understand it, *Dracula* returns to haunt me with what I do not know. Stoker's other novels are academic curiosities, but *Dracula* remains alive because Stoker discovered what haunts modern readers: that Evil — whether the compulsion to destroy what is different or the difficulty of breaking from conventional thinking — exists despite human attempts to eliminate it. Telling Gladstone that *Dracula* was cathartic, Stoker apparently believed readers would be purged of the fear and terror they experienced. As a woman reader, I am haunted by Mina's silence. Her son will learn the old ways because male mentors will teach him the ways of patriarchy. More than a century after *Dracula*, I see that violence, along with blindness and insanity, are unfortunately part of being human.

3

Ongoing Work with the Gothic in Miss Betty, The Mystery of the Sea and The Jewel of Seven Stars

଼ଉଓ଼

Although nothing Stoker wrote in the years following *Dracula* received the critical attention that *Dracula* did, *The Mystery of the Sea* (1902) is notable for its Gothic elements,[1] *The Jewel of Seven Stars* (1903), another Gothic tale, is generally considered Stoker's second-best work.[2] *Miss Betty* (1898), Stoker's only historical novel, receives almost no critical attention.[3]

Miss Betty

Miss Betty, published immediately after *Dracula*, has few Gothic elements and is regarded as one of Stoker's weakest works. Andrew Maunder describes it in *Bram Stoker* as 'one of the least-known of Stoker's novels' but adds that it 'provoked the most enthusiastic response from reviewers when first published'.[4] William Hughes explains in *Bram Stoker: A Bibliography* that Stoker published it against the advice of,

> the Bristol-based publisher J. W. Arrowsmith, to whom the author had presumably first offered the manuscript . . . Writing to Stoker in 1894, Arrowsmith asserts 'I do not think that there would be the remotest chance of my getting any sale and I should do neither you nor myself any good by putting it on the market'.[5]

Because Stoker pursued publication despite that criticism, the novel had a relatively long history during which time he continued work on it. According to Murray, the manuscript in the Brotherton Collection reveals that it was written in 1891, submitted to Arrowsmith some time before October 1894, and published in 1898 by C.A. Pearson as the first in a series of 'Latter-Day Stories'.[6] Hughes observes in *Beyond Dracula* that Stoker rewrote the conclusion:

> In *Seven Golden Buttons*, Otwell dies on his quest. The novel elaborates on ... changes in the former reprobate's character through the speech of a galley slave whose freedom Rafe has purchased ... Rafe's final message to the now elderly Betty is triumphant ... 'tell her that had I lived I would have gone to her and claimed my wife as not unworthy' (*SGB* f. H15).
> Stoker ... revised this ending. In the more conventional romantic reconciliation that concludes *Miss Betty*, the youthful heroine not only learns of, but herself experiences, the regeneration of Rafe Otwell.[7]

That Stoker also dramatized it to protect his copyright suggests he believed in it despite the criticism he received.

Critics today take it seriously rather than dismiss it as a hurriedly written mistake, and Lisa Hopkins argues in *Bram Stoker: A Literary Life* that it is worth studying as it provides a context for *Dracula*:

> *Dracula* alone cannot give a full sense of ... the range of Stoker's interests or of the pressures and contexts that conditioned the creation of his most famous novel. Even the weakest and most disregarded of Stoker's other fictions – *The Shoulder of Shasta*, *Miss Betty*, *The Primrose Path* – are interesting in this respect.[8]

More accurately described as romance or historical fiction, *Miss Betty* includes a surprising number of Gothic elements, including a character who resembles the Gothic villain, a youthful heroine threatened by powerful outside forces, some terrifying episodes, awareness of the past and at least one instance of paranormal activity. Furthermore, examining how Stoker handles these elements allows readers to discern the difference between the past in historical fiction and the past in the Gothic.

The villain is a historical figure, Sir Robert Walpole, prime minister from 1721 to 1742. Significantly, he was also father of Horace Walpole, who wrote *The Castle of Otranto*, widely acclaimed as the first Gothic novel. Walpole was frequently accused of not sharing power and of using others to serve his purposes, characteristics that resemble the behaviour of the Gothic villain. Indeed, Maunder describes him as 'vampiric' though without exploring the political connections.[9] Nor does Stoker explore Walpole's politics – beyond describing him as 'the virtual ruler of England, since he controlled both the Treasury and the Exchecquer' (p. 51) – because he is interested in him as an impediment to the lovers, Betty Pole and Rafe Otwell. Walpole, however, is so appropriately manipulative that Roth describes the 'archetypally villainous' Walpole as 'the best element in *Miss Betty*'.[10]

Readers see that manipulation when he offers to help the impoverished Rafe if he marries someone of Walpole's choosing:

> When you . . . tell me that you are willing to carry out my project I shall appoint you forthwith to the post I spoke of but time does not stand still, and lacking you, I must choose some other suitor for my Lady Mary, and his must be the reward I reserved for you. (p. 52)

He thus offers knowledge and power if Rafe does his bidding: 'With such an alliance your fortune may yet be a greater one . . . You and I will be brought into very close relations, and many secrets of State . . . must become known to you. Knowledge is power . . . and nowhere is it more patent than in the world of politics' (pp. 65–6). Accepting such power, Rafe would lose Betty and sacrifice love for wealth and ambition.

Miss Betty demonstrates Stoker's consciousness of the past though his treatment of it in this novel differs from his presentation in Gothic fiction. For example, only Betty's great-grandfather is haunted by the past, and he is old and knows he will die soon: 'My child, it seems strange of me to talk of such things, but there is a spell upon me tonight. Mayhap that the old memories are awake and are growing stronger still as the end draws nearer' (p. 20).

Chapter II opens with the passing of time but does not suggest that the past is threatening:

In the ten years that had elapsed after her great-grandfather's death Betty Pole had many subjects for after-remembrance. Queen Anne had passed away; Marlborough had won glorious victories, had been a traitor twice told and had fallen . . . King George had come, and ruled in London a German Court by German ways. (p. 25)

While the passage, which reveals how great events impact on ordinary people, hints at history's dark side, it lacks the oppressive sense that the past haunts the present.

Fred Botting observes in *Gothic* that the Gothic is linked to the past and reinforces the darkness associated with the Gothic:

Gothic signifies a writing of excess. It appears in the awful obscurity that haunted eighteenth-century rationality and morality. It shadows the despairing ecstasies of Romantic idealism and individualism and the uncanny dualities of Victorian realism and decadence. Gothic atmospheres . . . have repeatedly signaled the disturbing return of pasts . . . and evoked emotions of terror and laughter. In the twentieth century . . . Gothic figures have continued to shadow the progress of modernity with counter-narratives displaying the underside of enlightenment and humanist values.[11]

Haunted by his past, Betty's great-grandfather confesses: 'All the faces I have loved seem gathered in yours tonight' (p. 21). As Maunder observes, however, most of *Miss Betty* treats the past with nostalgia:

As an example of 1890s historical fiction, *Miss Betty* has many of the outward features of this . . . sub-genre. It seems reactionary and glorifies the national past using reminders of a lost 'golden age' as an ideological weapon in the struggles of the present day.[12]

Moreover, because *Betty* is set in the past, it has little to say about the urban present. Unlike more Gothic works – *Dracula*, *Mystery*, *Jewel* and *Lair* – which are haunted by representations of a past that refuses to die, *Betty* is simply nostalgic about that past.

Maunder examines that nostalgia:

> *Miss Betty* is a love story but . . . it is also about the threats to the stability
> and order of the English family unit posed by outsiders. Miss Betty's
> fortune and its attendant responsibilities are bequeathed to her by her
> great-grandfather . . . as an act of faith in her abilities to carry on the
> honourable traditions of the family.[13]

Remaining true to her family's values, which include faith, duty
and truth, Betty offers Rafe money, and, when he turns highwayman rather than accept it, confronts him with his errors. Seeing the
gold buttons he has given her, Rafe recalls their message, 'El Amor
del infiel es como la espada destemplada' or 'The Love lacking faith
is as a sword untempered' (p. 56) and agrees to accept Betty's money
to reimburse his victims. From here on, the threats to their future are
not Gothic but military, including fighting the Turks and imprison-
ment on a Turkish galley.

One more element – occasional paranormal abilities – links *Betty*
to the Gothic. Hopkins mentions 'an intuition so strong it is like
second sight' after Betty's great-grandfather informs her of a special
fund she can use only when 'there is real want of it; that it can do
some good thing such as your heart tells you is good – when it can
avert some calamity' (p. 22).[14] Next morning, upon awakening, Betty
knows he has died. Similarly, the scene where she concludes Rafe had
turned highwayman resembles a nightmare from a more Gothic work:

> What Betty dreamed that night she could never remember. It seemed
> . . . that her sleeping thoughts had at first been happy enough, but that
> such dreams . . . were not all about Rafe. Suddenly, however she found
> herself broad awake, sitting up in bed with her hair damp with terror
> and a scream frozen on her lips. It was as though all her vague thoughts
> of months past had suddenly become clear – that her fears had found
> their source, and that henceforth there was nothing more left in the
> world that could give her new pain. And that source – Rafe! (p. 91)

Stoker explores this preternatural power in his next novel, *The
Mystery of the Sea*, where second sight figures prominently, as well
as in a later one, *The Lady of the Shroud*.

The Mystery of the Sea

Miss Betty is a historical romance with occasional Gothic elements, but *The Mystery of the Sea* (1902) is more difficult to classify. Phyllis A. Roth praises it in *Bram Stoker* for being 'as carefully constructed as *Dracula*' and argues that it is 'a more mature work'.[15] One of the most overtly political of Stoker's novels – it mentions the Spanish–American War as well as changes in the Scottish fishing industry – it also examines gender, race and class relationships. Roth, who classifies it as a romance, points to 'the use of the supernatural in the ideas of the Fates and of second sight' but argues it 'is by no means a Gothic novel'.[16] Glover describes it as 'Stoker's quasi-supernatural adventure story' while Hopkins argues that it is 'no more amenable to generic classification than the rest of Stoker's fiction. Part love story, part political tract, part treasure quest and part tale of the supernatural.'[17] This chapter demonstrates that what makes *Mystery* interesting is Stoker's use of Gothic details in a novel that is not obviously Gothic: paranormal abilities, characters who resemble Gothic villains, a medieval castle with mysterious underground passages, strange characters and uncanny events and the impact of the past.

Stoker's first-person narrator shares many of Stoker's traits. A barrister who falls in love with Cruden Bay, the athletic Archie Hunter had been an invalid child. Because Archie is a rationalist and a gadget freak, it is surprising when Stoker reveals the power the unseen world has over him. He first experiences second sight when he sees a man carrying a box, which he surmises is a coffin, and later learns a child has drowned. This event occurs on the first page, and Archie's life is filled with mystery until the last.

While he generally associates second sight with the uncanny Gormala MacNiel, Archie reveals that ordinary characters also have great gifts when, on Lammas Eve, a day 'connected with various superstitions' (p. 26), he watches a local fisherman struggle in the water. Archie rescues the body, which washes ashore; carrying it to the village, he sees 'a silent procession of ghostly figures' (p. 33) and concludes that 'these were the ghosts of the dead who had been drowned in the waters of the Cruden Skares' (p. 34). The scene is made more uncanny by Archie's recognition that he is close to the realm of the dead: 'Perhaps it was for the best; looking back . . . I know that no man can say what his mind may suffer in the aftertime who walks alone with the Dead' (p. 35). Paul Murray offers two explanations for this scene in *From the Shadow of Dracula*. The first is a college miscellany, edited by a friend, Robert Yelverton Tyrell:

> Stoker . . . would have read *Kottabos* and it is interesting that W. G. Wills's 'Ballad of Graf Brom' . . . featured a ghostly procession of dead women undone by a rake who had come to gloat over his death, rather like the procession of the dead in . . . *The Mystery of the Sea*.[18]

Another suggestion is a local legend 'that the bodies of those drowned in the previous twelve months rose from the waves to join their spirits in heaven or hell'.[19] Moreover, Stoker would have known the scene in *Macbeth* where Macbeth and Banquo observe Banquo's descendants stretching out from generation to generation. According to Murray, *Macbeth* 'interested Stoker the most of all the plays performed by Irving and it was a favourite subject of discussion between them from 1876 . . . until 1888 when it was performed at the Lyceum'.[20] One of Shakespeare's most ghostly plays, *Macbeth* was also set in Scotland.

If Stoker invests his hero with paranormal abilities, *Mystery* also features one of his most uncanny characters, Gormala MacNiel. Not literally supernatural, she has powers that frighten Archie and Marjory, and Murray observes that Stoker based her on an encounter in 1901, with 'an old woman, believed to have supernatural powers and so generally shunned by the locals'.[21] Stoker wrote 'The Seer' about her in 1901 and later incorporated her into *Mystery*.

Hopkins observes that Gormala's ancestry, of which she is proud, resembles Dracula's: 'They hae come doon to me through centuries. Frae mither to dochter, and from mither to dochter again, wi' never a break in the lang line o' the tellin'. Know ye, young master, that I am o' a race o' Seers' (p. 23). Consciousness of that strong female tradition also motivates the dying Gormala to help rescue Marjory, and Archie describes the experience of seeing through her eyes the boat to which the kidnappers take Marjory:

> With unconscious movement . . . I hung poised over this vessel . . . I could see through her, and down into the deep below her . . . till my

eyes rested on the patches of bare sand or the masses of giant seaweed which swayed with the tide above the rocks on which it grew. (p. 318)

The uncanny experience motivates Archie to swim to the ship, where he substitutes mundane skills with knives and guns for paranormal abilities.

If Archie and Marjory are twentieth-century people – both ride bicycles and use modern weapons – *Mystery* also reminds readers of the Gothic emphasis on the past, something Hopkins notes is characteristic of Stoker:

Stoker's book insistently recurs to the motif of the return of something from a distant past, a pattern repeated in *The Snake's Pass*, *The Mystery of the Sea*, *The Jewel of Seven Stars*, *Dracula* and *The Lair of the White Worm*. In these novels, what returns can, uncannily, be either monster or treasure, as if they were interchangeable.[22]

One wonders whether Stoker found the Gothic so congenial because the past haunted him.

Another element that links *Mystery* to traditional Gothic is Stoker's attention to nature's power over human beings. For example, although Archie falls in love with Cruden Bay and chooses to make his home there, he sometimes sees it as threatening. Indeed, his first description, which compares the bay to a mouth, makes it appear ominous: 'If Cruden Bay is to be taken figuratively as a mouth, with the sand hills for soft palate, and the green Hawklaw as the tongue, the rocks which mark the extremities are its teeth. To the north the rocks of red granite rise jagged and broken' (p. 9). A devouring maw that swallows numerous people, Cruden Bay eventually threatens Archie and Marjory. Who needs supernatural monsters when the natural world is both threatening and mysterious?

For half a mile or more the rocks rise through the sea singly or in broken masses ending in a dangerous cluster known as 'The Skares' and which has had for centuries its full toll of wreck and disaster. Did the sea hold its dead where they fell, its floor around the Skares would be whitened with their bones. (p. 9)

Stoker, who grew up near the sea and travelled widely, understood its dangers.[23] A strong swimmer, he invests the scene before Archie swims to the whaling vessel with nature's overwhelming power:

> At the foot of the cliff path the prospect was almost terrifying. The rocks were so washed with the churning water . . . that now and again only black tops could be seen rising out of the . . . white water; and a moment after, as the wave fell back, there would be a great mass of jagged rocks, all stark and grim . . . with the water streaming down them, and great rifts yawning between. Outside, the sea was a grim terror, a wildness of rising waves and lines of foam, all shrouded in fog and gloom . . . Nothing but the faith which I had in the vision of Marjory . . . could have carried me out into that dreadful gloom. All its possibilities of horror and danger woke to me at once, and for a moment appalled me. (p. 324)

Having seen Lauchland Macleod struggle unsuccessfully against the sea's overwhelming power in almost this same spot, Archie is justifiably terrified.

Stoker also demonstrates nature's power when Archie and Marjory seek the lost Spanish treasure in the caverns underneath his home, a scene that demonstrates Freud's idea of the transformation of the homely and familiar into the uncanny and terrifying since Archie was setting up his home when he decides to explore the caverns. Hopkins observes Radcliffe's influence:

> Indeed . . . it is virtually in his own bowels that he will . . . find it, since, as in . . . *The Sicilian Romance*, it proves to be in the cellarage of his own house that he finds the concealed entrance to the cave system . . . (Radcliffe may indeed have been an influence on Stoker, since her 1789 novel *The Castles of Athlin and Dunbayne* opens with . . . 'On the north-east coast of Scotland, in the most romantic part of the Highlands, stood the castle of Athlin', which comes close to the title of Stoker's *Lady Athlyne*.)[24]

He invites Marjory to join him, and the rising tide threatens them in a scene invested with all the claustrophobic terror of traditional Gothic: 'And now, in the darkness, the terror of the rising flood grew worse and worse. The chill water crept up, and up, and up; till . . . it was only by raising her head that Marjory could breathe' (p. 226). The scene evokes Poe's descriptions of premature burial, and readers experience the terror vicariously.

In addition to revealing people gripped by raw natural power, *Mystery* indicates that other powers exert control as well. A typical twentieth-century man, Archie believes in science and technology. However, bicycles, guns, windlasses and other instruments offer no protection against these powers. Carrying Macleod's body, Archie realizes he 'was becoming wrapped in the realisation of the mightier forces around me' (p. 33). Indeed, *Mystery* pits the consummate modern couple against primeval forces they cannot control:

> The Fates were at work upon us. Clotho was spinning the thread which was to enmesh Marjory and myself and all who were in the scheme of the old prophecy of the Mystery of the Sea and its working out.
>
> Once more the sense of impotence grew upon me. We were all as shuttlecocks, buffeted to and fro without power to alter our course. (p. 138)

Referring to Clotho, the youngest Fate who determines the length of an individual's life, personifies one of these forces.

Mystery is Gothic because it describes the terror of being in the hands of something uncontrollable: 'I was in the nightmare stage, when one can understand danger and realise terror; and when the only thing impossible to one is to *do* anything' (p. 338). Archie's feeling of paralysis before deciding to save Marjory is reminiscent of Burke's observations about terror in *A Philosophical Enquiry*: 'No passion so effectually robs the mind of all its powers of acting and reasoning as fear. For fear being an apprehension of pain or death, it operates in a manner that resembles actual pain.'[25]

Mystery includes other terrifying scenes, including one when Archie fears being buried alive:

> Here, though the roof came down in places dangerously low, there was still ample room, and the air came up sweet and cool. To any one unused to deep burrows . . . there is a dread of being underground. One is cut off from light and air; and burial alive in all its potential horrors is always at hand. (p. 191)

Later Marjory describes horror at an unexpected encounter:

> Whilst I was trying to look into the depth of the reservoir . . . I saw
> something white at the bottom. Just then the lamp . . . began to smoke,
> but as I looked in that last moment through the crystal pure water I
> recognised that the white object was a skull. (p. 196)

This scene reminds characters and readers they are vulnerable because
Death always has the last laugh.

If the setting and the references to overwhelming powers are reminiscent of traditional Gothic novels, the gloomy castle where Marjory
lives also harkens back to those reminders of the past. Angela Wright's
study, *Gothic Fiction: A Reader's Guide to Essential Criticism*, discusses
the importance of castles to the Gothic, noting that 'buildings are
as important as the protagonists in Gothic romance' and concluding
that 'the Gothic building as a symbol of fear and unyielding power
is ubiquitous'.[26] Describing Crom, Marjory hints at its gloom and
mystery:

> It is in reality an old castle, built about two or three hundred years ago
> . . . an interesting old place, but awfully gloomy. There are steel trellis
> gates, and great oak doors bound with steel, that rumble like thunder
> when you shut them. There are vaulted roofs; and windows in the thick-
> ness of the wall . . . I will take you all over it; that is, over all I can, for
> there are some parts of it shut off and locked up. (p. 133)

Marjory's description emphasizes age and strangeness. Not only is it
gloomy as befits an old castle, but something discouraged others from
renting it. Eventually discovering that its owner is the descendant of
the family who funded the Armada against Queen Elizabeth I, Archie
and Marjory see the power of the past reinforced by the building and
the fact that so many people seek the lost treasure.

Crom appears more mysterious because of its isolation, locked
rooms and hidden passages. Seeing it for the first time, Archie notes
the darkness and isolation that make Marjory's abduction easy for
her kidnappers: 'It was cut off altogether from the outer world; one
might remain in it for a life-time unknown. Inside it was, if possible,
more gloomy' (p. 146). Their exploration reminds readers that the

typical Gothic dwelling includes mysterious hidden spaces: 'Marjory showed me the parts which were barred up and the rooms which were locked . . . here was something unknown and forbidden. She being a woman, it became a Tree of Knowledge and a Bluebeard's Chamber in one' (p. 151). The locked doors remind readers of similar doors in Dracula's castle, behind which lie threats to Jonathan Harker, while the reference to Bluebeard reinforces that the Gothic villain, frequently the castle's owner, threatens the curious maiden over whom he has absolute control. As Wright summarizes, 'Thus a castle – even a ruined one – becomes the imaginative catalyst for contemplating power.'[27]

Finally, it includes a ruined chapel, 'manifestly a relic of the older castle on whose site Crom was built. It may have been used for service early in the sixteenth century' (pp. 176–7). A relic of a more distant past, the chapel is eerie because of 'some kind of superstition amongst the servants regarding this place. None of them would under any circumstances go near it at night; and not even in daytime if they could decently excuse themselves' (p. 177). Hearing voices while they are in the chapel, Archie and Marjory believe there is 'some secret vault or hiding place in the chapel; or it might be that there was some subterranean passage' (p. 181). Because there is also a secret passage behind the bookcase, people come and go without being seen by anyone, including the American Secret Service, which has sworn to protect Marjory.

In addition to Crom, Archie's cottage contains a mystery, that it is built over the caverns where Don Bernardino's ancestor hid the treasure, and Archie, Marjory and the kidnappers probe its inner mysteries to uncover vast riches.

The buildings in *Mystery* resemble buildings of early Gothic novels with their labyrinthine passages, and several characters resemble characters from these works. The bicycle-riding, gun-toting Marjory is more New Woman than persecuted maiden although, like heroines of early Gothic literature, she requires the hero's help to escape. Stoker uses other traits to encourage readers to think about the changing role of women and the changing dynamic between women and men. She is much like the independent and assertive Mina in this way.

More in keeping with their Gothic originals are the villains. Even though Don Bernardino redeems himself by working to rescue

Marjory (and loses his life in the process), he resembles the traditional villain as defined by Chris Baldick and Robert Mighall in
'Gothic criticism':'Gothic villains derive their "Gothic" status princi-
pally from their out-of-placeness, their dissynchronicity with the
modern Victorian world of technology and progress into which they
intrude.'[28] As Archie describes him, he looks out of place in nineteenth-
century Scotland:

> Don Bernardino, with his high aquiline nose and black eyes of eagle
> keenness, his proud bearing and the very swarthiness which told of
> Moorish descent, was, despite his modern clothes, just such a picture
> as Velasquez would have loved to paint, or as Fortuny might have made
> to live again. (pp. 204–5)

Not only does Stoker present him as a relic from the past and as racially
Other, he also invests him with the same animal characteristics as
Dracula:

> As he spoke, the canine teeth began to show. He knew that what he had
> to tell was wrong; and being determined to brazen it out, the cruelty
> which lay behind his strength became manifest . . . Spain was once the
> possession of the Moors, and the noblest of the old families had some
> black blood in them . . . The old diabolism whence sprung fantee and
> hoo-doo seemed to gleam out in the grim smile of incarnate, rebellious
> purpose. (p. 247)

Despite suggestions he is primitive and cruel – especially by references
to his animal nature and connection to African folk magic – Stoker
redeems him because his civilized behaviour and concern for Marjory
trump his desire for the treasure.

While redeeming Don Bernardino, Stoker creates thoroughly
vicious villains and singles out the unnamed African American,
Marjory's message revealing she will commit suicide rather than be
defiled by him: 'Frightful threats to give me to the negro if any
trouble, or letters to friends. Don't fear, dear, shall die first' (p. 298).
Archie, glimpsing him for the first time, is filled with revulsion:'All
but one I surveyed calmly . . . but this one was a huge coal-black negro,
hideous, and of repulsive aspect. A glimpse . . . made my blood run

cold, and filled my mind . . . with hate and fear' (pp. 319–20). Stoker's characters respond similarly to Native Americans in *Shasta* and 'The Squaw', and he depicts another villainous African in *Lair of the White Worm*. More significant is that Stoker's treatment of the racial Other resembles that of the earliest Gothic novels, which Murray observes, focused on a different kind of Other, Roman Catholics: 'The anti-Roman-Catholic, anti-Spanish sentiments so evident in Lewis's work are also to be found in John Dryden's play, *The Spanish Fryar, or, The Double Discovery* (1680), a copy of which was in Stoker's library.'[29] Evolving over time, the Gothic allows writers to personify whatever they fear most. From the perspective of someone living in the twenty-first century, what horrifies me is the ease with which the otherwise civilized Archie is overcome by hatred. Even considering that he is protecting his new wife, his rage is excessive, ultimately horrifying. After killing one man to retrieve the key to Marjory's cabin, Archie describes his joy at killing another:

> Never before did I understand the pleasure of killing a man. Since then, it makes me shudder when I think of how so potent a passion, or so keen a pleasure, can rest latent in the heart of a righteous man. It may have been that between the man and myself was all the antagonism that came from race, and fear, and wrongdoing; but the act of his killing was to me a joy unspeakable. It will rest with me as a wild pleasure till I die. (p. 329)

This scene, like the scene in which Seward describes joy at the thought of killing the vampire Lucy, reminds readers that the mere presence of the Other produces negative behaviour.

The Gothic arose during a period when people were becoming familiar with a scientific world-view and provides an alternative to that world, one in which humans lack the control promised by science. Stoker's attention to the cipher brings this tension to the fore-ground. Referring to it initially as a mystery, 'this new labyrinth of figures, words and symbols' (p. 74), Archie confesses he is haunted by it: 'Hitherto . . . my only experience of haunting had been that of Gormala; but even that experience failed before the ever-hopeful, ever-baffling subject of the cryptograms' (p. 76). On the other hand, Archie observes that scientific principles allow him to solve it:

At one time I had been an invalid ... and had taken from my father's
library a book ... Herein were given accounts of many of the old
methods of secret communication, ciphers, string writing, hidden
meanings, and many of the mechanical devices employed ... when
the correspondence of ambassadors, spies and secret agents was mainly
conducted by such means. This experience had set my mind somewhat
on secret writing, and ever after when ... I came across anything relating
to the subject I made a note of it. I now looked over the papers to see
if I could find traces of the methods with which I was acquainted; before
long I had an idea. (p. 73)

Archie determines that the cipher is based on the 'Biliteral Cipher' of
Francis Bacon (p. 73). Referencing the philosopher, statesman and
essayist credited with 'inventing' the scientific method as well as
developing a secret code while he was a diplomat in France, Stoker
hints at the power of science. Nonetheless, despite the power of science
and technology in *Mystery*, Stoker never shows science to be all-
powerful.

The Jewel of Seven Stars

Stoker also blends science and the Gothic in *The Jewel of Seven Stars*
(1903), which keeps romance at its centre with the love of Margaret
Trelawny and another barrister narrator, Malcolm Ross. *Jewel* has
never achieved *Dracula*'s popularity, but scholars respond favourably,
and Leatherdale's introduction to his annotated edition argues that
Jewel might have received more attention had it preceded *Dracula*.[30]
Dalby and Hughes describe it, in *Bram Stoker: A Bibliography*, as
'Stoker's best supernatural novel after *Dracula*', while Daniel Farson
places it 'next to *Dracula* for suspense and readability. The climax is
grand.'[31] Maunder observes that it matches *Dracula* 'in its complexity,
scale and scope'.[32] Roth, Belford and Murray praise Stoker's research;
admitting that *Jewel* is not as good as *Dracula*, Roth nonetheless praises
'Stoker's talents as a researcher and his skill in employing the fruits
of his research [which] serve him well in creating the uncanniness of
his tale.'[33] Belford demonstrates that Stoker wove together research
and personal experience: 'From the time Stoker heard Sir William

Wilde expound on his Egyptian adventures, he had in mind a book about mummies and curses; he borrowed the plot from Wilde, who had found a mummy . . . and brought it back to Merrion Square.'[34] While Belford emphasizes Stoker's relationship with the Wildes, Murray explores his knowledge of Egyptology:

> Through the character of Mr Corbeck . . . Stoker was able to display his considerable knowledge of ancient Egyptian religion and . . . the work of the great Egyptologists, including Wallis Budge, the Keeper of Egyptian and Assyrian antiquities in the British Museum. Stoker was a keen student of Budge's work and had in his library Budge's *History of Egypt* in nine volumes, his *Egyptian Ideas of the Future Life, Easy Lessons in Egyptian Hieroglyphics* and *The Egyptian Book of the Dead*.[35]

Replete with references to Egyptology, *Jewel* demonstrates that Stoker wove his own creative impulses in with his research. For example, *Jewel* includes a manuscript, 'a folio in Dutch, printed in Amsterdam in 1650' (p. 116) attributed to the fictitious Nicholas van Huyn of Hoorn:

> In the preface he told how, attracted by the work of John Greaves of Merton College, *Pyramidographia,* he himself visited Egypt, where . . . he devoted some years . . . to visiting strange places, and exploring the ruins of many temples and tombs. He had come across many variants of the story of the building of the Pyramids as told by the Arabian historian, Ibn Abd Alhokin. (p. 117)

While Huyn and his manuscript are Stoker's inventions, Greaves was a professor of astronomy, who published *Pyramidographia* in 1646, and Ibn Abd Alhokin, the first historian of Islamic Egypt, died in 871. Elsewhere in *Jewel*, Stoker refers to Young, Champollion, Birch, Lepsius, Rosellini, Salvolini, Mariette Bey, Budge and Flinders Petrie, all expert Egyptologists. Murray mentions that Trinity was 'a principal centre for the study of Orientalism in Britain and Ireland, with scholars like Edward Hincks (1792–1866) . . . among the leading pioneers in the field of Assyriology and Egyptology'.[36] Stoker's careful research explains why *Jewel* is a different kind of Gothic work, which Maunder describes as 'an Orientalist, Gothic novel, which exploits the mystique and exoticism of Ancient Egypt'.[37]

As usual, Stoker experimented with existing genres to comment on his world. Not only does his reference to Arabi Pasha in 'Chapter XI: A Queen's Tomb' sympathize with colonies attempting to overthrow their rulers, but it reminds readers that the story takes place in their own time.[38] Although Roth and others read Stoker's apprehension of powerful fathers and powerful women psychologically, these issues are concerns he shared with contemporaries who were attempting to rid themselves of the pressures of tradition and adjust to a new kind of life.

Jewel also resembles a detective story, and Murray observes that Stoker's notes for *Dracula* had included a detective who does not appear in the finished novel: 'The opening . . . has the distinct feel of a Sherlock Holmes story . . . a messenger arrives with a summons for . . . Ross . . . the narrator of the novel . . . The character of Superintendent Dolan. . . suggests the same provenance.'[39] As a friend of Arthur Conan Doyle, author of the Holmes stories, Stoker undoubtedly knew them, and his own works often feature characters seeking answers to pressing problems. Indeed, the Crew of Light in *Dracula*, Betty Pole, Archie and Marjory serve as detectives; and *Mystery* also includes the American Secret Service and its British equivalent. *Jewel* has the distinction of being the first Stoker work to feature a professional detective of the type familiar in detective fiction.

That Stoker experiments with various conventions and genres should come as no surprise, and Glover demonstrates how he uses these genres to address contemporary issues rather than personal demons:

> I read Stoker's fiction as public and primarily conscious fantasies, narratives that are formally structured and designed for popular consumption, despite the occasional intrusion of recherché elements or references belonging to the author's individual myth. Indeed, it is essential to see that the anxieties that animate these novels are inextricably bound up with the most deeply rooted dilemmas facing late Victorian culture.[40]

That is a view with which I concur.

Although this study focuses on Stoker as a Gothic writer, he used other popular genres, generally putting his own unique stamp on them rather than adopting them in their entirety. These popular genres also reveal profoundly different ways of imagining the world. Gothic and romance emphasize mystery, the Gothic focusing on occurrences that overpower humans and produce fear and horror. Romances, on the other hand, end happily and suggest love conquers external obstacles. Detective fiction, which is linked to the growing power of science, implies that rational people can solve most mysteries that confront them. That Stoker alternates between romance and Gothic and thus between two different ways of seeing the world, weaving into both genres generous references to science and technology, reveals a desire that science and rationality would ultimately solve overwhelming problems and a hope that individuals would find personal satisfaction. Coupled with this optimism, however, is fear that some mysteries may remain overwhelming.

The most grim and hopeless of Stoker's novels, *Jewel* is the only one (with the exception of the possible open ending of *Dracula*) that portrays modern human beings at the mercy of forces against which they have no control. As is evident in *Dracula* and *Mystery*, Stoker usually suggests that science and technology are useful, even against powerful supernatural forces. Stoker is thus allied with other nineteenth-century progessionists who argue that human beings are moving toward a better, more civilized and more comprehensible future.

Jewel reveals little evidence of that future. Stoker's original conclusion, published in 1903, is stark and hopeless.[41] The last chapter, whose title 'The Great Experiment' hints at systematic exploration reveals a scientific endeavour gone horribly wrong:

> Sick at heart, and with a terror which has no name, I went down into the cavern
> . . . I found them all where they had stood. They had sunk down on the floor, and were gazing upward with fixed eyes of unspeakable terror . . . I did what I could for my companions; but there was nothing that could avail . . . It was merciful that I was spared the pain of hoping. (p. 250)

Hughes explains in *Beyond Dracula* that this conclusion, in which everyone dies except the narrator, 'is pervaded by a hopelessness unique in Stoker's fiction'.[42] Not only does Ross lose the woman he loves, he must accept that modern science is powerless against the ancient past.

Glover demonstrates that the second edition, issued in 1912, is more positive:

> When *The Jewel of Seven Stars* was republished . . . one of its more speculative chapters (16) was deleted and a 'happy ending' substituted in which all the characters survive with the sole exception of Queen Tera, who through a kind of metempsychosis merges with the personality of Margaret . . . The 1912 edition is almost invariably used in modern reprints.[43]

Although it is possible to read the 1912 ending as ambiguous, most readers see it as positive. After revealing the failure of the resurrection, Ross marries Margaret and observes, 'there is no other life in all the world so happy as my own' (p. 256). Stoker was perfectly capable of creating a romance, and either he or someone else substituted the original dark and terrible ending with something brighter and more simplistic.

Both endings emphasize mystery since Stoker holds off revealing what happens until the final pages. While Gothic fiction is not necessarily experimental, it is often associated with ambiguous narration. Indeed, readers can think of Gothic works in which narration contributes to the mystery, with *Frankenstein*, *Wuthering Heights*, *The Turn of the Screw* and *Dracula* among the most famous. As Roth observes, the narration 'is far simpler than the journal-letter format Stoker employs in *Dracula* and elsewhere, though the innocent-I account of Malcolm Ross is highly effective in building and sustaining suspense'.[44] In fact, *Jewel*'s narrative resembles that of *Mystery*: both narrators are barristers who describe themselves as rational and modern, and both confront mysterious forces beyond their control.

Jewel opens with Ross awakening from dreaming of a young woman he had recently met:

> It seems that there is never to be any perfect rest. Even in Eden the snake rears its head among the laden boughs of the Tree of Knowledge. The silence of the dreamless night is broken . . . Waking existence is

prosaic enough – there was somebody knocking and ringing at some one's street door. (p. 20)

Although the scene hints at mystery and overwhelming power, Malcolm nonetheless emphasizes his very ordinary life:

A very few minutes sufficed to wash and dress; and we were soon driving through the streets . . . It was market morning, and when we got out on Piccadilly there was an endless stream of carts coming from the west; but for the rest the roadway was clear, and we went quickly. (p. 22)

Stoker follows the format he used in *Dracula* and *Mystery*, of confronting an ordinary modern character with an embodiment of Gothic mystery. However, Ross does not need to travel to an exotic location because Stoker has him encounter mystery and excess in his own backyard.

Much of that mystery occurs when he and his acquaintances confront powers from the ancient past. Like Dracula, Tera is a master of statecraft and military affairs befitting a monarch as well as a practitioner of magic. Opposed by the powerful Egyptian priesthood who wished to suppress her name and thus deny her immortality, Tera has herself buried, apparently intending future resurrection, an event that begins when Corbeck and Trelawney find her tomb in the Valley of the Sorcerers.

While they attempt to understand the writing on the walls of Tera's tomb, readers confront her potential for violence, when someone or something attacks Trelawney and tries to remove a gold bangle from his wrist. The detective notes that extreme power was required: 'This is no ordinary bangle. The gold is wrought over triple steel links; see where it is worn away. It is manifestly not meant to be removed lightly; and it would need more than an ordinary file to do it' (p. 27). Stoker emphasizes that power as Tera's mere presence causes people to enter a cataleptic state. The chief victims are Trelawny and Nurse Kennedy, but even Ross is affected:

These very mummy smells arise from the presence of substances . . . which the Egyptian priests, who were the learned men and scientists of their time, found . . . strong enough to arrest the natural forces of decay. There must be powerful agencies at work to effect such a purpose; and it is possible that we may have here some rare substance or combination whose qualities and powers are not understood in this later and more prosaic age. (p. 81)

Neither Trelawny nor Kennedy is permanently harmed by their encounter, although Ross suspects Tera's influence may be ultimately malicious:

Nine dead men, one of them slain manifestly by the Queen's own hand! And . . . several savage attacks on Mr Trelawny in his own room, in which . . . she had tried to open the safe and to extract the Talisman jewel. His device of fastening the key to his wrist . . . had wellnigh cost him his life. (p. 216)

Not only does Ross suspect Tera of causing death or injury he also believes she has possessed the woman he loves, at one point observing: 'Margaret was changing . . . Now she was generally *distraite*, and at times in a sort of negative condition as though her mind – her very being – was not present' (p. 211). Indeed, the closer they come to the Great Experiment, the more he believes they are making a mistake. Readers share that suspicion, noting that even Margaret's cat shares Ross's apprehensions. Because Ross and Silvio are unfortunately in the minority, the 1903 version unleashes this representative of the past on modern England, her past behaviour suggesting she will stop at nothing to achieve her desires.

As with *Dracula* and *Lair*, Stoker transforms the representations of the past into supernatural monsters against which humans have limited control. Maunder describes this transformation in terms of Gothic conventions:

Showing the terrifying eruption of the supernatural and other spectres of monstrosity – demonic females, doubles, taboo desires, themes of infectious disease, unlawful (sexual) desires, subterranean spaces – all packaged together in a fragmented narrative and sometimes confusing narrative structure, Stoker uses many of the conventions of what we have come to recognize as Gothic writing.[45]

What makes Tera so overwhelming is her violence and ability to over-power the assembled experts. Sir James Frere refuses to address the case; Nurse Kennedy is immediately overpowered; and Doctor Winchester succumbs during the Great Experiment as do Trelawny and Corbeck. A polymath, Corbeck reveals his expertise in almost all fields: 'I am a Master of Arts and Doctor of Laws and Master of Surgery of Cambridge; Doctor of Letters of Oxford; Doctor of Science and Doctor of Languages of London University; Doctor of Philosophy of Berlin; Doctor of Oriental Languages of Paris' (pp. 88–9). Neither expert training nor love nor religion is sufficient. The most religious of Stoker's heroes, Ross falls on his knees in prayer and acknowledges God's power: 'There could be no going back now! We were in the hands of God!' (p. 228). Stoker suggests, however, that God has turned his back on humanity.

Jewel leaves readers with – at least in its original and more horrify-ing version – a profound sense of the mummy's materiality, as Ross observes before the resurrection:

> Then, and then only, did the full horror of the whole thing burst upon me! There, in the full glare of the light, the whole material and sordid side of death seemed staringly real . . . The coverings were evidently many, for the bulk was great. But through all, showed that unhidable human figure . . . What was before us was death, and nothing else. All the romance and sentiment of fancy had disappeared. (p. 238)

This materiality becomes more evident when the storm intrudes. Thinking he is taking Margaret to safety, Ross carries Tera's body out of the cavern, her very name suggesting she is earthly (from the Latin *terra*, earth) like Dracula, who must rest in native soil at day's end.[46] Returning to rescue the others, Ross is surrounded by dead bodies. The 'glassy stare' of Margaret's eyes 'was more terrible than an open glare' (p. 250).

Stoker reinforces Tera's corporeality in the same way he reminded readers of Dracula's physical presence, through smell. Robert Mighall, one of the only scholars to comment on the Gothic use of smell, ob-serves in *A Geography of Victorian Gothic Fiction* that early Gothic novels, including *Castle of Otranto, A Sicilian Romance* or *Melmoth* do not mention smell but that it becomes an important part of *fin de siècle* Gothic:

In contrast, one of the first things which Jonathan Harker notes about Count Dracula is his bad breath. And in ... *The Lair of the White Worm*, Stoker describes the smell of the eponymous terrain ...Within a hundred years Gothic fiction has become more fastidious about smell.[47]

Burke mentions smell briefly in 'Section XXI: Smell and Taste. Bitters and Stenches', noting only that 'no smells or tastes can produce a grand sensation, except excessive bitters, and intolerable stenches'.[48] Mighall, as noted earlier, links odours in *fin de siècle* Gothic literature to social changes:

> In Stoker, the narrator gropes for analogies gleaned from 'clinical' or sanitary situations and experiences to evoke that which cannot quite be described ...The new Gothic landscape of the slum ... demands an appropriate language to evoke its horrors, and employs the familiar Gothic trope of the unspeakable.[49]

Anyone who reads contemporary Gothic literature knows that writers and readers are still horrified by bad smells. While readers in previous centuries may have been surrounded by odours caused by poor sanitation and generalized pollution, the developed world now has sanitary sewers that remove waste from sight and smell as well as re-frigeration that preserves both food and bodies. Nonetheless, unpleasant smells remind readers what ultimately happens to our physical bodies: sickness, death and decomposition. While Ancient Egyptians and modern undertakers attempt to deny this, putting the bodies of the dead through elaborate procedures, ultimately dead is dead. In 'Comic Gothic', Avril Horner and Sue Zlosnik comment on what humans fear and argue that the Gothic intends to 'generate fear: the serious Gothic work challenges the reader with the question "What are you afraid of?" and, in so doing, evokes feelings of horror, terror and revulsion'.[50] Adding that the Gothic deals with boundaries, Horner and Zlosnik suggest why vampires and mummies evoke fears:

> Gothic writing always concerns itself with boundaries and their in-stabilities, whether between the quick/the dead, eros/thanatos, pain/pleasure, 'real'/'unreal', 'natural'/'supernatural', material/transcendent, man/machine, human/vampire or 'masculine'/'feminine'. Serious

Gothic writing manifests a deep anxiety about the permeability of such boundaries. The serious Gothic writer deliberately exploits the fear of the 'Other' encroaching upon the apparent safety of the post-Enlightenment world and the stability of the post-Enlightenment subject.[51]

Smell reminds readers of the instability of boundaries. Indeed, Ross is haunted by these smells:

> You may put a mummy in a glass case and hermetically seal it . . . but all the same it will exhale its odour. One might think that four or five thousand years would exhaust the olfactory qualities of anything; but . . . these smells remain, and . . . their secrets are unknown to us. Today they are as much mysteries as they were when the embalmers put the body in the bath of natron . . .
>
> All at once I sat up. I had become lost in an absorbing reverie. The Egyptian smell had seemed to get on my nerves – on my memory – on my very will. (p. 46)

In short, such overwhelming smells remind Ross and readers of matters over which they have no control, in particular two especially powerful fears, of death and the impact of the past. Even love – often a powerful force in Stoker's work – cannot overcome death, and it has little control over tradition either.

If his emphasis on smell indicates that Stoker is moving toward a new kind of Gothic, his setting demonstrates what he learned from his predecessors. There are no castles because there are no aristocrats, but Trelawny's ancestral home resembles castles in early Gothic literature:

> [T]he house is absolutely shut out from public access or even from view. It stands on a little promontory behind a steep hill, and except from the sea cannot be seen. Of old it was fenced in by a high stone wall, for the house which it succeeded was built . . . in the days when a great house . . . had to . . . defend itself. (p. 197)

At its heart is the underground cavern where the Great Experiment occurs. Both Hopkins and Roth comment on the significance of this spot. Roth observes that 'the labyrinthine path to the cave followed by the initiates' duplicates 'Trelawny's earlier journeys to Queen Tera's rock-tomb in Egypt'.[52] Hopkins comments that Stoker often sets portions of his works in dark subterranean places, which reveal 'the darker side of Stoker's fiction, especially its obsessions with sex, gender, disease, and various forms of secret knowledge'.[53]

The conclusion, which returns to the ancestral home, pays homage to Stoker's predecessors and also suggests that Trelawny, who is both the father and the leader of the quest to bring Tera back, is corrupt or mad. Because he does not question the wisdom of resurrecting the dead queen and unleashing her on the modern world, horrors come to civilized London, which Maunder describes as 'a place of danger':

> Both *Dracula* and *The Jewel of Seven Stars* convey this in fairly lurid and 'fantastic' ways, starting off in the strange and alien worlds of Transylvania and Ancient Egypt but then depicting how their monsters ... find their way to London, the supposed impregnable centre of the modern world.[54]

No longer is the Gothic relegated to exotic locations or set safely in the past so readers can conclude: 'These things can't happen, certainly not here.' Indeed, Stoker's Gothic works evoke fear because he sets them in a world that resembles their own.

That Stoker originally concluded *Jewel* with an apocalyptic ending suggests his uncertainty about the potential for modern science to overcome ancient evils. Faced with the exciting future that science and technology seemed to promise, Stoker sometimes imagined a future full of infinite possibilities though he could never entirely ignore the violence and irrationality he and his contemporaries associated with the past and with primitive people closer to home. Although Stoker's works often embody the power of the modern scientific and technological age and, therefore, conclude happily, *Jewel* does not, and Tera's ghost haunts even the revised, supposedly happy ending, making *Jewel* not Stoker's best-known novel but his most Gothic.

4

Gothic-tinged Romances:
The Man, Lady Athlyne *and*
The Lady of the Shroud

&OCR&

Following *Jewel*, his most Gothic work, Stoker's next works take
radically different directions. He wrote *Personal Reminiscences of Henry
Irving* (1906) out of obligation to his friend as well as for fans of the
great actor. Pure romances with occasional Gothic hints, *The Man*
(1905) and *Lady Athlyne* (1908) feature small casts of characters and
conclude with happy marriages.[1] More panoramic, *The Lady of the
Shroud* (1909) includes numerous Gothic references, including a
heroine who sleeps in a coffin and is reputed to be a vampire.[2]
However, references to the supernatural turn out to be false, and
the novel, which begins with a reported vampire sighting in *The
Journal of Occultism* (a fictionalized version of the journal of the
Society for Psychical Research) and features its hero's midnight
marriage, concludes with the founding of a unified Balkan Federation. While it might be classified as a romance because it includes
the marriage of its central characters, David Glover calls it a 'liberal
utopia in its fullest, most developed form', in *Vampires, Mummies, and
Liberals*, because of its emphasis on politics.[3] He cites Krishan Kumar,
who defined the genre in *Utopia and Anti-Utopia in Modern Times*, and
observes:[4]

> For the end of the nineteenth century saw a revival of literary utopias,
> a trend both inspired by and in reaction against precisely the sorts of
> spectacular . . . technological achievements . . . that Stoker loved . . .

At opposite poles, stories of 'advanced mechanical civilizations jostled those of simple, back-to-nature utopias,' and on this spectrum *The Lady of the Shroud* is positioned neatly in the middle.[5]

Although Stoker includes Gothic conventions in all three novels, he replaces Gothic mystery with political and technological certainty in *Lady*, and with love in *The Man* and *Athlyne*. It is nonetheless useful to analyse Stoker's adaptation of Gothic elements in novels rarely classified as Gothic.

The Man

Most scholars characterize *The Man* as a romance. In *A Biography of Dracula*, Harry Ludlam describes it as 'a pure and unashamed romance'.[6] In *Bram Stoker*, Phyllis A. Roth, one of the few scholars to treat it at length, calls it 'Stoker's most leisurely and sophisticated romance; indeed, with regard to characterization, it is his most painstaking and satisfying novel'.[7] Comparing it with *Miss Betty* in *Bram Stoker: A Bibliography*, William Hughes describes it as 'equally deficient in Gothic content'.[8]

The few Gothic conventions in *The Man* are subtle: strong suggestions of mystery in descriptions of the natural world and the greedy and amoral Everards, who resemble villains of early Gothic literature. Finally, his depiction of Stephen's experience in her family crypt is reminiscent of terrifying experiences in earlier Gothic novels. Maunder describes this episode as 'a gruesome, almost Gothic, scene in which the adolescent girl discovers her mother's coffin'.[9] These Gothic notes temper the sweetness of the story and remind readers that even the happiest lives include moments of pain and suffering. Indeed, those moments are especially poignant here, for Stephen and Harold lose their parents before they are adults, and Stephen also loses her beloved aunt while she is still a young woman. Nonetheless, despite the presence of death, *The Man* focuses on the present and the future. It is not haunted by the past; its villains are ordinary human beings not supernatural monsters; and it includes few of the dark and inscrutable mysteries generally associated with the Gothic.

The novel opens with a 'Fore-Glimpse', set in the churchyard at Normanstand, Stephen's family estate, where she and Harold An Wolf overhear children discussing various supernatural creatures. The day is sunlit, but the setting evokes earlier Gothic fiction:

> Round it [the church] clustered many tombstones seemingly decrepit from age, tilted and slanted in all directions; amongst them a few stately monuments, rising patrician fashion amongst the crowd and grave with the hoary dignity of years. Behind the church a line of ancient yews so gnarled and twisted in their thick brown stems, so worn and broken and wasted with time and storm, that one could well imagine that long ago from them came the furnishing of battle when the bowstrings twanged and the clothyard shafts whistled on their deadly way. (p. 1)

While the churchyard reminds readers of the past and of death, the sunny scene features childish innocence and Stephen's and Harold's debate about justice. It is thus typical of *The Man*, a romance in which the Gothic is a distant memory and the pain of losing loved ones a dull ache rather than acute pain.

One of the few terrifying scenes occurs when eleven-year-old Stephen asks Leonard to accompany her into her family crypt. When the children drop their candles, Stephen faints, and Leonard runs away. Explaining her hysteria to Harold, she admits it stemmed from her sudden awareness of death:

> I never thought . . . that my poor dear mother was buried in the crypt. And when I went to look at the name on the coffin that was nearest to where I was, I knocked away the dust, and then I saw her name: 'Margaret Norman, ætat 22.' I couldn't bear it. She was only a girl herself, only just twice my age – lying there in that terrible dark place with all the thick dust and the spiders' webs . . . How shall I ever bear to think of her lying there, and that I shall never see her dear face? Never! Never! (p. 66)

No doubt the grisly setting contributes to her fears (Stoker uses a similar setting to full Gothic effect in *Lady*), but Stephen suddenly realizes death is real, the crypt a conclusion for everyone. Nonetheless, this scene is an anomaly in *The Man*. Even though characters face death (the deaths of Stephen's father and uncle resulting from an accident), *The Man* features the sadness of losing loved ones rather than Gothic horror.

While nature in *The Man* is generally sunlit and balmy, Stoker occasionally uses it to remind readers that life has a dark side over which human beings have no control. On two occasions Harold faces storms at sea that remind readers of human fragility. In the first, while travelling to Canada, he rescues Pearl Stonehouse who is swept overboard. In the second, he brings a burning ship safely to the harbour. Both scenes emphasize Harold's strength and masculinity – he is, of course, the eponymous man of the title – while they demonstrate nature's power. As Roth notes, the rescue scenes, while 'ripe for melodrama, are instead noteworthy for dramatic depictions of the natural forces'.[10] Indeed, the second rescue is especially dramatic because the storm follows a pleasant ocean crossing:

> After some days the fine weather changed; howling winds and growing seas were the environment. The great ship, which usually rested even-keeled on two waves, and whose bilge keels under normal conditions rendered rolling impossible, began to pitch and roll like a leviathan at play. (p. 356)

The passage demonstrates that nature, while generally benign, has a dark and terrifying side. Other passages point to nature's overwhelming power:

> And The Man, away in the wilds of Alaska, was feeling ... the chastening and purifying influences of the wilderness. The towering mountains, the great wooded valleys that vanished in curving distance, the eternal snowfields and the glaciers that mocked at time seemed to dwarf anything that was of man. Fears and hopes and memories and misgivings gave way before the ... overwhelming vastness. How could the passions or regrets of man seem to hold a discernible place, when man himself was of such manifest insignificance? (p. 322)

The references to nature's sublime power and human insignificance might have come straight from Burke.

Even though several scenes suggest that nature is vast and mysterious and human beings as powerless against it as they are against death, relatively few scenes focus on death and nature. Indeed, the element most reminiscent of the Gothic is its villains, Leonard Everard and his father Jasper, though the Gothic is an echo, for Leonard is not a supernatural monster like Dracula, Tera or Arabella or even a criminal like the kidnappers in *The Mystery of the Sea*. Instead, he is a craven young man whose greed and inability to curb his desires suggest his Gothic ancestors. Because he abandons Stephen in the crypt, seduces a young village woman only to abandon her when she becomes pregnant and wishes he could kill his father so he could pay his debts, Stoker presents him as an ordinary human being, not a monster:

> His egotism was so colossal and his selfishness so abysmal that he did not realize what a magnificent possibility had opened itself to him without effort or seeking on his own part. He was in truth that perfect selfish egotist who lives in the moment and whose impelling force is his immediate desire. (p. 137)

Andrew Maunder, in *Bram Stoker*, describes Leonard as 'one of Stoker's social villains; a serial seducer driven on in pursuit of self-gratification'.[11] William Hughes, in *Beyond Dracula*, discusses his family and suggests that Gothic villains can become domesticated – though they are still destructive to those over whom they have control:

> Jasper Everard ... provides a particularly acute example. Emphatically a bourgeois who has recently bought himself into the gentry circles ... Everard is represented as 'a gentleman, retired partner of a bank, who had not long before purchased a moderate estate between Norcester and Normanstand' (*TM* 41) ... In contrast to Stephen's assumption of the role of Lady Bountiful ... an extension of her father's position as 'a sort of power to help them' (*TM* 85), Everard brings the 'precise, cold, exact' ethics of the urban bourgeoisies to bear upon his retainers.[12]

Hughes compares him to Mendoza, the money lender in *The Watter's Mou'*, and readers may also compare him to Murdock in *The Snake's Pass*, works that replace supernatural power with ordinary greed and selfishness.

That Stoker sets *The Man* in his own day and peoples it with ordinary characters suggests he is considering contemporary social issues.

That concern is especially clear in references to the Boer War and to changes in the economic and social status of women.[13] Stephen's horror at the loss of life she reads about in the newspaper will be repeated in *Athlyne*:

> Towards Christmas . . . the Boer war had reached its climax of evil. As the news of disaster after disaster was flashed through the cable she . . . felt appalled at the sacrifices exacted by the God of War. In the early days the war was an 'officers'' war . . . Many names there were which she knew, for before the war was three months old nearly every great house . . . was in mourning. (pp. 323–4)

More than a century later, readers feel what it meant for England to lose a generation of young men, and Stoker dramatizes the impact of that loss of life and changed gender roles by having Stephen succeed to an earldom because the war wiped out the younger males in her family and because the earl de Lannoy 'never recovered from the shock of hearing that his two sons and his nephew had been killed in an ambush by Cronje' (p. 324). When real horrors intrude, there is no reason to manufacture monsters.

Maunder, acutely aware of Stoker's interest in contemporary issues, summarizes legislation that changed English ideas about gender:

> The waning of Victorianism, the impetus which the 'Woman Question' seemed to be gathering, after the passing of the Married Women's Property Act (1882) and the Matrimonial Causes Acts of (1882; 1893), the sudden 'plague', as it seemed to many, of New Women, homosexuals and 'inverts' like Oscar Wilde, the continuing impact of urbanizaton and the recruiting campaigns for the Boer War which revealed that 60 per cent of men were physically unfit for military service – all meant that it was easy to regard . . . standards of masculinity . . . in a state of transition and decay.[14]

There is no question that *The Man* and *Athlyne* address questions that dominated discussions at the turn of the twentieth century. That Stephen's father raises her as the son he had wanted leads her to question traditional gender roles and adopt male prerogatives. Among these is her desire to accompany her father to the Petty Sessions Court, a wish that horrifies her maiden aunt. Reading this scene, Roth suggests it reveals Stoker's sympathy towards women:

> Stoker has come some distance since *Dracula* in which Mina Harker, the perfect Victorian woman, reviles those of her sex who ... might even ... dare to propose to men! By 1905 Stoker is not so unsympathetic as Mina. In a series of discussions between Stephen and her aunt Laetitia, Stephen avers the equal responsibility of men for pregnancies.[15]

He is moving away from the idea that women's desire for equality is frightening. Nonetheless, Stephen's decision to propose to Leonard causes her great pain. She suffers for more than two years because of her impulsive proposal, which she almost immediately regrets, and her equally impulsive rejection of Harold. Because Stephen and Harold mature over the two years they are separated, learning about themselves and the world, *The Man* concludes with their reunion and anticipates their long and happy life together: 'When the two saw each other's eyes there was no need for words. Harold came close, opening wide his arms. Stephen flew to them. In that divine moment, when their mouths met, both knew that their souls were one' (p. 436). Remembering that Stoker frequently punishes aggressive women, readers often see the conclusion as sanctioning traditional gender roles and heterosexual marriage.

The Man is less traditional than it may initially appear. While it and *Athlyne* conclude with happy marriages, it also demonstrates other possibilities for women. Stephen's aunt is an assertive spinster with a rich and fulfilling life, and Maunder mentions 'other important kinds of women in the novel':

> These include Mrs Egerton, a lecturer and political activist at the women-only Somerville College, Oxford (whose name is presumably meant to remind us of the well-known New Woman writer, George Egerton) and whose charity work ... Stephen sees at first hand.[16]

Furthermore, because marriage will not strip Stephen of her title or the power that goes with it, *The Man* is less conventional than it sometimes appears, more aware of present circumstances and future possibilities.

Indeed, Maunder discusses Stoker's treatment of the imprisoning force of tradition:

> His novels also validate female intelligence and initiative, and question the sexual double standard. They suggest that female fulfilment and a sense of self is desirable. Thus ... Stephen Norman is represented losing her moral bearings but also as trapped in that part of the new twentieth century, still governed by Victorian assumptions ... Indeed, sympathy for Stephen's social and moral confusion, her intelligence, her resourcefulness, and her feelings of imprisonment increase the more she sublimates herself within approved kinds of behaviour and does so in a rather confused and cheerless way.[17]

Stoker does not present Stephen or Joy in *Athlyne* as wrong or monstrous because they desire equality with the men they love and want more than is sanctioned by women's traditional roles. Certainly, Stephen, who is raised as her father's 'son' and inherits a title because there are no male heirs, is no ravening vampire-bride.

The absence of monsters does not mean the absence of problems, though evil in *The Man* comes from ordinary people. Leonard, for example, is a seducer, and Susan Mings, who had gone into service in Oxford and become pregnant, kills herself because of his indifference. Elsewhere he reveals his desire for mastery:

> His debts being now paid, the fear which was his restraining influence was removed, and all the hectoring side of the man, which was ... based on his masculinity, was aroused ... He knew something of the value of a whip with the weaker sex. (p. 260)

That women were gaining economic rights and demanding political power probably exacerbated Leonard's desire for mastery. Like other men at the beginning of the twentieth century, he knew he had lost his absolute and unquestioned authority.

Much of the unhappiness in the novel – the evil with a small 'e' – comes from ordinary youthful impulsiveness. Stephen proposes to Leonard without seeing that he is unsuitable and rejects Harold equally impulsively. After Stephen's rejection, Harold immediately leaves for Alaska. That the subsequent years are lonely is due to their impetuosity rather than to the monstrous external forces evident in Stoker's Gothic works.

Lady Athlyne

Although Stoker interrupted his novel writing to prepare *Personal Reminiscences* and *Snowbound*, his next novel returned to the same issues as *The Man*, the impact of the Boer War and concern over women's growing independence. The biggest difference is that *The Man* includes dark elements, including a cold and manipulative family, while *Lady Athlyne*, Stoker's sunniest work, concludes happily with the marriage of the main characters (and anticipates another wedding between Joy's Aunt Judy and the Sheriff of Galway) and is set in a benign natural world that lacks the mystery and violence associated with the Gothic. The single character who might remind readers of the Gothic is the heroine's irascible father who threatens violence and serves as an impediment to the young lovers.

Putting the text under a microscope reveals a few moments of Gothic unease and suggests that Stoker, whose Gothic tales generally include romance at the centre, cannot totally eliminate the Gothic. While most of the novel takes place in sunny Italy or the Lake District, where the Ogilvie family is on holiday, *Athlyne* opens with nature's overwhelming power:

> On . . . a day in February 1899, the White Star S.S. *Cryptic* forced her way . . . out into the Hudson River through a mass of floating ice, which made a moving carpet over the whole river . . . For three whole weeks the great city had been beleaguered by cold; held besieged in the icy grip of a blizzard which . . . had begun on the last day of January to devastate the central North American States. In one place, Breckenridge in Colorado, there fell in five days—and this on the top of an accumulation of six feet of snow—an additional forty-five inches. In the track swept by the cold wave, a thousand miles wide, record low temperatures were effected, ranging from 15° below zero in Indiana to 54° below at White River on the northern shore of Lake Superior.
>
> In New York city the temperature had sunk to 6.2° below zero, the lowest ever recorded . . . The city itself was in a helpless condition, paralyzed and impotent. (p. 15)

The same power is evident in *Snowbound*, published at roughly the same time. Both reveal nature at its most brutal, a force against which human beings are powerless. Indeed, one has only to look at Stoker's word choice – 'beleaguered', 'besieged', 'icy grip', 'devastate', 'extraordinary temperature', 'helpless', 'paralyzed' and 'impotent' – to see that human beings only think they are masters of all they survey. While the opening section is dramatic, a more subtle passage about Italy emphasizes both beauty and power:

> The whole day was spent on the road, for the beauty was such that the stoppages were endless. Joy ... could hardly contain her rapture as fresh vistas ... burst upon her. When the curve of the promontory began to cut off the view of Vesuvius ... she got out of the carriage and ran back to ... have a full view. Underneath her lay the wonderful scene of matchless beauty. To the right rose Vesuvius a mass of warm colour, with its cinder cone staring boldly into the blue sky ... Below it was the sloping plain dotted with trees and villas and villages, articulated in the clear air like a miniature map. Then the great curve of the bay, the sapphire sea marked clearly on the outline of the coast from Ischia which rose like a jewel from a jewel. Past Naples ... and the buried Herculaneum ... To the left, a silhouette of splendid soft purple, rose the island of Capri from the sea of sapphire which seemed to quiver in the sunshine. (pp. 34–5)

Stoker paints a scene that is picture-postcard perfect, the narrator observing that 'Naples is always at spring time' (p. 37). That he mentions Vesuvius and Herculaneum, ancient cities destroyed by nature at its most powerful, nonetheless reminds readers of over-whelming power.

Another manifestation of nature's power is that the heroine's mother, Sarah Ogilvie, has travelled to Ischia for her health. Much improved, she is still troubled by nightmares:

> This evening Mrs. Ogilvie was very quietly inclined to be tearful. She too had had a bad night; constant wakings from vague apprehensions, horrible imaginings of unknown dangers; dread that she could not localise or specify. Altogether she was upset, something as one is in the low stage following an attack of hysteria; nervous, weak, apprehensive, inclined to misunderstand things on the melancholy side. (p. 77)

In Gothic novels, references to 'a bad night', 'constant wakings from vague apprehensions', 'horrible imaginings', 'unknown dangers' and 'dread' might prepare readers for something terrible. In *Athlyne*, the passage simply reinforces Mrs Ogilvie's invalidism.

Her husband is decidedly more Gothic although the romance plot gives him little opportunity to do more than bluster and threaten. There is, however, the suggestion of his dark and violent past, mostly connected to duelling. Athlyne learns of one instance from an American soldier: 'He called it an unforgivable outrage and insisted on fighting over it. I tell you it nearly cost the joker his life. He was drilled right through, and only escaped death by a miracle' (p. 91). Judy, Mrs Ogilvie's spinster sister, hints that Colonel Ogilvie killed her former lover in a duel:

> Please God may you never know what it is to be in or on the fringe of a Feud . . . My own life that years ago was as bright and promising as any young life can be; when the Love that had dawned on my girl-hood rose and beat with noonday heat on my young-womanhood made it seem as if heaven had come down to earth. And then the one moment of misunderstanding – the quick accusation – the quicker retort – and my poor heart lying crushed between . . . two men whom I loved each in his proper way. (p. 123)

In this way, Judy warns Athlyne about her brother-in-law's temper, and the omniscient narrator suggests his devious side as well:

> Colonel Ogilvie was skilled in the deadly preliminaries to lethal quarrel. More than once when a foe had been marked down for vengeance had he led him on to force the duel . . . There was in his nature something . . . of the Red Indian which enables him to enjoy the torture of his foe . . . Perhaps the very air of the 'dark and bloody, ground' of Kentucky was so impregnated with the passions of those who made it so that the dwelling of some generations had imbued the dwellers with some of the old Indian spirit. (pp. 190–1)

Like Hutcheson in 'The Squaw', Colonel Ogilvie is comfortable with torture; like Hutcheson, Quincey Morris and Grizzly Dick, he retains something of the primitive. Although Stoker eventually

redeems him – *Athlyne* is as sparkling and ultimately as joyous as
Shakespearean comedy – this American has a dark and sinister side.

If the colonel is a descendant of the Gothic villain, Joy resembles
the persecuted maiden. Ordinarily independent and self-confident,
she meets Athlyne who saves her from a runaway horse, and she is
frightened at the prospect of driving his car to her hotel. That the
dangers are real is reinforced by the fact that Athlyne, a more experienced motorist, is frightened for her:

> She might get into any one of many forms of trouble . . . She was . . .
> not a practiced [*sic*] driver; and was in control of the very latest type of
> machine of whose special mechanism she could know nothing. If she
> should break down far from any town she would be in the most difficult
> position possible: a girl all alone in a country she did not know. And all
> this apart from the possibility of accident, of mischance of driving; of
> the act of other travellers; of cattle on the road; of any of the countless
> mishaps which can be with so swift and heavy a machine as a motor.
> And then should she not arrive in time, what pain or unpleasantness
> might there not be with her father . . . He might be angry with her for
> going out on such a long excursion with a man alone. (pp. 154–5)

Stoker connects Joy even more to the persecuted maiden by presenting danger from her perspective:

> To start with, she was full of fears; some of them natural, others of that
> class which is due to the restrictions and conventions of a woman's life.
> She was by no means an expert driver. She merely had some lessons
> and was never in an automobile by herself before. Moreover she was not
> only in a country strange to her . . . In addition . . . she was – as an
> American – handicapped by the difference in the rules of the road. In
> America they follow the French and drive on the off side: in England
> the "on" rule is correct. (p. 157)

As night falls, she becomes more frightened, and the atmosphere,
with its emphasis on darkness, cold and mist, becomes more Gothic:

> It was a shock . . . to see how different were her surroundings from
> her thoughts. Those hours when they sat together where the sunbeams

stole through the trees would afford her many a comparison . . . All was now dark and dank and chill. The mist was thickening every instant; she could hardly see the road ahead of her. (p. 158)

Before she crashes Athlyne's car, Joy is terrified both for herself and the man she loves:

Everything around her was new and strange and unknown, and so was full of terrors . . . She knew that unless she got home in something like reasonable time her father would be . . . furiously angry – and all that anger would be visited on Him . . . It was too frightful to contemplate what might happen should she have to be out all night . . . and after having gone out with a man against whom her father had already a grievance. (p. 160)

The passage alternates between general fright and fear of the all-powerful father, subtle reminders why Stoker is known as a Gothic writer.

Roth, who says almost nothing about *Athlyne*, comments on the awkward presence of Joy's father: 'The plot . . . is based . . . on a case of falsified identity which is condoned and resolved . . . through the romance of the two protagonists whom we last see locked in a triangular embrace including the heroine's father.'[18] In a Gothic work, the father would be more sinister largely because other characters rebel against exploitative father figures and attempt to escape. In *Athlyne*, Joy adores her biological father and also discovers value in other representatives of the past: 'In Italy Joy Ogilvie learned to the full, consciously and unconsciously, all the lessons which a younger civilisation can learn from an elder' (p. 38).

While the Gothic is haunted by the past, *Athlyne* focuses on the present and, because of its interest in technology and greater autonomy for women, looks to the future. It also reminds readers that the Boer War has caused cultural shifts. Athlyne is a veteran of that conflict and his heroism is revealed to Joy through newspaper accounts. A decorated cavalry officer, he has been imprisoned in the 'Bird-cage' at Pretoria, an experience that diminished his confidence. Thus the war is not merely part of Athlyne's past but an influence on his present because he returns from the war with no clear sense of what to do with his life.

References to the war occur only in the opening chapters, where they reinforce Athlyne's unquestionable masculinity. If *Dracula* presents readers with a Gothic sense that sexuality is mysterious and dangerous, *Athlyne* focuses on sexuality as an affirmation of individual identity. Scholars emphasize that Stoker, in *Dracula* and 'The censorship of fiction', criticizes writers, including the New Women writers, who treat sexuality openly, and some even argue that these works demonstrate Stoker's hostility towards feminism or even towards women.[19] *Athlyne*, on the other hand, celebrates the open expression of female sexuality, and Glover comments that Stoker's letters reveal friendships with 'New Women writers, including George Egerton, Elizabeth Robins, and Grant Allen, the controversial author of the *Woman Who Did* (1895).'[20] Ludlam indicates Stoker's complexity when he observes that *Athlyne* was published at the same time as Stoker wrote on censorship for *The Nineteenth Century*: '"Lady Athlyne", published at this time was a happy parcel of romantic reading with plenty of love and blushes and . . . a motoring episode to speed along the plot.'[21] Paul Murray, in *From the Shadow of Dracula*, demonstrates that technology impacted on gender roles, noting how the automobile allows his lovers to escape the prying eyes of family and servants.[22] Stoker's narration also emphasizes their passion:

> Athlyne loved Joy in all ways . . . His was no passing fancy which might or might not develop, flame up, and fade away. He had . . . found the other half of him, lost in the primeval chaos; and he wanted the union to be so complete that it would outlive the clashing worlds in the final cataclysm. Healthy people are healthy in their loves and even in their passions. These two young people were both healthy, both red-blooded, both of ardent, passionate nature; and they were drawn together . . . by all the powers that rule sex and character. To say that their love was all of earth would be as absurd as to say that it was all of heaven. It was human, all human, and all that such implies. Heaven and earth had both their parts in the combination; and perhaps, since both were of strong nature . . . Hell had its due share in the amalgam. (p. 130)

Despite the reference to hell, nothing suggests the predatory sexuality evident in *Dracula* or even the desire for mastery that characterizes

Leonard. In fact, *Athlyne* focuses on mutuality. The following passage, in which Joy responds to Athlyne's suggestion that they celebrate their marriage in Westminster Abbey, hints at a significant difference between *Dracula* and *Athlyne*, between the paradigmatic Gothic text and the perfect romance:

> 'Anywhere you choose – darling!' she spoke the last word shyly 'will be what I wish. I am glad I am to be married three times to you' . . . 'Because darling' she spoke the word now without shyness or hesitation. 'I love you enough for three husbands; and now we must have three honeymoons!' (p. 222)

Lucy's desire for three husbands suggests a thoughtless and uncontrollable sexuality for which she and the other vampires are punished. In *Athlyne* Joy's desire for three marriages reflects her love of one man, and the novel concludes by affirming their mutual love, including its physical manifestations: 'Then she closed his mouth in the very best way that a young wife can do – the way that seems to take his feet from earth and to raise him to heaven' (p. 237).

Both *The Man* and *Athlyne* conclude with joyous celebrations of young heterosexual love, and both exorcize the haunting presence of the past so characteristic of the Gothic. Changing attitudes toward female sexuality are also evident in Mrs O'Brien, Athlyne's old nurse, whose earthy references to future offspring and cheerful memories of her wedding night remind readers that Stoker's romances are forward looking. *The Lady of the Shroud* is even more future oriented, concluding not with the promise of children but with Little Rupert, son of the protagonists.

The Lady of the Shroud

If *The Man* and *Athlyne* focus on their protagonists and the limited cast of characters surrounding them, *The Lady of the Shroud* is multi-faceted. Not only does it include more characters as well as a political conflict that involves whole nations, its more complex narrative suggests its Gothic heritage. Ludlam, Maunder and Roth assert that it follows essentially the same narrative strategy as *Dracula*. Ludlam notes that it is written 'in the form of journals kept by the principal characters', while Maunder observes that it 'is told through a series of supposedly "real" documents (journals, letters, newspaper reports, travel narratives)' and adds that it 'returns to some of the same ground mapped out in *Dracula*, taking in not only the occult and supernatural but also the clashes between past and present and between cultures'.[23] Commenting on the narrative, Roth describes a strategy that makes *Lady* more panoramic than its immediate predecessors but argues that it is less satisfactory than *Dracula*:

> Moreover, although it employs a variety of narrative devices similar to those . . . in *Dracula,* the motivation for them . . . is not internally justified; rather, in the second half . . . after the mystery has been explained, the story becomes . . . an adventure tale, with the narrative devices serving only to provide information . . . As a consequence, many of the narrators . . . are incidental characters in whom the reader is interested only for the information they provide.[24]

Roth's assessment stems from her preference for Stoker's horror tales, which *Lady*, despite obvious Gothic elements, clearly is not.

Indeed, *Lady* demonstrates that Stoker is more interested in contemporary problems than in the past, and scholars examine his interest in politics, which is much in evidence. Ludlam points to its interest in aviation:

> 'The Lady of the Shroud' was published in 1909. It was only in the last months of the previous year that the Wright brothers had made their most successful flights; and only as the book was published did Bleriot successfully fly the Channel . . . His fantastic last scene . . . written . . . before the start of World War I now reads prophetically.[25]

Maunder observes that reviewers remarked on its contemporary resonance and mentions specifically a review in *The Bookman* that admired Stoker's patriotism: 'A huge prophetic melodrama of the near East: he [Stoker] creates in outline . . . that Balkan Federation, which . . . certainly seems essential to the curbing of Austrian ambitions on the one hand and Turkish pretensions on the other.'[26] Murray explores works that inspired Stoker and explains that Robert Kane's

The Industrial Resources of Ireland (1844) may have influenced his thinking about economic development in the Balkans:

> Kane was concerned with the ... potential of Irish natural resources – for example the harnessing of water power through turbines – which he saw as being facilitated by the marriage of English capital and of Irish enterprise. This ... is precisely the solution adopted in *The Snake's Pass* and, years later in the Balkan context, *The Lady of the Shroud*. Kane's ideas were adopted by the mid-nineteenth-century Irish nationalist leader, Thomas Davis, who was, like Stoker, a Protestant educated at Trinity College ... and they became a staple element in the Irish nationalist economic thinking which informed Stoker's views on his native country for the rest of his life.[27]

Murray, Hughes, Jimmie Cain and Victor Sage examine the literary context of *Lady*.[28] Murray compares it to *The War in the Air*:

> Stoker's accurate appreciation of the ... importance of air power may have been inspired by H.G. Wells's *The War in the Air* ... published ... in 1908. Like Wells's work too, Stoker's is a political novel, attempting to anticipate coming strategic trends and alliances. Rupert dreams ... of a Balkan Federation. This will counter the aggression of ... Austria-Hungary, behind which lay a 'German lust for enlargement'. Russia too is seen as expansionist.[29]

Hughes comments on its 'shift from a Gothic mystery to a political adventure narrative with a conventional romantic closure', while Cain observes that *Dracula* and *Lady* may be read 'as political, imperial travelogues'.[30] In one of the most complete examinations of the novel, Sage describes it as a conflation of the 'Gothic novel and the Empire adventure story'.[31]

Many readers miss its economic and political message because Stoker's conclusion is missing from many editions. Indeed, Glover comments that in 'modern editions one-third of the text has been excised, entirely removing the novel's utopian finale'.[32] Consequently, readers may see it as more Gothic than Stoker intended.

Lady cannot be classified as Gothic because its interest in contemporary politics and insistence on rational explanations point forward rather than backwards. Nonetheless its Gothic elements are worth exploring: a young woman whom people believe is a vampire, the threat of rape, several characters who resemble the Gothic villain, a medieval castle, a darkened underground crypt and paranormal abilities.

In addition, Claire Simmons, in 'Fables of continuity: Bram Stoker and medievalism', observes Stoker's sly inside references to other Gothic novels, including *Dracula*, which 'read as jokes for the vigilant reader':

> Rupert's aeroplane is sent from Whitby via Otranto, a name recalling Horace Walpole's first 'Gothic' novel ... and Ernest Melton's mother goes to live at Carfax ... By the end ... when Rupert says to his wife, 'Of course, darling, you will wear your shroud'. . . the Gothic has become almost comic.[33]

Whitby is the port where Dracula lands in England, and Carfax the name of his London estate next to Seward's mental hospital. These echoes reinforce that the Gothic in *Lady* is a distant memory.

The title definitely hints at its Gothic ancestry and refers to the fact that the heroine is perceived to be a vampire for the first portion of the book. (The book is divided into nine chapters plus an excerpt from *The Journal of Occultism*, but only four chapters touch on genuinely Gothic matters.) Indeed, readers do not learn that Teuta is human until the novel is more than half over, at which point she reveals that she has pretended to be a vampire to protect herself from the Turks who wanted to take over her country: 'The vampire legend was spread as a protection against partial discovery ... and other weird beliefs were set afoot and fostered' (p. 215). The vampire thus protects her against Turkish aggression and gives her countrymen a powerful symbol of nationhood around which to rally.

Until the point when Teuta reveals herself to her lover, Stoker encourages readers to regard *Lady* as a sequel to *Dracula* or at least another novel in a similar vein. It opens with a vampire sighting by an expert in occult affairs, 'Mr Peter Caulfield, whose reports of Spiritual Phenomena in remote places are well known to the readers of "The Journal of Occultism"' (p. 20): 'Presently I made out that the boat ... was none other than a Coffin, and that the woman ... was clothed in a shroud' (p. 21). Later, on his way to Vissarion, Rupert Sent Leger, the hero, encounters one of the witnesses who saw the woman floating in the coffin. Because Rupert and his Scottish relatives are presented as having paranormal abilities and because Rupert had examined various 'worlds of thought, of spiritual import, of psychic phenomena – speaking generally, of mysteries' (p. 66), readers are prepared to accept his belief in the vampire's existence.

While references to the vampire are present from the first page, the first two books take place in the ordinary world (the reading of the will and Rupert's discussion of his new home at Vissarion). 'Book III: The Coming of the Lady', however, opens with a suggestion of Gothic mystery:

> I have waited till now – well into midday – before beginning to set down the details of the strange episode of last night. I have spoken with persons whom I know to be of normal type. I have breakfasted . . . and have every reason to consider myself in perfect health and sanity. So that the record following may be regarded as not only true in substance, but exact as to details. I have investigated and reported on too many cases for the Psychical Research Society to be ignorant of the necessity for absolute accuracy in such matters of even the minutest detail. (p. 103)

Readers familiar with Gothic novels recognize a familiar pattern: a character encounters something that causes him or her to question his sanity but takes care to get all the details right while mulling over the strange phenomenon. Here Rupert details his first experience with the mysterious vampire/woman:

> There . . . in the now brilliant moonlight, stood a woman, wrapped in white grave-clothes . . . Attitude and dress and circumstances all conveyed the idea that, though she moved and spoke, she was not quick, but dead. She was young and very beautiful, but pale, like the grey pallor of death. (p. 107)

The grave clothes and the pallor suggest she is a vampire, and Rupert emphasizes details that convince him she is not of this world. Indeed, like Van Helsing, he consults experts on the occult, including Aunt

Janet's books 'on odd subjects . . . Second Sight, Ghosts, Dreams . . . superstitions, Vampires, Wehr-Wolves, and all such uncanny folk and things' (p. 102):

> The effect of this brooding was that I was . . . struck by the similarity of circumstances bearing on my visitor, and the conditions apportioned by tradition and superstition to such strange survivals from earlier ages as these partial existences which are rather Undead than Living – still walking the earth, though claimed by the world of the Dead. Amongst them are the Vampire, or the Wehr-Wolf. (p. 119)

Readers familiar with *Dracula* are likely to jump to a Gothic conclusion here.

Nonetheless, *Lady* is a different kind of work, for Rupert is never horrified by his mysterious visitor. Instead, like many of Stoker's other heroes, he falls in love with her, almost at first sight, and contemplates saving her from her vampire existence, eventually going to the Church of St Sava to see where she might be buried. His discovery of her grave hints at Gothic horror but also suggests she is not dead but, like Snow White and Sleeping Beauty, awaiting a hero to awaken her:

> Naturally curious to know what might be within such a strange receptacle, I raised the lantern . . . so that the light might fall within.
> Then I started back with a cry, the lantern slipping from my nerveless hand and falling with a ringing sound on the great sheet of thick glass.
> Within, pillowed on soft cushions . . . lay the body of a woman – none other than my beautiful visitor. (p. 138)

Focusing on her beauty, he considers reviving her rather than driving a stake through her heart, and his thoughts touch on deep-seated psychological reasons for our ongoing fascination with the Gothic:

> Surely the old myths were not absolute inventions; they must have had a basis somewhere in fact. May not the . . . story of Orpheus and Eurydice have been based on some deep-lying principle or power of human nature? There is not one of us but has wished . . . to bring back the dead. Ay, and who has not felt that in himself or herself was power

in the deep love for our dead to make them quick again, did we but know the secret of how it was to be done? (p. 143)

Although it will be another hundred pages before Teuta explains the hoax, there is no doubt that, if Gothic, *Lady* is a very different kind of Gothic with Teuta sharing more with the persecuted maiden than with Stoker's monstrous women. Rupert is relieved to learn the truth: 'My wife! My wife! Not a Vampire; not a poor harassed creature doomed to terrible woe, but a splendid woman, brave beyond belief, patriotic in a way which has but few peers even in the wide history of bravery!' (p. 219). He and the reader later see that the truth about his bride is even more complex when she brandishes a weapon to battle with her Turkish kidnappers, more evidence that Stoker is adapting Gothic conventions to explore something new and different.

On the other hand, while Teuta bears little resemblance to the persecuted Gothic maiden, the Sultan and Rupert's despicable cousin, Ernest Roger Halbard Melton, resemble the Gothic villain. Both political monster and rapist, the Sultan plans to invade the Land of the Blue Mountains, and kidnapping Teuta causes Rupert to fear she will also become an unwilling member of his harem. Hughes, in *Beyond Dracula*, links the threat of rape, 'present in virtually all of Stoker's novels', to the Gothic tradition:

> [It] . . . provides an opportunity . . . for display and titillation. Such is its frequent function in the Gothic tradition – whether in the uncertainty of the relationship between Ann Radcliffe's Emily and Montoni. Or in the actual violence inflicted by M. G. Lewis's Ambrosio on his sister Antonia. Stoker's most compulsive and protracted scenes of attempted or potential rape appear in his first-person narratives, where the immediacy of the writing permits the reader to identify with a sense of outrage based more on the portrayed emotions of the propriety male than on those of the threatened woman herself.[34]

Hughes correctly points out Stoker's debt to the Gothic, but readers should also recognize that he adapts Gothic ideas to explore contemporary needs, including the need in the modern world for strong and independent men and women, not individuals trapped by their past.

In fact, *Lady* criticizes characters like Rupert's cousin Ernest, who are trapped by their past. Even though Ernest's greed and malicious behaviour hint at the Gothic tradition, he is generally presented as a comic figure rather than a serious threat. Like Leonard Everard, he is an ordinary and rather small man, not a powerful threat.

Throughout *Lady*, Stoker adapts traditional Gothic elements to explore contemporary issues. That adaptation is especially clear as turbines, airplanes, automobiles and other accoutrements of the modern world transform the medieval setting. The initial descriptions of Vissarion resonate with Gothic imagery, however, and Hughes demonstrates how much Stoker owes to his predecessors:

> The appreciation of vastness and obscurity, premised in part upon . . . Burke's *A Philosophical Enquiry* . . . is central to the Gothic. The obscure and massive are awesome and seemingly powerful, inspiring . . . a sense of personal insignificance, a pleasurable feeling of fear . . . The castle thus presents . . . a tantalizing glimpse of that which is to come, a suggestion that within the vastness lies some secret yet to be revealed.[35]

Writing to Aunt Janet, Rupert describes their new home in much the same way that Harker describes Dracula's castle, as an embodiment of the past: 'On the western shore of that creek is the Castle, a huge pile of buildings of every style of architecture, from the Twelfth century to where such things seemed to stop in this dear old- world land – about the time of Queen Elizabeth' p. (81). Its age leads him and readers to anticipate something mysterious and uncanny:

> So you see . . . that our new home is not without superstitious interests . . . It is rather a nice idea . . . to have a dead woman cruising round our promontory in a coffin . . . and it will save us the trouble of importing some of your Highland ghosts to make you feel at home . . . I don't know, but we might ask the stiff to come to tea. (p. 82)

The last sentence, complete with its rather jarring use of the American slang 'stiff', points observant readers to the conclusion that *Lady* is not Gothic.

Reinforcing his description of the medieval setting is Rupert's presentation of the natural environment, which threatens to overwhelm the castle's human inhabitants:

> Nature has been doing her own work . . . in enforcing the survival of the fittest. The shrubs have grown and grown, and have overtopped flower and weed, according to their inherent varieties of stature; to the effect that now you see irregularly scattered through the garden quite a number . . . of vegetable products which from a landscape standpoint have something of the general effects of statues without the cramping feeling of detail. (p. 90)

As happens so often in Gothic literature, Stoker hints that human beings are in the presence of something over which they have very little control, of natural forces running amuck. The reference to 'survival of the fittest' is, like Rupert's use of the word 'stiff', jarringly modern.

Before concluding this chapter on Stoker's romances, it is important to mention his use of the supernatural. Even though *Lady* slips gradually from something that seems Gothic to something that feels modern, there are examples of unexplained paranormal activity. Aunt Janet has a vision in which she sees Rupert marry Teuta in the Church of St Sava, mistaking the Orthodox marriage for a heathen rite. Rupert also hears a voice at the time that Teuta is kidnapped by the Turks.

While the final three books of *Lady* – even their titles 'The Empire of the Air', 'The Flashing of the Handjar' and 'Balka' suggesting their political orientation – focus on material solutions to human problems, Stoker occasionally reminds readers why the Gothic emphasis on mystery remains so important. For example, still thinking his visitor is a vampire, Rupert muses on psychological reasons for belief in the supernatural, including the desire to reunite with the dead. Rupert, who lost both parents while he was a boy, seems especially concerned to reconnect with the dead. He records in his journal, 'I love my mother so much – I always think of her in the present – that I cannot think of her as dead' (p. 73), and Roth attributes Stoker's desire to bring back the dead to the recent deaths of both Irving and his mother.[36] However, while the Gothic is haunted by frightening parental figures who refuse to die, *Lady* is confident and forward looking. Death remains a mystery, and Rupert will never resurrect his parents or the uncle whose will sets the entire tale in motion. He can, however, live his own life and begin his own family, as his aunt records happily: 'The baby ... is much too precious ... to be spoken of except with love, quite independent of the fact that he will be, in natural course, a King!' (p. 331). In contrast, Mina's baby has an ambiguous connection to the past because Dracula is one of his fathers. Stoker's romances look forward. Rupert's children and the children of Joy and Athlyne will not be haunted by the past but will move confidently forward.

As a result, the novel that began with a vampire sighting ends with the promise of a bright future, related by correspondents for 'Free America':

> The flight of aeroplanes was a memorable sight. It helped to make history. Henceforth no nation with an eye for either defence or attack can hope for success without the mastery of the air.
>
> In the meantime ... God help the nation that attacks 'Balka' ... so long as Rupert and Teuta live in the hearts of that people, and bind them into an irresistible unity. (pp. 351–2)

While the Gothic focuses on fears of being overwhelmed, Stoker's romances are confident about human ability to address present problems and move confidently forward. *The Man* and *Athlyne* conclude with personal fulfilment, *Lady* with political fulfilment. If *Dracula* is the history of the vampire count, *Lady* is the history of a modern man in a modern, technological world:

> There is enough of Rupert's work to make a lot of volumes, and we have an ambitious literary project of ... publishing an *edition de luxe* of his whole collected works ... But this is to be all about himself, so that in the future it may serve as a sort of backbone of his personal history. (p. 332)

One has only to compare this novel to *Dracula*, which remains very much in the shadow of the powerful past, to see exactly how Stoker adapts the Gothic to move in entirely new directions and consequently conquer the fears he occasionally evokes.

5

Stoker's Return to the Gothic in Famous Impostors *and* The Lair of the White Worm

಄ఇ

Looking at the first decade of the twentieth century, readers see an increasingly optimistic Stoker. *Mystery, The Man, Athlyne* and many of the stories in *Snowbound* and *Lady* exude confidence whether they concentrate on personal fulfilment, technological advances or political achievements. Such optimism flies in the face of Stoker's personal circumstances. Now that he had time to devote time to writing, health and financial problems plagued him. A paralytic stroke in 1906 incapacitated him for several months and damaged his eyesight, and he suffered several smaller strokes after that. Stoker remained optimistic, however, publishing two of his most confident works – *Lady Athlyne* and *The Lady of the Shroud* – after 1906. In his final years, his health continued to deteriorate as chronic gout turned into even more painful Bright's disease.[1] In 1911, after their son's marriage, the increasingly frail Stoker and Florence left Chelsea, where they had lived for thirty years, and moved into a smaller flat in Belgravia.

Around that time, Stoker's friend Lady Ritchie encouraged him to apply to the Royal Literary Fund for a grant and, according to Paul Murray in *From the Shadow of Dracula*, the application explained he had been 'unable to do any work, with the exception of completing a book begun some time before, the preparatory study for which had already been done'.[2] That nonfiction work, *Famous Impostors*, which Sidgwick & Jackson commissioned, was published in December 1910.[3] Stoker regained sufficient health to produce one more original –

and very Gothic – work, *The Lair of the White Worm*.[4] Barbara Belford provides this timeline in *Bram Stoker: A Biography of the Author of Dracula*:

> As his health failed, writing became an act of desperation, and for the first time he put himself on a schedule. He began writing *The Lair of the White Worm* on March 3, 1911, inscribing a date after each day's work, and completed it . . . on June 12.[5]

While he was writing *Lair*, he received a grant of £100 from the Royal Literary Fund. Apparently too ill to think about original work after *Lair*, he worked on short stories, intending to publish three collections.

Famous Impostors

Although his penultimate book is not typical of Stoker, it is nonetheless worth examining both for what it reveals about his interest in the Gothic and about his range as a writer. Largely ignored during the recent revival of interest except for brief references by Phyllis A. Roth, Lisa Hopkins and Murray, *Impostors* was reviewed enthusiastically in England and the United States, often receiving more attention than his fiction.[6] As one might expect, scholars today link it to *Dracula* or suggest that it reveals something about Stoker's psychological framework. For example, Roth describes it as 'another demonstration of Stoker's lifelong dualism' and points to 'his belief in the mysterious dimensions of persons and events and in the dichotomy between the empirical and the spiritual'. She also characterizes it as 'witty and vivid', observing that it 'reinforces the perspective of Stoker as one comfortable in both of his worlds: the practical and mundane on the one hand, the imaginative and often bizarre on the other'.[7] Hopkins explains that *Impostors* and *Personal Reminiscences* 'reveal much not only about Stoker's life but also about the concerns which dominate his fiction'.[8]

Murray reminds readers that, because the book was commissioned, readers should avoid reading too much biographical material into it. Discussing Stoker's work habits, he adds that Stoker spent time doing research in the Public Record Office and the British Museum, and argues that the quality of his research is 'evident in the impressive range of sources on Queen Elizabeth I used in the book'.[9] Because Stoker's works are difficult to locate, Murray's reference to the un-published preface is intriguing for the insights it provides about Stoker's mind in his final years. Not only does Murray describe it as 'well written and closely reasoned', he argues that it demonstrates Stoker was not suffering from dementia (as has been claimed) before his death.[10] He adds that Stoker's notes reveal his desire to write further sections. It is impossible to know whether Stoker's health or the publisher prevented his expanding it.

Some material included in *Impostors* builds on research Stoker had done for previous works, including material on the Balkans, the setting for sections of *Lady* as well as a part of the world that was in the news while Stoker was preparing *Impostors*. Stoker devotes a chapter to Stefan Mali, who had posed as Peter III and mentions Vladika Sava, ruler of Montenegro. Indeed, Stoker may have modelled Peter Vissarion on Sava. In *Lady*, Vissarion abdicates power to his warlike son-in-law because, 'having spent some twenty years in monastic life', he was 'unfitted for the government of a turbulent nation always harassed by the Turks and always engaged in a struggle for bare existence' (p. 32). Murray also points to Stoker's 'considerable research into Tudor history' for *Mystery* and adds that *Impostors* uses 'an impressive range of sources on Queen Elizabeth I and reveal[s] a profound admiration for her'.[11] The final chapter, which received the greatest attention from Stoker's contemporaries, explores the Bisley Boy legend: that the real Princess Elizabeth died and was re-placed by a boy. Stoker, who learned of this legend from his friend Bertha Nicoll, examines specific details, including the facts that the skeleton of a young girl was found at Bisley and that Elizabeth refused to marry.

Imposters also reveals Stoker's research into other historical figures (Perkin Warbeck, Stefan Mali, the false dauphins), scientists and char-latans (Paracelsus, Cagliostro, Mesmer) and individuals whom today might be described as cross-dressers (in addition to the Bisley Boy, Stoker examines the Chevalier D'Eon and women who dressed as men to improve their economic situations). There are also chapters on more mysterious subjects, including the Wandering Jew, witchcraft, clairvoyance and hoaxes. Stoker concedes that imposture continues to flourish because 'society shows itself ready to be gulled' (p. v). Because Stoker's Preface opens by examining human interest in one kind of mystery, readers expect continued emphasis on Gothic material: 'imposture, even if unsuccessful may be very difficult to detect' (p. vi). For the most part, however, Stoker avoids the overtly Gothic aspects of his subjects and focuses on rational explanations. It is not surprising, however, that the writer who created such memorable Gothic villains as Murdock, Dracula and Lady Arabella was also interested in blood-thirsty historical figures, including Richard III, who 'literally carved his way to the throne of England. It would hardly be an exaggeration to say that he waded to it through blood' (p. 3). Another bloodthirsty historical figure is Stefan Mali, who pretended to be Czar Peter III of Russia. Scholars continue to debate whether Stoker knew about the historical Vlad, but his description of Stefan reveals that, like Vlad, he 'had men shot for theft' (p. 33).

Impostors also reveals Stoker's interest in social change as well as historical monsters and mixes stories of imposture with awareness of social change, including the violent and chaotic times that produced the false dauphins:

> France was in a state of social chaos. The fountains of the deep were stirred, and no human intelligence could do more than guess at what might result from any individual effort of self-advancement. The public conscience was debauched, and for all practical purposes the end justified the means. It was an age of desperate adventure, of reckless enterprise, of unscrupulous methods. (pp. 37–8)

In short, the very times might be described as Gothic.

More sympathetic to other figures, Stoker nonetheless hints at social circumstances that create Gothic behaviour. For example, he is ambivalent about Mesmer, describing him sometimes as a scientist, sometimes as a charlatan. Admiring Mesmer's scientific discoveries, Stoker observes chicanery in his equipment: 'Indeed the implement which he used in his practice, and which made him famous in fashionable and idle society, was set forth as having magic properties' (p. 95). Stoker even suggests that Mesmer uses his abilities to dupe foolish people, depicting him as manipulative like the Gothic villain:

Mesmer soon used the picturesque side of his brain for . . . fashionable success. So he invented an appliance which soon became the talk of the town . . . the famous *baquet magique* or magic tub, a sort of covered bath . . . To the bath were attached a number of tubes, each of which was held by a patient . . . After a while the patients began to get excited, and many of them went into convulsions. Amongst them walked Mesmer, clad in an imposing dress suggestive of mystery and carrying a long wand of alleged magic power; often calming those who had already reached the stage of being actually convulsed. (pp. 96–7)

Although Mesmer is a historical figure who shares some characteristics with the Gothic villain, he is not Dracula, Murdock or Arabella, and Stoker stresses that his treatments were sometimes effective. He is not even Leonard Everard or any of the other unscrupulous people who have been domesticated.

While Stoker's reputation today is based on his fiction, much of *Impostors* features well-documented people and events. As a result, references to Gothic subjects are rare. The exceptions are a section on the Wandering Jew, and another on witchcraft, neither of which examines their mysterious aspects. With the Wandering Jew, he emphasizes 'the possibility of human longevity beyond what is natural and normal' (p. 107) but indicates that there is no scientific reason for such belief and, therefore, suggests that it is a remnant of a primitive world. The same is true of witchcraft, which he describes as the mistaken belief of an earlier stage of civilization, caused by 'the superstitions of society which attributed powers of evil to innocent persons whose subsequent mock-trials and butchery made a public holiday for their so-called judges' (pp. vi–vii). In fact, he generally emphasizes the cruelty associated with such superstitions rather than the mystery.

Looking at *Impostors*, careful readers may conclude that Stoker is moving to something more rational and scientific, although he stops short of that conclusion, pointing out that some matters remain mysterious, beyond the reach of scientific inquiry:

In an age more clear-seeing . . . and less selfish we shall not think so poorly of primitive emotions . . . On the contrary we shall begin to understand that in times when primitivity holds sway, we are most in touch with the loftiest things we are capable of understanding, and our judgment, being complex, is most exact. (p. 150)

This observation transports readers again to the mysterious realm he had explored in *Dracula* and *Jewel* and to which he would return in *Lair*, a realm beyond the scientific and rational knowledge of the late nineteenth and early twentieth centuries.

The Lair of the White Worm

It is impossible to speculate where Stoker might have gone if his health had not deteriorated, but one thing is clear: *Lair* returns to the Gothic world where monsters supernatural and domesticated walk the earth, where nature threatens everything humans have created and where the primitive past occasionally dominates the scientific and rational present. Gone is the confidence of *Lady* or even the human dignity of the major romances. While *Lair*, like most Stoker novels, includes romance, Adam Salton's love for Mimi feels like an afterthought, a desire for normalcy in a monstrous world. Furthermore, the human characters seem confused by the forces that they face, their attempts to describe them strangely unsatisfying. That Adam marries Mimi and anticipates economic prosperity may even be undermined by the possibility that other monsters lurk beneath the surface. Indeed, the monsters in *Lair* – Lady Arabella March and Edgar Caswall – are more inscrutable than monsters who retain some semblance of their human selves and thus motives readers can understand.

Even though Stoker returns to the Gothic in *Lair*, his second most popular work, scholars and critics give it little positive attention. Roth observes that it 'initially received favorable reviews and has been successful enough apparently to warrant reissue', but adds that it is 'the weakest of all his novel-length fictions, revealing impatience with plotting and characterization, inconsistency in action and tone, and a lack of overall vision or design organizing and unifying the story elements'.[12] Murray concurs, describing *Lair* as Stoker's weakest novel 'full of incredible and fantastic subplots, with little overall coherence or consistency'.[13] The Dalby and Hughes bibliography points out, however, that this incoherence stems from the fact that many editions are seriously abridged.

Hughes and Farson attribute its strangeness to psychological problems or to medication. Hughes observes that *Lair* 'bears all the hallmarks of hasty (and at times, repetitive) writing and equally hasty revision, though such things may all too easily be interpreted in modern criticism as the consequences of a guilty conscience, a chronically ill mind or an imagination affected by hallucinatory medication'.[14] Farson speculates that it 'might have been written under the influence of drugs' most specifically those used 'to alleviate the painful Bright's Disease which corroded him in his last years'.[15] Other scholars speculate that Stoker's apparent confusion stemmed from dementia associated with syphilis. Somewhat more generously Harry Ludlam, in *A Biography of Dracula*, looks at the physical difficulties Stoker overcame simply to get *Lair* down on paper: 'But the words that he put to paper then, sitting up in bed, poring over his manuscript with a magnifying glass to determine what he had written, evinced his bitter struggle against a wretched disease and failing powers.'[16]

A few scholars are complimentary. Kate Hebblethwaite describes the novel as a 'product of deep thought, research and a profound understanding of the society in which he lived' and recommends ongoing study:

> The Lair of the White Worm . . . is . . . an intensely intriguing novel, working on mythic, historical, social and sexual levels, whilst also responding to nineteenth- and early twentieth-century shifts in artistic expression. In short, Stoker was a popular fiction writer of significant aptitude, in tune with the undercurrents of the social though and creative articulation of his time.[17]

David Glover comments in *Vampires, Mummies, and Liberals* that *Lair* reveals Stoker's continued professionalism:

> Despite his poor health . . . the manuscript is fluently written, with very few revisions and only a handful of minor errors. If it is hardly his best book . . . Stoker clearly tackled it with his usual professional aplomb, taking a keen interest in its illustrations and sending out copies.[18]

Andrew Maunder, even more appreciative in *Bram Stoker*, shares my view of what *Lair* offers:

> For the most part, critics have tended to ignore these novels, viewing them as second-rate, or — as far as *The Lair of the White Worm* is concerned — rather embarrassing. If these texts have any interest at all, the argument goes, it is as . . . hack work . . . by a man who was careless . . . or, in the case of *The Lair of the White Worm*, was in the advanced stages of syphilitic-induced dementia. As novels they . . . are written with an eye to what Stoker thought would sell but . . . they . . . demonstrate Stoker's mastery of different narrative techniques; they demonstrate his concern with morality.[19]

Maunder also observes that *Lair* has 'only very recently . . . begun to attract the . . . critical attention bestowed on its more famous fore-runner'.[20]

In addition to Maunder, Hopkins and Glover, all of whom provide insights because they examine everything Stoker wrote, two excellent studies explore *Lair* in detail: David Punter, 'Echoes in the animal house: *The Lair of the White Worm*', and David Seed, 'Eruptions of the primitive into the present: *The Jewel of Seven Stars* and *The Lair of the White Worm*'.[21] Punter focuses on architecture, noting that the 'central landscape consists of five "great houses"' and pointing to legal issues in the novel.[22] He does not address *Lair* as a Gothic work, but he touches on issues that are generally considered Gothic and concludes by noting: '*The Lair of the White Worm* can thus be seen . . . as a novel about order and chaos, about reason and the unconscious; but it can also be seen as a text about territorialisation.'[23] Seed, on the other hand, is concerned with an issue of particular relevance to the Gothic: the impact of the past on the present. He observes that contemporary issues are 'complicated by the apparent coming to life . . . of archaic legend'.[24] He emphasizes 'obsessive atavism', reveal-ing how it plays out in several characters: 'Lilla, the fair-skinned maiden . . . comes from "old Saxon stock" (p. 358); Caswall embodies the qualities of endurance and imperiousness typical of his Roman line (p. 387); and so on.'[25]

This chapter builds on insights included in these thoughtful essays along with observations by scholars like Maunder and Hopkins who, like me, are interested in evaluating the complete Stoker oeuvre. It emphasizes Gothic elements, including its confusing narration, the haunting presence of an ancient – sometimes primeval – past that threatens to dominate the scientific and technologically sophisticated present, the existence of diabolical people and supernatural monsters that elicit fear and the overwhelming power of nature. Even though Murray observes that 'the White Worm does not have supernatural powers', Lady Arabella's ability to transform into a gigantic creature falls into the realm of the supernatural.[26] Above all, what makes *Lair* Gothic is the sense that life cannot be explained by rational, scientific means and that the world is generally mysterious.

Lair is also mysterious because Stoker creates a new kind of monster rather than adapting a monster such as the vampire or mummy for which readers have certain expectations. Readers hardly know how to interpret a woman who becomes a gigantic antediluvian monster, and Edgar, a modern incarnation of the Gothic villain, is more formidable because of access to technology.

Lair is made more difficult by the narration, which differs from what Stoker uses successfully in other Gothic works. His frequent use of first-person narration immerses readers in mysterious events even as his characters are immersed, and scholars comment on the effective use of letters, diaries and newspaper clippings in *Dracula*, most of which feature a writer's confrontation with terrible events that he or she cannot understand. Stoker also uses straightforward first-person narration in *Mystery* and *Jewel* as well as in the sections of *Lady* that replicate Rupert's journal or letters between characters. The narration in these works encourages readers to share his characters' confusion at being in the presence of something large and powerful. Commenting on the narration of *Lair*, Hopkins attributes its difficulty to 'a jolting and entirely unheralded switch of narrative perspective roughly a third of the way through', but the difficulty stems less from a narrative switch than to Stoker's confronting readers with something for which there is no established Gothic vocabulary.[27] Furthermore, not only are Lady Arabella and Edgar new, Stoker also has difficulty describing them in terms that readers can understand, a difficulty made evident in Mimi's reflections on an encounter with Lady Arabella:

From this she went into all sorts of wild fancies. What sort of tea did dragons prefer? What was it that essentially tickled their palates? Who did the washing for dragons' servants? Did they use starch? If, in the privacy of their houses ... dragons were accustomed to use knives and forks and teaspoons? Yes, that at any rate was true; she had seen them used herself. (p. 246)

Mimi has just come from Lady Arabella's home and has, in the middle of tea, barely avoided being swept into the worm's lair. Attempting to create a complex situation, featuring a character that is both human and monstrous, Stoker does not provide a strong alternative to the monsters that dominate this novel. Neither personal love nor the explosive conclusion quite satisfies, and readers suspect that human beings are ill equipped to confront those fearful presences. Having come to expect catharsis from the Gothic experience, readers may feel confused and overwhelmed.

Not everything in *Lair* is new or revolutionary, of course, for Stoker continues to work through problems he had previously explored, including the overpowering presence of the past. In addition, he uses Gothic excess to critique contemporary social evils, to present monstrous individuals who exert their control over others and to demonstrate that nature is an overwhelming presence.

Readers of Stoker's fiction know he is acutely interested in the relationship of the present to a powerful past that threatens to dominate it. It is perhaps the single most important Gothic topic as well as the subject of almost everything Stoker wrote. Indeed, Seed demonstrates how characters in *Lair* are linked to the past, noting that 'the action . . . is constantly being displaced from turn-of-the-century England into a legendary past which, Stoker implies, is not anywhere near as remote as we imagined'.[28] Stoker emphasizes that connection by linking characters to their homes and the land on which those homes are built. Even more than Dracula or Tera, these individuals are identified with their ancestral homes. Punter's essay noted the importance of 'five "great houses"', and the novel suggests these dwellings hold enormous power over their residents.[29] Castra Regis is, according to local historian and president of the Mercian Archæological Society, Sir Nathaniel de Salis, the 'great house and estate in this part of the world' and 'the family seat of the Caswall family' (p. 11). He also associates the Caswalls whose 'family is coeval with that of England' (p. 15) with the Roman inhabitants of Britain when he relates their history to Adam, who has recently arrived from Australia:

> The history of the Castle has no beginning so far as we know. The furthest records or surmises or inferences simply accept it as existing . . . there was some sort of structure there when the Romans came, therefore it must have been a place of importance in Druid times. (p. 25)

According to Sir Nathaniel, the Caswalls adhere 'to the early Roman type' (p. 18) and have 'prevailing characteristics' that are 'well preserved and unchanging . . . cold, selfish, dominant, reckless of consequences in pursuit of their own will . . . If they should make a mistake someone else should bear the burthen of it' (p. 17). These characteristics are negative but nonetheless human, although Sir Nathaniel also explains their cruelty by bringing in the supernatural: 'With such strange compelling qualities, is it any wonder that there is . . . an idea that . . . there is some demoniac possession, which tends to a . . . belief that certain individuals have . . . sold themselves to the Devil?' (p. 19). On this occasion, the Gothic vocabulary breaks down. Because there is little evidence of the Devil, Caswall's evil behaviour is all the more inscrutable.

The second great house, Diana's Grove, is older still, its human owner more mysterious, and Sir Nathaniel relates the history of the property as if its history explained the incomprehensible events that transpire there. He tells Adam that Diana's Grove is built on the 'location of a Roman temple, possibly founded on a pre-existing Druidical one. Its name implies the former, and the grove of ancient oaks suggests the latter' (p. 24). Its current owner is Lady Arabella March whose husband purchased it before his death, possibly a suicide. Even more important, Diana's Grove is built over an enormous well from which emerges the antediluvian monster known as the White Worm. The precise relationship between Lady Arabella and the Worm is never made clear although other characters conflate the lady with the monster.

Of lesser importance are Doom Tower, Sir Nathaniel's residence; Lesser Hill, the Salton ancestral home; and Mercy Farm, home of

Michael Watford and his granddaughters Lilla and Mimi. Watford is Caswall's tenant, and Mercy Farm was built on land where Queen Bertha had previously founded a nunnery 'in memory of Columba, which was named *Sedes misericordiæ*, the House of Mercy' (p. 80). Indeed, Sir Nathaniel links the nunnery and the current residents of Mercy Farm:

> In process of time this religious house again fell into desuetude; but before it disappeared it had achieved a great name for good works ... if deeds and prayers and hopes and earnest thinking leave anywhere any moral effect, Mercy Farm and all around it have almost the right to be considered holy ground. (p. 81)

At the conclusion, the two great houses and their respective owners are destroyed: 'Castra Regis was a shapeless huddle of shattered architecture ... As for Diana's Grove, they looked in vain for a sign which had a suggestion of permanence' (pp. 319–20). Only the freeholdings – Lesser Hill and Doom Tower, as well as Mercy Farm – remain, and Punter analyses their significance: 'What survives are Mercy Farm and the equally aptly named Lesser Hill, both places which have already made, as it were, some kind of compromise with the aspirations – to power, to immortality – which have proved the "doom" of the two more looming edifices' (p. 178).

Because Stoker frequently draws parallels between these dwellings and their human occupants, readers should ponder the significance of those parallels as well as the apocalyptic conclusion that destroys Edgar and Lady Arabella and leaves Adam, who has recently purchased Diana's Grove, even wealthier. It is difficult to argue, however, that Stoker is recommending a spiritual response. Unlike Mina, who pities Dracula, the characters remaining at the conclusion reveal little pity for their opponents.

Since both Lady Arabella and Caswall and their dwellings are associated with the past, it might also be argued that the conclusion signifies the triumph of modernity, a reading consistent with the fact that the future seems to belong to Adam and his bride. Seed comments on the name of Stoker's young protagonist: 'Although the last of his line, Adam's Christian name signifies fresh beginnings once he takes up his inheritance, and *The Lair of the White Worm* depicts this inheritance as a representation in miniature of England.'[30] The problem is that this reading is not completely satisfying. Certain remnants of the past, including the Saltons, Sir Nathaniel and the Watfords (except for the sacrificial Lilla), survive the apocalyptic conclusion. Why they survive and others perish is less clear.

Like Dracula, Edgar is connected to his past. Not only does he bear the same Christian name as his ancestors, but, like Dracula, he seems incapable of learning anything new. Even more primitive is Lady Arabella who is transformed into a primeval serpent; thus, like Dracula, she is literally a relic from the past though a past infinitely more distant and less human than his. She also seems to be trapped in two separate bodies: one is the body of the carnivorous white worm, the other an impoverished gentlewoman who, having lost one husband to suicide, hopes to find and marry another. Usually presented as monstrous, a human temptress or a primeval serpent, Lady Arabella occasionally appears as a human being for whom readers can feel sympathy, a circumstance that makes their ultimate response to her more difficult.

As he had done with *Dracula*, Stoker has representatives of the past impact the modern world. Edgar returns to his ancestral home, and the White Worm (for reasons that are never adequately explained) returns after centuries of dormancy to wreak havoc on the country-side. In fact, the only explanation offered suggests that, like Dracula, she had been resting. She 'has been in the habit of sleeping for a thousand years at a time . . . However . . . her ladyship is now nightly on the prowl . . . in her own proper shape that she used before the time of the Romans' (p. 218). Because Lady Arabella has only recently come into possession of Diana's Grove, it is also unclear whether she came under the control of the White Worm when she moved there or whether she awakened it when she came to the Grove and summoned it to do her bidding. The explanations for monstrous behaviour in *Lair* remain shrouded in mystery, but one thing unites the characters who are identified with the primitive past: all are selfish, seeing the world and its inhabitants only in terms of their own needs.

The representatives of modernity, on the other hand, believe they are acting for the good of the whole and see their behaviour as progressive. Even though Sir Nathaniel frequently reminds his followers of their relationship to the past, Adam is a new kind of hero. For example, he feels obligated to acquire Diana's Grove legally before he stuffs the well with dynamite to destroy the Worm. This attention to law and decorum suggests that the modern world depends on shared values. No longer can a single heroic individual use force to take what he or she needs. Even Lady Arabella is caught in the modern paradigm that requires her to have a husband. While she can assume the body of the White Worm and roam the world, she cannot do what she wants when she wants. Having dragged Oolanga, Caswall's African servant, to his death in the well, she feels obliged to send Adam a note explaining that she is 'upset and unnerved by all that has happened in this terrible night' (p. 178). One of the few scholars to write about this odd juxtaposition, Punter comments on repeated references to law in *Lair*: 'To ignore the legal aspects would be to sink into the pit, to abandon the decencies of civilized life and to relapse into the condition of worm or native.'[31] He does not recognize that Lady Arabella, despite her supernatural powers, is bound by the conventions of civilized life and cannot surmount the legal and economic requirements of the twentieth century. Continuing to explore the great Gothic subject, the haunting presence of the past, Stoker presents readers with more mystery than answers. People and houses, science and legend are conjoined in ways that are not entirely clear to either characters or readers, perhaps not to Stoker himself who was attempting to make sense of a topic with which he had wrestled for most of his literary career.

Stoker also continues to use Gothic excess to explore contemporary problems, including the fact that representatives of other, more primitive races are coming to England and women are gaining social and economic power. Oolanga allows Stoker to explore fears Europeans felt regarding the dark-skinned inhabitants of Africa and Asia. Indeed, describing him, other characters become almost hysterical:

> Caswall looked ... a savage – but a cultured savage. In him were traces of the softening civilization of ages – of some of the higher instincts and education of man, no matter how rudimentary these might be. But ... Oolanga ... was pure pristine, unreformed, unsoftened savage, with ... all the hideous possibilities of a lost, devil-ridden child of the

forest and the swamp – the lowest and most loathsome of all created things which were in some form ostensibly human. (p. 35)

Not content to leave Oolanga as a primitive human, however, Adam explains his revulsion by investing him with otherworldly powers, observing that Oolanga was 'originally a witch-finder' and 'became an Obi-man, which gives an opportunity to wealth *via* blackmail'. From this point, readers might conclude he is not human: 'Monsters such as he is belong to an earlier and more rudimentary stage of barbarism' (p. 69). The problem for twenty-first-century readers is that Oolanga really *does* very little to deserve such vituperation. Dressed in grotesque cast-off clothing, he is objectively more pitiful than evil:

His dress, which was a grotesque mixture . . . seemed absurd. He had on evening dress of an ill cut, an abnormally efflorescent white shirt with exaggerated cuffs and collar, all holding mock jewels of various colours. In his nose was a silver ring, and in his ears large ornaments composed of trophies of teeth. He wore a tall hat, which had once been of a shape of some kind . . . Altogether he looked like a horrible distortion of a gentleman's servant. All those around grinned or openly jeered. (p. 37)

The teeth decorating his ears suggest he once had power, but he seems stripped of that power in England. That so many people respond with hostility, however, suggests racism. Both Adam and Lady Arabella agree that Oolanga is hardly worth shooting, and his death is nothing if not undignified:

In another instant she had seized Oolanga and . . . had drawn him . . . down into the gaping aperture . . . Adam saw a medley of . . . lights blaze in a whirling circle, and as it sank down into the well a pair of blazing green eyes became fixed, sank lower and lower with frightful rapidity, and disappeared, throwing upward the green light which grew more and more vivid every second. As the light sank into the noisome depths, there came a shriek which chilled Adam's very blood—a prolonged agony of pain and terror which seemed to have no end. (pp. 174–5)

Many readers assume Stoker shared the racial prejudices of his day because his dark-skinned villains are summarily dismissed from their respective stories. Glover, for example, refers to 'the apoplectic racist invective of his last novel . . . one of whose villains . . . is described as a "Negroid of the lowest type"'.[32] Glover forgets, however, that Mimi is dark skinned. The daughter of an English soldier and a Burmese woman, she is 'almost as dark as the darkest of her mother's race'.[33]

While *Lair* occasionally presents fear of the racial other, it also reveals fear of women who deviate from traditional roles. Representing such fears is Lady Arabella who is both a down-on-her-luck aristocrat and a primeval monster. Stoker's use of such excess is sometimes surprisingly effective, sometimes a little silly. That he wanted readers to consider contemporary issues (as he had done in *Dracula* when Mina refers to the New Woman) becomes clear when Sir Nathaniel compares her to a suffragette:

> Our opponent has pretty well all the trumps. I never thought this fighting an antediluvian monster was such a complicated job. This one is a woman, with all a woman's wisdom and wit, combined with the heartlessness of a cocotte and the want of principle of a suffragette. She has the reserved strength and impregnability of a diplodocus. We may be sure that in the fight that is before us there will be no semblance of fair-play. (p. 206)

The passage demonstrates the complexity of the male response to Lady Arabella. The word 'cocotte' implies flirtatiousness while 'diplodocus' suggests physical size and primitiveness. Oddly enough, although his reference to the women's suffrage movement might remind readers of contemporary issues, Lady Arabella shares little with women who actively campaigned for economic and political rights. Maunder names Emmeline Pankhurst, who formed the Women's Social and Political Union in 1903, and observes that the union had begun to 'step up its militant approach' in '1911, the year of the novel's publication', but Lady Arabella is not interested in political equality.[34] As a woman, she desires a husband who will keep her in the fashion to which she had become accustomed. As a primeval monster, she takes whatever she wants although she occasionally regrets such impulsive behaviour. That Sir Nathaniel and Adam compare her to a suffragette reveals more about their fears than her powers.

Because Stoker created such appealing women characters as Mina, Marjory, Stephen, Joy and Teuta, readers must disagree with Glover's conclusion that Stoker is 'staunchly antifeminist'. Nonetheless, readers should explore some of what, according to Glover, makes Lady Arabella and her monstrous alter ego so terrifying:

> Moreover, whereas Stoker's ... brand of Liberal politics seems always to have been staunchly antifeminist, his convictions hardened appreciably as the decade wore on. Where *Dracula* pokes dismissive fun at the New Women, *The Lair of the White Worm* (1911) back-handedly sums up Lady Arabella March's monstrous feminine resourcefulness ... The gratuitous connection drawn between women's suffrage and sexual promiscuity is quite deliberate here.[35]

Certainly, much of the commentary on Lady Arabella focuses on her voracious sexuality. Maunder comments on the novel's 'heavy emphasis on "phallic" snakes and cavernous openings', one of the reasons it 'has proved so enticing to psychoanalytic critics'.[36] Unlike Glover, however, Maunder questions whether Stoker shares his characters' misogynistic views:

> How far Stoker endorses these is a more complex question ... Stoker wrote too much on this [prejudices and anxieties held by many Victorian men] for us not to think that he shared some of them. Nonetheless ... Stoker is also concerned with the corresponding lives of women and it is this which can give Stoker's work a very different feel from other male writers of adventure romances.[37]

The radical change in gender roles that confronted Stoker and his contemporaries is so new and overwhelming that readers suspect Stoker is wrestling with issues for which he knows there are no easy answers. Thus Lady Arabella sometimes appears to be a vulnerable woman who desires economic security in the form of a new husband *and* a powerful, larger-than-life creature, both a woman and the incarnation of ancient legend. If the combination is occasionally a bit silly, it also touches on real issues.

While Stoker's presentation of Lady Arabella takes him in new directions, his portrait of Edgar derives from the traditional Gothic villain. The same is true of his depiction of the overwhelming power of the natural world. One of the best discussions of Edgar is by Roth, who refers to him as 'a sort of Count Dracula manqué', although she explains why he is Dracula's inferior:

> In *The Lair* the existence of two villains reflects a bifurcation or diffusion of the threat and the horror: both Edgar Caswell as mono-maniac and rival and Lady Arabella as primeval monster must be destroyed. Nevertheless the threat posed by Edgar is . . . more per-functorily and unsatisfactorily portrayed. The locus of the real horror and evil . . . is the white worm, and on it Stoker spends far more time.[38]

Although Lady Arabella dominates, Edgar is another representative of the past who is incapable of adapting to the modern world of science, technology and capital. Indeed, like Lucy, Edgar wreaks havoc primarily in his sleep. The narrator observes him with Mesmer's trunk: 'In his sleep in the darkness he arose, and, as if in obedience to some influence beyond and greater than himself, lifted the great trunk and set it on a strong table at one side of the room' (p. 116). And, again, 'He was conscious of being still asleep, and of acting rather in obedience to some unseen and unknown command than in accordance with any reasonable plan to be followed by results which he understood and was aiming at' (pp. 116–17). Readers might logically conclude that he is either possessed or insane.

Caswall's actions bring about evil, and the fact that he is an aristocrat most clearly aligns him with the traditional Gothic villain. Having returned to England from abroad, he lords it over his tenants, especially Lilla with whom he seems to be infatuated. Their relationship, which is presented as the relationship of predator to prey, is reinforced by their social positions. Indeed, because her grandfather is Caswall's tenant, Lilla believes she must be courteous: 'If it was only for her father's sake, she [Lilla] must not refuse him [Caswall] or show any disinclination which he might construe into incivility' (p. 264). Such deference makes her physically ill: 'And as she had been brought up to consider duty as first, she braced herself to go through . . . what was before her' (p. 265). This confrontation, which results in

Lilla's death, replicates an earlier meeting in which Caswall is compared to a hawk, and Lilla his prey. The symbiotic nature of their relationship is a tepid version of Dracula's vampirism: 'The weaker Lilla seemed the stronger he seemed to get, just as if he was feeding on her strength' (p. 67). Caswall never achieves Dracula's horrifying power, however.

In addition, Stoker continues to be fascinated with the overwhelming power of nature. As both readers and characters await the final conflagration, Stoker provides a reminder of that power:

> Strange to say, they [Adam and Mimi] both enjoyed . . . the tumult
> of Nature's forces . . . Had their nervous strain been less, the sense of
> æstheticism . . . would have had more scope. Even as it was, the dark
> beauties of sky and landscape appealed to them; the careering of the
> inky-black clouds; the glimpses of the wind-swept sky; the rush and
> roar of the tempest amongst the trees; the never-ceasing crackle of
> electricity . . . claimed their interest and admiration, forming . . . a
> background of fitting grandeur and sublimity to the great tragedy . . .
> which was being enacted in their very midst. (pp. 309–10)

Elsewhere Stoker reminds readers that humans cannot understand nature, for example, by portraying the effect Edgar's kite has over animals: 'All the birds were cowed; their sounds stopped. Neither song nor chirp was heard—silence seemed to have taken the place of the myriad voices of bird life. But that was not all. The silence spread to all animals' (p. 101). And impacts on the rest of the world:

> From this infliction of silence there was no relief. Everything was
> affected; gloom was the predominant note. Joy appeared to have passed
> away . . . and this creative impulse had nothing to take its place. That
> giant spot in high air was a plague of evil influence. It seemed like a
> new misanthropic belief which had fallen on human beings, carrying
> with it the negation of all hope. After a few days, men began to grow
> desperate; their very words as well as their senses seemed to be in chains.
> (p. 102)

Readers are thus reminded that human beings are part of a natural world that they can neither understand nor control.

One other aspect of Stoker's treatment of nature is worth noting: his use of evolutionary science to depict a process that is random and beyond the control of either God or humans. Various characters use evolution to explain the White Worm and other 'survivals from earlier ages, preserved by some special qualities in their habitats' (p. 51). What is more important here, however, is the suggestion that other monstrous creatures exist (Sir Nathaniel, for example, mentions a giant snake about which an Indian acquaintance had told him) which may also prey on human beings.

In addition, Stoker continues to use disgusting visual and olfactory descriptions to confront readers with something that is overwhelming or, as Robert Mighall reminds us in *A Geography of Victorian Gothic Fiction,* 'the familiar Gothic trope of the unspeakable'.[39] As he had done in *Dracula* and *Jewel,* Stoker demonstrates that smells can be overpowering. There are countless examples in *Lair,* but the following description of the well is representative:

> It was like nothing that Adam had ever met with. He compared it with . . . the drainage of war hospitals, of slaughter-houses, the refuse of dissecting rooms. None of these were like it, though it had something of them all, with, added, the sourness of chemical waste and the poisonous effluvium of the bilge of a water-logged ship whereon a multitude of rats had been drowned. (p. 172)

If nauseating odours were not enough, Stoker also assaults readers' vision, describing snakes the mongoose had killed: 'They all lay in a row, straight and rigid, as if they had been placed by hands. Their skins seemed all damp and sticky, and they were covered all over with ants and all sorts of insects. They looked loathsome' (p. 70). The novel concludes with an even more horrifying visual image:

> The worst parts to see were the great masses of the flesh of the monstrous Worm in all its red and sickening aspect . . . Now the whole mass seemed to have become all at once corrupt. But that corruption was not all. It seemed to have attracted every natural organism which was in itself obnoxious. The whole surface of the fragments, once alive, was covered with insects, worms, and vermin of all kinds. The sight was horrible enough, but, with the awful smell

added, was simply unbearable. The Worm's hole appeared to breathe
forth death in its most repulsive forms. Both Adam and Sir Nathaniel
. . . turned and ran to the top of the Brow, where a fresh breeze . . .
was blowing up. (p. 323)

The conclusion is as sudden as the conclusions to *Dracula* and *Jewel*,
and readers' reaction to it is important. Adam's name suggests a new
beginning and the resurrection of the Saltons in England as does the
suggestion of a fresh breeze and Sir Nathaniel's confident response:
'But all's well that ends well' (p. 324). That haunting reference to one
of Shakespeare's darkest and least satisfying romances undermines
the jaunty conclusion. Moreover, the initial conclusion to *Jewel* and
the fact that Dracula's castle remains a haunting presence reinforce
Seed's cautious reading: 'Even here, though, the language is shot
through with qualifications. Has the evil merely been concealed? And,
given that the novel contains a very local narrative, might there not
be other "worms" or allied monsters waiting to make their presence
felt?' (p. 202). The ultimate fear is that the evil remains and that his
human characters are too smug to face it. While Sir Nathaniel and
Adam go off to join Mimi for breakfast, I remain haunted by evil the
characters fail to see.

I am also troubled that characters with whom readers are expected
to identify justify their violence in legal terms. Here is Stoker's
description of Sir Nathaniel, the Van Helsing-like figure to whom
other characters look for guidance:

> But he was an elderly man with much experience and knowledge of
> law and diplomacy. It seemed to him to be a stern duty to prevent
> anything irrevocable taking place till it had been thought out and all
> was ready. There were all sorts of legal cruxes to be thought out, not
> only regarding the taking of life, even of a monstrosity in human form,
> but also of property. Lady Arabella, be she woman or snake or devil,
> owned the ground she moved in, according to British law, and the
> law is jealous and swift to avenge wrongs done within its ken. (p. 202)

Because they value the law, they must avoid being charged with
murder: 'What are we to do? We cannot manifestly take and murder
Lady Arabella off-hand. Therefore we shall have to put things in

order for the killing, and in such a way that we may not be taxed with a base crime' (p. 205). That supposedly ethical people rely on violent and/or exploitative behaviours undermines any sense that Gothic mystery is replaced by something positive and affirmative. Consequently, readers await an answer that never appears and a catharsis that never occurs.

Looking back over everything Stoker wrote between 1875 and 1911, readers see a variety of genres – fiction, non-fiction, memoir, adventure tale, romance, Gothic horror – as well as works of varying lengths. Stoker wrote all these forms over the course of his life. Nonetheless, his obituary identified him as a Gothic writer, and that characterization continues to this day despite his efforts in other genres. Although Stoker was one of the greatest Gothic writers, he was more. Even when he used Gothic conventions, he often did so in the service of understanding his own times. He did not use Gothic details only to shock and horrify but to enable readers to examine issues that frightened them. Reading Stoker's works carefully can produce catharsis or greater self-understanding, at the worst revulsion or titillation. Often forgotten except for *Dracula*, all of Stoker's works deserve our attention for what they reveal about the Gothic and our world.

Notes

ജ്യ

Introduction: Tracing the Gothic through Stoker's Short Stories

1   'Bram Stoker', *The Times*, 22 April 1912, 15.
2   Andrew Maunder attributes 'almost half Stoker's fictional output . . . to the last seven years of his life', in *Bram Stoker* (Devon: Northcote House Publishers Ltd, 2006), p. 7.
3   Bram Stoker, *Personal Reminiscences of Henry Irving*, vol. I (New York: Macmillan, 1906), p. 32. Despite Stoker's disparaging comments, Harry Ludlam observes, in *A Biography of Dracula: The Life Story of Bram Stoker* (London: Foulsham, 1962), that the '248-page volume did in fact come to be regarded in the civil service as a standard reference book', p. 63.
4   For example, Bram Stoker, *Best Ghost and Horror Stories*, ed. Richard Dalby, Stefan Dziemianowicz and S. T. Joshi (Mineola, NY: Dover, 1997); Bram Stoker. *The Judge's House and Other Weird Tales* (Doylestown, PA: Wildside Press, undated); and *Dracula's Guest and Other Stories* (London: Wordsworth, 2006).
5   Bram Stoker, 'The Crystal Cup', in *Dracula's Guest and Other Stories*, pp. 147–57. Future references will be included in the text.
6   Bram Stoker, *The Primrose Path* (Westcliff-on-Sea, Essex: Desert Island Books, 1999). According to editor Richard Dalby, *The Primrose Path* and *Buried Treasures*, which is also published in this volume, 'have never been reprinted anywhere since . . . 1875 until now', p. 6. Future references in this chapter to *The Primrose Path* will be included in the text.
7   Stoker, *Best Ghost and Horror Stories*, p. 9.
8   Stoker's biographer Paul Murray observes that 'Stoker had not yet seen Irving play this role when he wrote this story', in *From the Shadow of Dracula* (London: Jonathan Cape, 2004), p. 67. It was, however, a role that made Irving famous:

Notes

The Lyceum production of Faust opened in December 1885. It ran for 792 performances and made over £250,000 – the Lyceum's greatest ever financial success ... Stoker is therefore more likely to have been influenced by Irving's performances in his great horror roles ... and his Faust may have been the most potent of these. (p. 183)

9 JosephValente discusses the allegorical nature of 'Death and Devil' in *Dracula's Crypt: Bram Stoker, Irishness, and the Question of Blood* (Chicago: University of Illinois Press, 2002), pp. 30–1.

10 It is easy to see similarities between Katey and Radcliffe's heroines as they are defined in *The Harper Handbook to Literature*: while Radcliffe's 'English girls ... encounter spooky French or Italian castles and ruined abbeys', Stoker's Irish heroine encounters the Other in an urban setting. Northrop Frye, Sheridan Baker, George Perkins and Barbara M. Perkins (eds), *The Harper Handbook to Literature*, 2nd edn (New York: Longman, 1997), pp. 224–5.

11 Maunder, *Bram Stoker*, p. 43.

12 Bette B. Roberts, 'Gothic fiction', in Sally Mitchell (ed.), *Victorian Britain: An Encyclopedia* (New York: Garland, 1988), p. 334.

13 Northrop Frye et al. (eds), *The Harper Handbook to Literature*, p. 225.

14 Bram Stoker, *The Primrose Path*, p. 106. Future references will be included in the text.

15 Bram Stoker, 'The Chain of Destiny', in *Dracula's Guest and Other Stories*, pp. 159–196. All references to this story will be included in the text.

16 Chris Morash, 'The time is out of joint (O cursèd pite!): towards a definition of a supernatural narrative', in Bruce Steward (ed.), *That OtherWorld:The Supernatural and the Fantastic in Irish Literature and its Contexts*, vol. I (Gerrards Cross: Colin Smythe Ltd, 1998), pp. 123–42.The actual quotation occurs on p. 126.

17 Bram Stoker, *Under the Sunset*, with an Introduction by Douglas Menville (North Hollywood, CA: Newcastle Company, 1978). All references to *Under the Sunset* will be included in the text.

18 Maunder, *Bram Stoker*, p. 22.

19 Phyllis A. Roth, *Bram Stoker* (Boston: Twayne, 1982), p. 52.

20 Clive Leatherdale, *Dracula: The Novel and the Legend* (Wellingborough, North-amptonshire: Aquarian, 1985), p. 63.

21 Roberts, 'Gothic fiction'.

22 Murray, *From the Shadow of Dracula*, p. 150.

23 Richard Dalby, 'Introduction', in Richard Dalby et al. (eds), Bram Stoker, *Best Ghost and Horror Stories*, p. ix.

24 Bram Stoker, 'The Dualitists', in *Dracula's Guest and Other Stories*, pp. 197–209. Quotations are from this edition and references are included in the text.

25 Murray, *From the Shadow of Dracula*, p. 152,

26 Valente devotes an entire chapter to this work in *Dracula's Crypt: Bram Stoker, Irishness, and the Question of Blood*: '"The Dualitists": prelude to *Dracula*', pp. 42–50.

27 Bram Stoker, 'The Judge's House', in *Dracula's Guest and Other Stories*, pp. 29–46. The story was originally published on 5 December 1891, in *The Illustrated Sporting*

and Dramatic News, 10–11. References for quotations from 'The Judge's House' will be included in the text.

28 Bram Stoker, *Dracula's Guest and Other Weird Stories with The Lair of the White Worm*, ed. Kate Hebblethwaite (London: Penguin, 2006), p. xvii.

29 According to Stephen King, rats are a recurrent Gothic image. King describes his personal fears in ascending order of importance – fear *for* someone else, fear of others, fear of death, fear of insects, fear of closed-in places, fear of rats, fear of snakes, fear of deformity, fear of 'squishy' things, and fear of the dark in 'The Horror Writer and the Ten Bears', in Tim Underwood and Chuck Miller (eds), *Kingdom of Fear: The World of Stephen King* (New York: NAL/Plume Trade Paperback, 1986), pp. 11–22.

30 Bram Stoker, 'The Secret of the Growing Gold', in *Dracula's Guest and Other Stories*, pp. 59–70. Quotations in this study are from this edition and references are included in the text. The story was originally published in *Black and White*, 3, 23 (January 1892), 118–21.

31 Maunder, *Bram Stoker*, p. 133.

32 Ibid., p. 140.

33 Ibid., p. 135.

34 Bram Stoker, *The Fate of Fenella*, ed. Andrew Maunder (Kansas City, MO: Valancourt Books, 2008). Quotations from the novel are from this edition and references are included in the text. The original appeared between 29 November 1891 and 7 May 1892, with Stoker's chapter published in vol. 4, 30 January 1892. Other contributors were Frances Eleanor Trollope, Arthur Conan Doyle, Hall Caine, Florence Marryat and Clement Scott. Richard Dalby and William Hughes describe *The Fate of Fenella* in *Bram Stoker: A Bibliography* (Southend-on-Sea, Essex: Desert Island Books, 2004):

> A novel with twenty-four authors, commissioned by J. S. Wood, editor and proprietor of *The Gentlewoman*, 'the Illustrated Weekly Journal for Gentlewomen'. Stoker's contribution . . . was advertised as 'The tenth chapter of the most extraordinary novel of modern times. Every chapter has been written by a well-known writer of fiction, without consulting his or her collaborateurs . . .' he serial was subsequently printed in volume form, first as a 'triple decker' and latterly in cheaper one-volume editions. (p. 113)

35 Maunder, *Bram Stoker*, p. 105.

36 Bram Stoker, 'The Squaw', in *Dracula's Guest and Other Stories*, pp. 47–58. Quotations from 'The Squaw' come from this edition and references will be included in the text. 'The Squaw' originally appeared in *The Illustrated Sporting and Dramatic News*, 2 (December 1893), 24–5. The first to feature the United States is *A Glimpse of America*, published in 1886 by Sampson Low, Marston & Co. Obviously fascinated with the American frontier and the rugged individualism he saw there, Stoker would continue to feature the United States and American characters throughout his writing career.

³⁷ Given the emphasis on an American character, it is interesting that Stoker sets the story before 1885, when the Lyceum began to play *Faust*.

³⁸ Lillian Nayden, 'Virgin territory and the Iron Virgin: engendering the Empire in Bram Stoker's "The Squaw"', in Claudia Nelson and Ann Sumner Holmes (eds), *Maternal Instincts: Visions of Motherhood and Sexuality in Britain 1875–1925* (London: Macmillan, 1997), pp. 75–97.

³⁹ Lisa Hopkins, *Bram Stoker: A Literary Life* (New York: Palgrave Macmillan, 2007), p. 93.

⁴⁰ Maunder discusses 'The Squaw' in *Bram Stoker*, pp. 126–31.

⁴¹ Ibid., p. 131.

⁴² Ibid.

⁴³ Bram Stoker, 'The Man from Shorrox', in *The Judge's House and Other Weird Tales* (Doylestown, PA: Wildside Press, undated), pp. 95–108. The story originally appeared in *Pall Mall Magazine*, 2 (February 1894), 656–69.

⁴⁴ Bram Stoker, 'A Dream of Red Hands', in *Dracula's Guest and Other Stories*, pp. 117–26. Quotations are from this edition and references will be included in the text. It originally appeared in *The Sketch*, 6 (11 July 1894), 578–80.

⁴⁵ Murray, *From the Shadow of Dracula*, p. 154.

⁴⁶ Bram Stoker, 'The Red Stockade', in *Dracula's Guest and Other Stories*, pp. 211–24. Quotations are from this edition and references will be included in the text. It was originally published in *Cosmopolitan Magazine*, 17 (October 1894), 619–30.

⁴⁷ Bram Stoker, 'Crooken Sands', in *Dracula's Guest and Other Stories*, pp. 127–45. Quotations are from this edition and references will be included in the text. This story was originally published in *The Illustrated Sporting and Dramatic News*, 1, December 1894, 28, 29, 32.

⁴⁸ While 'Crooken Sands' has not elicited much critical commentary; what little there is hints at the story's subtle anti-Semitism: see, for example, Lisa Hopkins, *Bram Stoker: A Literary Life*, p. 85; and Murray, *From the Shadow of Dracula*, p. 155.

⁴⁹ Bram Stoker, *Snowbound: The Record of a Theatrical Touring Party*, annotated and edited by Bruce Wightman [1908] (reprint Westcliff-on-Sea, Essex: Desert Island Books, 2000). Quotations are from this reprinted edition.

⁵⁰ Stoker is so moved by rugged landscape that it is surprising few scholars notice his appreciation of nature, especially since a logical connection exists between Stoker and Edmund Burke, author of *A Philosophical Enquiry into the Origin of our Ideas of the Sublime and Beautiful*. Both were born in Dublin and attended Trinity College.

⁵¹ The title refers to a bit of theatrical equipment, which Wightman's footnote explains:

> A star trap is an opening in the stage which propels an actor upwards through the floor at great speed. Each segment is triangular, the points of the star meeting in the middle. The wedges are hinged to the circumference, which enables them to fly upwards as the body is catapulted through the trap. The wedges fall back in place so quickly that the audience cannot see what has happened, the actor materializing as if by magic. The star trap was so dangerous it was eventually

banned. If the pieces of the star failed to open and close properly, a performer could jump short and be impaled round the waist. (p. 138)

52   Bram Stoker, 'The Eros of the Thames: The Story of a Frustrated Advertisement', *The Bram Stoker Society Journal*, 2 (1990), 24–33. It was originally printed in *The Royal Magazine*, 20 October 1908, 566–70. Bram Stoker, 'The Way of Peace', *The Bram Stoker Society Journal*, 1 (1989), 34–41. Quotations are from this edition and references will be included in the text. It was originally printed in *Everybody's Story Magazine*, December 1909, 204–9.
53   Bram Stoker, *Dracula's Guest and Other Stories* (London: Wordsworth, 2006).
54   Richard Dalby and William Hughes (eds), *Bram Stoker: A Bibliography*, p. 27.
55   Stoker, *Dracula's Guest and Other Weird Stories with The Lair of the White Worm*, ed. Kate Hebblethwaite (London: Penguin, 2006), p.371.
56   Murray, *From the Shadow of Dracula*, p. 170.
57   Bram Stoker, 'The Gypsy Prophecy', *Dracula's Guest & Other Stories* (London: Wordsworth, 2006), pp. 71–8. Quotations are from this edition and references will be included in the text. The correct spelling of the title of this story is 'The Gipsy Prophecy', but for consistency here I have used the spelling given in this Wordsworth edition.
58   Bram Stoker, 'The Coming of Abel Behena', *Dracula's Guest & Other Stories*, pp. 79–94. Quotations are from this edition and references will be included in the text.
59   Murray, *From the Shadow of Dracula*, p. 153.
60   Maunder, *Bram Stoker*, p. 100.
61   Ibid., pp. 137, 136.
62   Bram Stoker, 'The Burial of the Rats', *Dracula's Guest and Other Stories*, pp. 95–116. Quotations are from this edition and references will be included in the text.
63   Murray, *From the Shadow of Dracula*, p. 48.
64   Bram Stoker, 'Dracula's Guest', *Dracula's Guest and Other Stories*, pp. 17–27. Quotations are from this edition and references will be included in the text.

1   Gothic Material in *The Snake's Pass*, *The Watter's Mou'* and *The Shoulder of Shasta*

1   William Hughes, *Beyond Dracula: Bram Stoker's Fiction and Its Cultural Context* (New York: St Martin's Press, 2000), pp. 7–8.
2   Bram Stoker, *The Snake's Pass* (Dingle, Co. Kerry, Ireland: Brandon, 1990). All references will be to this edition and will be included in the text.
3   Phyllis A. Roth, *Bram Stoker* (Boston: Twayne, 1982), pp. 22–3, p. 23. Roth characterizes the romances (*The Snake's Pass*, *Miss Betty*, *The Man* and *Lady Athlyne*) as 'far weaker' but adds that they are nonetheless important in terms of Stoker's corpus.
4   Joseph Valente, *Dracula's Crypt: Bram Stoker, Irishness, and the Question of Blood* (Chicago: University of Illinois Press, 2002); Nicholas Daly, 'Incorporated

bodies: *Dracula* and the rise of professionalism', *Texas Studies in Literature and Language*, 39 (1997), 181–203; David Glover, *Vampires, Mummies, and Liberals: Bram Stoker and the Politics of Popular Fiction* (Durham, NC: Duke University Press, 1996).

5   Valente defines this convention as 'an Anglocentric framework for projecting gendered, hierarchically disposed stereotypes of Englishness and Irishness under the sign of a harmonious reconciliation of the two lands and peoples', in *Dracula's Crypt*, p. 12.

6   Glover, *Vampires, Mummies, and Liberals*, p. 31.

7   Ibid., p. 35.

8   Carol Margaret Davison, 'The ghost of genres past: theorizing the Gothic in the Victorian novel', in Karen Sayer and Rosemary Mitchell (eds), *Victorian Gothic* (Leeds: Leeds Centre for Victorian Studies, 2003), pp. 23–40, p. 28.

9   Paul Murray, *From the Shadow of Dracula* (London: Jonathan Cape, 2004).

10   Ibid., pp. 138–9.

11   Ibid., p. 156. For a thorough discussion of Stoker's interest in science and engineering, see Carol A. Senf, *Science and Social Science in Bram Stoker's Fiction* (Westport, CT: Greenwood, 2002). The most relevant chapter is 'Chapter IV: technological salvation in *The Snake's Pass, The Mystery of the Sea, Lady Athlyne, The Lady of the Shroud*, and *The Lair of the White Worm*', pp. 97–126.

12   Edmund Burke, *A Philosophical Enquiry into the Origin of our Ideas of the Sublime and Beautiful*, ed. Adam Phillips (Oxford: Oxford University Press, 1998).

13   Roth, *Bram Stoker*, p. 32.

14   Hughes, *Beyond Dracula*, p. 60.

15   Andrew Maunder, *Bram Stoker* (Tavistock: Northcote House Publishers Ltd, 2006), p. 78.

16   Murray, *From the Shadow of Dracula*, p. 157.

17   Alison Milbank, '"Powers old and new": Stoker's alliances with Anglo-Irish Gothic', in William Hughes and Andrew Smith (eds), *Bram Stoker: History, Psychoanalysis and the Gothic* (New York: St Martin's Press, 1998), pp. 12–28, p. 15.

18   At least one character observes that Murdock 'has nayther law nor the fear iv law' (p. 27). I disagree. While Murdock may be amoral, he stays within the limits of the law, which he uses to his advantage.

19   William Hughes, *Beyond Dracula: Bram Stoker's Fiction and Its Cultural Context* (New York: St Martin's Press, 2000), p. 192, n. 17. The review appeared in 'New books and magazines', *Labour World*, 29 November 1890.

20   Murray, *From the Shadow of Dracula*, pp. 158–9.

21   The following scholars have explored the Irish penchant for the Gothic: Seamus Deane, *Strange Country: Modernity and Nationhood in Irish writing since 1790* (Oxford: Clarendon Press, 1997); Brian Cosgrove (ed.), *Literature and the Supernatural* (Dublin: Columba Press, 1995); Patricia A. Lynch, Joachim Fischer and Brian Coates (eds), *Back to the Present, Forward to the Past: Irish Writing and History since 1798* (New York: Rodopi, 2006); Margot Gayle Backus, *The Gothic Family Romance: Heterosexuality, Child Sacrifice, and the Anglo-Irish Colonial Order* (Durham, NC: Duke University Press, 1999); and Patrick R. O'Malley, *Catholicism, Sexual Deviance, and Victorian Gothic Culture* (New York: Cambridge University Press, 2006).

22 Maggie Kilgour, 'The curious case of the Miltonic vampire', in Andrew Smith, Diane Mason and William Hughes (eds), *Fictions of Unease: The Gothic from Otranto to The X-Files* (Bath: Sulis Press, 2002), pp. 58–73.

23 Ibid., p. 69; Kilgour is citing Ian Duncan, *Modern Romance and the Transformations of the Novel: The Gothic, Scott, Dickens* (Cambridge: Cambridge University Press, 1992), pp. 22–3.

24 Bram Stoker, *The Watter's Mou'*, in Charles Osborne (ed.), *The Bram Stoker Bedside Companion: 10 Stories by the Author of Dracula* (New York: Taplinger, 1973), pp. 166–224. Quotations are from this edition and references will be included in the text.

25 Hughes follows this reference with the observation that 'it is with *Dracula* (1897) that Stoker becomes associated with the generically "lurid and creepy" first and foremost' (Hughes, *Bibliography*, p. 19).

26 Murray, *From the Shadow of Dracula*, p. 28; here Murray cites an original review in *Literary World*, 15 November 1905.

27 Peter Haining and Peter Tremayne, *The Un-Dead: The Legend of Bram Stoker and Dracula* (London: Constable, 1997), p. 149.

28 In *Bram Stoker: A Literary Life* (New York: Palgrave Macmillan, 2007), Lisa Hopkins notes that 'the interest in danger at sea will also have been fed by the fact that on 13 April 1887 Florence and Noel were shipwrecked and fetched ashore at Féchamp' (p. 94).

29 Murray, *From the Shadow of Dracula*, pp. 160–1.

30 Ibid., p. 161.

31 Bram Stoker, *The Shoulder of Shasta*, ed. and annotated by Alan Johnson (Westcliff-on-Sea, Essex: Desert Island Books Limited), 2000. Quotations are from this edition and references will be included in the text.

32 Roth, *Bram Stoker*, p. 22.

33 Ibid.

34 Harry Ludlam, *A Biography of Dracula: The Life Story of Bram Stoker* (London: Foulsham, 1962).

35 Murray, *From the Shadow of Dracula*, p. 161.

36 Ibid., p. 27.

37 Louis S. Warren, 'Buffalo Bill meets Dracula: William F. Cody, Bram Stoker, and the frontiers of racial decay', *American Historical Review*, 107 (October 2002), 1124–57. Richard Dalby observes in the Bibliographical Note to *The Shoulder of Shasta* that 'Stoker's only American novel . . . has never been published in that country', p. 6.

38 Hughes, *Beyond Dracula*, p. 95.

39 Hopkins, *Bram Stoker*, p. 1.

40 Ibid., pp. 3, 21.

41 Massimiliano Demata, 'Discovering Eastern horrors: Beckford, Maturin and the discourse of travel literature', in Andrew Smith and William Hughes (eds), *Empire and the Gothic: The Politics of Genre* (New York: Palgrave Macmillan, 2003), pp. 13–34, p. 14.

42 Edmund Burke, *A Philosophical Enquiry into the Origin of our Ideas of the Sublime and Beautiful*, ed. Adam Phillips (Oxford: Oxford University Press, 1998), pp. 66, 71.

Notes

43   Clive Bloom (ed.) *Gothic Horror: A Guide for Students and Readers*, 2nd edn (New York: Palgrave Macmillan, 2007), p. 11.

44   Joseph Grixti, *Terrors of Uncertainty: The Cultural Contexts of Horror Fiction* (New York: Routledge, 1989); Lynda Dryden, "'The coming terror":Wells's outcast London and the modern Gothic', in Karen Sayer and Rosemary Mitchell (eds), *Victorian Gothic* (Leeds: Leeds Centre for Victorian Studies, 2003), pp. 41–55.

45   Grixti, *Terrors of Uncertainty*, p. 18.

46   Dryden, "'The coming terror"', p. 41.

47   Tim Underwood and Chuck Miller (eds), *Bare Bones: Conversations on Terror with Stephen King* (New York: McGraw-Hill, 1988), pp. 49–50.

48   Robert Mighall, *A Geography of Victorian Gothic Fiction: Mapping History's Nightmares* (New York: Oxford University Press, 1999), pp. 66, 68.

2 *Dracula*: Stoker's Gothic Masterpiece

1   Andrew Maunder, *Bram Stoker* (Tavistock, Devon: Northcote House Publishers Ltd, 2006).

2   Bram Stoker, *Dracula Unearthed*, ed. Clive Leatherdale (Westcliff-on-Sea, Essex: Desert Island Books, 1998). All references to *Dracula* will be to this edition and will be included in the text.

3   Barbara Belford, *Bram Stoker: A Biography of the Author of Dracula* (New York: Alfred A. Knopf, 1966), pp. 260–1.

4   The seven years that Stoker worked on *Dracula* contrasts with the three weeks it took him to write *Miss Betty*, according to David Glover in *Vampires, Mummies, and Liberals: Bram Stoker and the Politics of Popular Fiction* (Durham, NC: Duke University Press, 1996), p. 7, or the three months that Belford observes it took him to write *The Lair of the White Worm* (pp. 317–18)

5   Robert Eighteen-Bisang and Elizabeth Miller, *Bram Stoker's Notes for Dracula: A Facsimile Edition* (Jefferson, NC: McFarland & Company, Inc., 2008).

6   Leslie S. Klinger (ed.), *The New Annotated Dracula* (New York: W. W. Norton, 2008), p. xii.

7   Ibid., p. 540. Klinger cites Elizabeth Miller (ed.), *Bram Stoker's Dracula: A Documentary Volume* (Detroit: Thomson Gale, 2005).

8   Klinger (ed.), *The New Annotated Dracula*, pp. 537–46.

9   Bram Stoker, *Dracula*, ed. John Paul Riquelme (Boston: Bedford/St Martin's, 2002), pp. 358–75, 359.

10   Paul Murray, *From the Shadow of Dracula* (London: Jonathan Cape, 2004), p. 202.

11   Quoted in ibid., p. 204.

12   Scott Vander Ploeg, 'Stoker's Dracula: a neo-Gothic experiment', in James Craig Holte (ed.), *The Fantastic Vampire: Studies in the Children of the Night. Selected Essays from the Eighteenth International Conference on the Fantastic in the Arts* (Westport, CT: Greenwood Press, 1997), pp. 37–44. Vander Ploeg argues that, while 'Dracula is full of Gothic conventions, Stoker does not rely on Gothic belief in the supernatural to structure the novel', p. 40.

13   Scott Brewster, 'Seeing things: Gothic and the madness of interpretation', in David Punter (ed.), *A Companion to the Gothic* (Malden, MA: Blackwell Publishers, 2000), pp. 281–92; the exact quotation appears on p. 287.

14   Clive Bloom, 'Introduction: death's own backyard', in *idem* (ed.), *Gothic Horror: A Guide for Students and Readers*, 2nd edn (New York: Palgrave Macmillan, 2007), pp. 1–24, p. 1.

15   Jerrold E. Hogle, 'Theorizing the Gothic', in Anna Powell and Andrew Smith (eds), *Teaching the Gothic* (New York: Palgrave Macmillan, 2006), pp. 29–47, p. 31.

16   Robert Mighall, *A Geography of Victorian Gothic Fiction: Mapping History's Nightmares* (New York: Oxford University Press, 1999), p. 267.

17   Here again, the exception proves the rule, with Jenna Harris arguing that 'Count Dracula is too familiar now to frighten us' (p. 52) and that today's readers do not share 'the cultural anxieties and fears of Victorian England' (p. 51), including reverse colonization, the New Woman, homosexuality and secularization, in 'Why Dracula no longer frightens us', *Journal of Dracula Studies*, 3 (2001), 50–2.

18   Phyllis A. Roth, *Bram Stoker* (Boston: Twayne, 1982), pp. 106–11, p. 106.

19   Among studies of Stoker's narrative methodology are the following: Susan M. Cribb, '"If I had to write with a pen": readership and Bram Stoker's diary narrative', *Journal of the Fantastic in the Arts*, 10 (1997), 133–41; David Seed, 'The narrative method of *Dracula*', *Nineteenth Century Fiction*, 40, 1 (1985), reprinted in Margaret L. Carter (ed.), *Dracula: The Vampire and the Critics* (Ann Arbor, MI: UMI Research Press, 1988), pp. 195–206; Carol Senf, 'The unseen face in the mirror', *Journal of Narrative Technique*, 9 (1979), 160–70; Geoffrey Wall, '"Different from writing": *Dracula* in 1897', *Literature and History*, 10 (1984), 15–23; and Jennifer Wicke, 'Vampiric typewriting: *Dracula* and its media', *ELH*, 59 (1992), 467–93.

20   Seed, 'The narrative method of *Dracula*', p. 200.

21   Andrew Maunder *Bram Stoker*, p. 30. Maunder analyses the importance of London in several Stoker novels:

> *The Primrose Path* is a temperance . . . novel . . . *Dracula* is a vampire novel, and also uses some of the tropes of the imperial Gothic and the fantastic; and *The Jewel of Seven Stars* is an Orientalist, Gothic novel, which exploits the mystique and exoticism of Ancient Egypt. (p. 29)

22   Ibid., p. 29.

23   Jean Marigny, 'Secrecy as strategy in *Dracula*', *Journal of Dracula Studies*, 2 (2000), 3–7, 3.

24   'Bram Stoker's Preface to the Icelandic Edition of *Dracula* (1901)', *Journal of Dracula Studies*, 2 (2000), 46.

25   He uses a similar strategy in *Snowbound* in which he clearly identifies himself by name in the Forward and asks readers to contemplate the relationship between truth and fiction: 'The Truth – or rather Accuracy – of these Stories may be accepted or not as the Reader pleases. They are given as Fiction.' (Bram Stoker,

Snowbound, ed. Bruce Wightman (Westcliff-on-Sea, Essex: Desert Island Books, 2000).

26 'Bram Stoker's Preface to the Icelandic Edition of *Dracula*', 46.

27 Ibid.

28 This letter is reprinted in the *Journal of Dracula Studies*, 1 (1999), 48.

29 Judith Halberstam, 'Technologies of monstrosity: Bram Stoker's *Dracula*', *Victorian Studies*, 36 (spring 1993), 333–52, 335.

30 Glennis Byron, 'Gothic in the 1890s', in David Punter (ed.), *A Companion to the Gothic* (Malden, MA: Blackwell Publishers, 2000), pp. 132–42. Byron cites Kathleen Spencer, 'Purity and danger: Dracula, the urban Gothic, and the late Victorian degeneracy crisis', *ELH*, 59, 1 (1992), 197–225.

31 Jerrold Hogle mentions *Doom* and *Resident Evil* in 'Theorizing the Gothic'. By the time the current study is published, there will undoubtedly be many others.

32 Avril Horner and Sue Zlosnik, 'Comic Gothic', in David Punter (ed.), *A Companion to the Gothic* (Malden, MA: Blackwell Publishers, 2000), pp. 242–54, p. 243.

33 According to Chris Baldick and Robert Mighall, this 'out-of-placeness, their dissynchronicity with the modern Victorian world of technology and progress into which they intrude' is a characteristic of Gothic villains. Their article, 'Gothic criticism', is included in David Punter (ed.), *A Companion to the Gothic*, pp. 209–28.

34 Judith Halberstam, 'Technologies of monstrosity: Bram Stoker's *Dracula*', and *Skin Shows: Gothic Horror and the Technology of Monsters* (Durham, NC: Duke University Press, 1995); H. L. Malchow, *Gothic Images of Race in Nineteenth-century Britain* (Stanford: Stanford University Press, 1996); Carol Margaret Davison, *Anti-Semitism and British Gothic Literature* (New York: Palgrave Macmillan, 2004). Davison observes that Jewish nationalism was also born in the 1880s and 1890s during the period of burgeoning British right-wing nationalism and was thus cause for concern for some Britons (p. 131).

35 Davison, *Anti-Semitism and British Gothic Literature*, p. 131.

36 Clive Leatherdale, *Dracula: The Novel and the Legend* (Wellingborough: Aquarian, 1985), p. 473.

37 Ibid., p. 473, n. 47.

38 William Hughes, 'A singular invasion: revisiting the postcoloniality of Bram Stoker's *Dracula*', in Andrew Smith and William Hughes (eds), *Empire and the Gothic: The Politics of Genre* (New York: Palgrave Macmillan, 2003), pp. 88–102; Stephen Arata, 'The occidental tourist: *Dracula* and the anxiety of reverse colonization', *Victorian Studies*, 33 (1990), 621–45; Patrick Brantlinger, 'Imperial Gothic', in Anna Powell and Andrew Smith (eds), *Teaching the Gothic* (New York: Palgrave Macmillan, 2006), pp. 153–67. 'Imperial Gothic' is a much shorter version of Brantlinger's *Rule of Darkness: British Literature and Imperialism, 1830–1914* (Ithaca, NY: Cornell University Press, 1988).

39 Bratlinger, 'Imperial Gothic', p. 156.

40 Jimmie E. Cain, Jr, *Bram Stoker and Russophobia: Evidence of the British Fear of Russia in Dracula and the Lady of the Shroud* (Jefferson, NC: McFarland, 2006);

Notes

Athena Vrettos, *Somatic Fictions: Imagining Illness in Victorian Culture* (Stanford: Stanford University Press, 1995).

41 Cain, *Bram Stoker and Russophobia*, p. 8.

42 Vrettos, *Somatic Fictions*, p. 218, n. 35.

43 The following are thought-provoking treatments of Stoker's treatment of women in *Dracula*: Salli J. Kline, *The Degeneration of Women: Bram Stoker's Dracula as Allegorical Criticism of the Fin de Siècle* (Rheinbach-Merzbach: CMZ-Verlag, 1992); Matthew C. Brennan, 'Knowledge and saving souls: the role of the "New Woman" in Stoker's *Dracula* and Murnau's *Nosferatu*', *Studies in the Humanities*, 19 (1992), 1–10; Alison Case, 'Tasting the original apple: gender and the struggle for narrative authority in *Dracula*', *Narrative*, 1 (October 1993), 223–43; Stephanie Demetrakopoulos, 'Feminism, sex role exchanges, and other subliminal fantasies in Bram Stoker's *Dracula*', *Frontiers* (1977), 104–13; Gail B. Griffin, '"Your girls that you all love are mine": *Dracula* and the Victorian male sexual imagination', *International Journal of Women's Studies*, 3 (1980), 454–65; Cyndy Hendershot, 'Vampire and replicant: the one-sex body in a two-sex world', *Science-Fiction Studies*, 22 (1995), 373–98; Phyllis Roth, 'Suddenly sexual women in Bram Stoker's *Dracula*', *Literature and Psychology*, 27 (1977), 113–21; Marie Mulvey-Roberts, '*Dracula* and the doctors: bad blood, menstrual taboo and the New Woman', in William Hughes and Andrew Smith (eds), *Bram Stoker: History, Psychoanalysis and the Gothic*, pp. 78–95; Carol A. Senf. '*Dracula*: Stoker's response to the New Woman', *Victorian Studies*, 26 (1982), 33–49; Judith Weissman, 'Women and vampires: *Dracula* as a Victorian novel', *Midwest Quarterly*, 18 (1977), 392–405.

44 Senf, '*Dracula*: Stoker's Response to the New Woman', 34.

45 Garrett Stewart reminds readers that Mina must have read New Woman novels to be able to draw conclusions about their sexual forwardness and questioning of traditional gender roles, in '"Count me in": *Dracula*, hypnotic participation, and the late Victorian Gothic of reading', *Literature Interpretation Theory*, 5 (1994), 1–18. A number of scholars have written books and articles on the New Woman movement that are worth reading for the light that they shed on Stoker: Gail Cunningham, *The New Woman and the Victorian Novel* (New York: Barnes and Noble, 1978); Lloyd Fernando, *'New Women' in the Late Victorian Novel* (University Park: Pennsylvania State University Press, 1977); Sally Ledger, *The New Woman: Fiction and Feminism at the Fin de Siècle* (Manchester: Manchester University Press, 1997); Lyn Pykett, *The 'Improper Feminine': The Women's Sensation Novel and the New Woman Writing* (New York: Routledge, 1992). Leatherdale's footnote provides a succinct definition of the New Woman for readers who do not want a comprehensive view:

> The New Woman was the popular name given to proto-feminists, who challenged restrictions imposed by male dominance and prejudice. They objected . . . to being encased in whalebone, and some dared to pedal around on bicycles, which required dispensing with petticoats and chaperones. Others turned their backs on their 'rightful' place, in the home, opting for greater independence, careers

of their own and sexual liaisons outside marriage. (Leatherdale, *Dracula*, p. 151, n. 2)

[46]   Roth, *Bram Stoker*, p. 33; Arata, 'The occidental tourist', 62–4.

[47]   Several scholars comment on the significance of her surname, Westenra. According to Eighteen-Bisang and Miller, it 'could be a pun on "West End," for both Lucy and Mina, who inhabit the fashionable part of London are contrasted with the vixens from the East who resemble the prostitutes in the East End' (*Bram Stoker's Notes for* Dracula, p. 281). Milbank notes that Westenra was the name 'of the Anglo-Irish barons of Rossmore in County Monaghan' (Alison Milbank, '"Powers old and new": Stoker's alliances with Anglo-Irish Gothic', in William Hughes and Andrew Smith (eds), *Bram Stoker: History, Psychoanalysis and the Gothic* (New York: St Martin's Press, 1998), p. 20). Even if her name did not evoke wealth and power, it would evoke the West as opposed to the East.

[48]   Leatherdale, *Dracula*, p. 252, n. 32.

[49]   Brennan, 'Knowledge and saving souls', 3.

[50]   Elizabeth Miller, 'Shapeshifting Dracula: the abridged edition of 1901', in James Craig Holte (ed.), *The Fantastic Vampire: Studies in the Children of the Night. Selected Essays from the Eighteenth International Conference on the Fantastic in the Arts* (Westport, CT: Greenwood Press, 1997), pp. 3–10, pp. 8, 9.

[51]   Roth, 'Suddenly sexual women in Bram Stoker's *Dracula*', 47.

[52]   William Patrick Day, *In the Circles of Fear and Desire: A Study of Gothic Fantasy* (Chicago: University of Chicago Press, 1985), p. 145; the passage is quoted in Carol A. Senf, *The Critical Response to Bram Stoker* (Westport, CT: Greenwood, 1993), p. 70.

[53]   Milbank, '"Powers old and new"', p. 21.

[54]   Maurice Richardson, 'The psychoanalysis of ghost stories', *Twentieth Century*, 166 (1959), 419–31, 427 .

[55]   Nina Auerbach, *Our Vampires, Ourselves* (Chicago: University of Chicago Press, 1995), p. 7.

[56]   Talia Schaffer, '"A Wilde desire took me": the homoerotic history of *Dracula*', *ELH*, 61 (1994), 381–425.

[57]   Lisa Hopkins, *Bram Stoker: A Literary Life* (New York: Palgrave Macmillan, 2007), p. 20.

[58]   Schaffer, '"A Wilde desire took me"', 398.

[59]   Ibid., 409.

[60]   Julian Wolfreys, 'Victorian Gothic', in Anna Powell and Andrew Smith (eds), *Teaching the Gothic* (New York: Palgrave Macmillan, 2006), pp. 62–77; Lynda Dryden, '"The coming terror": Wells's outcast London and the modern Gothic', in Karen Sayer and Rosemary Mitchell (eds), *Victorian Gothic* (Leeds: Leeds Centre for Victorian Studies, 2003), pp. 41–55.

[61]   'Review of *Dracula*', *Spectator*, 79 (31 July 1897), 150–1, 151.

[62]   Among the best commentaries on Stoker's use of the modern are the following: Manuel Aguirre, 'Narrative structure, liminality, self-similarity: the case of Gothic fiction', in Bloom (ed.), *Gothic Horror*, pp. 226–47; Nicholas Daly,

'Incorporated bodies: *Dracula* and the rise of professionalism', *Texas Studies in Literature and Language*, 39 (summer 1997), 181–203; Joel Feimer, 'Bram Stoker's *Dracula*: the challenge of the occult to science, reason and psychiatry', in Michele K. Langford (ed.), *Contours of the Fantastic* (New York: Greenwood, 1994), pp. 165–71; John L. Greenway, 'Seward's folly: *Dracula* as a critique of "normal science"', *Stanford Literature Review*, 3 (1986), 213–30; Jenna Harris, 'Why Dracula no longer frightens us', 50–2; Rosemary Jann, 'Saved by science? The mixed messages of Stoker's *Dracula*', *Texas Studies in Literature and Language*, 31 (summer 1989), 273–87; Carol Senf, *Science and Social Science in Bram Stoker's Fiction* (Wesport, CT: Greenwood, 2002), and *Dracula: Between Tradition and Modernism* (New York: Twayne, 1998); Clare Simmons, 'Fables of continuity: Bram Stoker and medievalism,' in William Hughes and Andrew Smith (eds), *Bram Stoker*, pp. 29–46; and Jennifer Wicke, 'Vampiric typewriting: *Dracula* and its media', *ELH*, 59 (1992), 467–93.

63 Harris, 'Why Dracula no longer frightens us', 50–1.
64 Clare Simmons, *Reversing the Conquest: History and Myth in Nineteenth Century British Literature* (Piscataway, NJ: Rutgers University Press, 1990), p. 34.
65 Aguirre, 'Narrative structure, liminality, self-similarity', p. 243.
66 Byron, 'Gothic in the 1890s', p. 134.
67 John L. Greenway, 'Seward's folly: *Dracula* as a critique of "normal science"', *Stanford Literature Review*, 3 (1986), 230.
68 Clive Bloom (ed.), *Gothic Horror: A Guide for Students and Readers*, 2nd edn (New York: Palgrave Macmillan, 2007), pp. 291–7, p. 291.
69 Eighteen-Bisang and Miller (eds), *Bram Stoker's Notes for Dracula*, p. 15.
70 I made this point a number of years ago in '*Dracula*: The unseen face in the mirror', *Journal of Narrative Technique*, 9 (1979), 160–70. Apparently others share my perception as the article was reprinted by Margaret L. Carter (ed.), *Dracula and the Critics* (Ann Arbor: UMI, 1988); Nina Auerbach and David J. Skal (eds), *Dracula* (New York: Norton, 1997). Harold Bloom (ed.), *Bram Stoker's Dracula* (Philadelphia: Chelsea House Publishers, 2003).
71 J. P. Riquelme (ed.), *Dracula: Complete, Authoritative Text with Biographical, Historical, and Cultural Contexts, Critical History and Essays from Contemporary Critical Perspectives* (Boston: Bedford/St Martin's Press, 2002).
72 J. P. Riquelme, 'Toward a history of Gothic and Modernism: dark modernity from Bram Stoker to Samuel Beckett', *Modern Fiction Studies*, 46, 3 (2000), 585–605, 585–6.
73 Belford, *Bram Stoker*, p. 228.
74 Leatherdale, *Dracula*, pp. 463–4, n. 111.
75 David Punter, *The Literature of Terror: A History of Gothic Fictions from 1765 to the Present Day* (London: Longman, 1980), p. 257.
76 Raymond T. McNally, 'Bram Stoker and Irish Gothic', pp. 11–12. McNally is partially responsible for the rebirth of interest in *Dracula* during the 1970s: McNally and Radu Florescu, *In Search of Dracula* (New York: Graphic Society, 1972). They revised and reissued it as *In Search of Dracula: History of Dracula and Vampires* (Boston: Houghton Mifflin, 1994). McNally also wrote *Dracula Was*

a Woman (London: Hale, 1984), which explores the connection between *Dracula* and the historical Elizabeth Bathory.

77 McNally, 'Bram Stoker and Irish Gothic', p. 13.
78 Eighteen-Bisang and Miller (eds), *Bram Stoker's Notes for Dracula*, p. 287.
79 Belford, *Bram Stoker*, p. 267.
80 Ibid., p. 268.
81 Vander Ploeg, 'Stoker's Dracula', p. 42.
82 Claire Simmons, 'Fables of continuity: Bram Stoker and medievalism', p. 30.
83 Glover, *Vampires, Mummies, and Liberals*, p. 61.
84 Ibid., p. 65.
85 Eighteen-Bisang and Miller, *Bram Stoker's Notes for Dracula*, p. 285.
86 Kate Ferguson Ellis, 'Can you forgive her? The Gothic heroine and her critics', in D. Punter (ed.), *A Companion to the Gothic* (Malden, MA: Blackwell Publishers, 2000), pp. 257–68, p. 263.
87 Eighteen-Bisang and Miller, *Bram Stoker's Notes for Dracula*, p. 117, n. 250.
88 Vander Ploeg, 'Stoker's Dracula', p. 42.
89 Hopkins, *Bram Stoker*, p. 150.

3 Ongoing Work with the Gothic in *Miss Betty*, *The Mystery of the Sea* and *The Jewel of Seven Stars*

1 Bram Stoker, *The Mystery of the Sea* (Kansas City, Missouri: Valancourt, 2007). All references will be to this edition and will be included in the text.
2 Bram Stoker, *The Jewel of Seven Stars* (Westcliff-on-Sea, Essex: Desert Island Books, 1996). All references will be to this edition and will be included in the text.
3 Bram Stoker, *Miss Betty* (London: New English Library, 1974). While the volume does not include the date of publication, Richard Dalby and William Hughes, in *Bram Stoker: A Bibliography*, include this information: '"First New English Library Edition" (London: New English Library, 1974), 160p.' All references will be to this edition and will be included in the text.
4 Andrew Maunder, *Bram Stoker* (Tavistock, Devon: Northcote House Publishers Ltd, 2006), pp. 109–10.
5 William Hughes, 'Reviewing Stoker's Fiction', in Richard Dalby and William Hughes (eds), *Bram Stoker: A Bibliography* (Southend-on-Sea, Essex: Desert Island Books, 2004), pp. 20–1, quotes a letter from J. S. Arrowsmith to Bram Stoker, 8 October 1894 (Brotherton Collection, Leeds University Library). David Glover comments on the speed with which Stoker wrote *Miss Betty* and cites the manuscript, dated from 22 March 1891 to 10 April 1891 in *Vampires, Mummies, and Liberals: Bram Stoker and the Politics of Popular Fiction* (Durham, NC: Duke University Press, 1996), p. 155, n. 29. Glover also points to what this manuscript reveals about Stoker's writing habits:

Notes

His habit of dating each day's output shows just how concentrated his work
could be: for example, the original draft of *Seven Golden Buttons* . . . that eventually
appeared under the title *Miss Betty* . . . was completed in slightly less than three
weeks. (p. 7)

6   Paul Murray, *From the Shadow of Dracula* (London: Jonathan Cape, 2004), p. 218.
7   William Hughes, *Beyond Dracula: Bram Stoker's Fiction and Its Cultural Context*
    (New York: St Martin's Press, 2000), pp. 81–2.
8   Lisa Hopkins, *Bram Stoker: A Literary Life* (New York: Palgrave Macmillan, 2007),
    p. 1.
9   Maunder, *Bram Stoker*, p. 111.
10 Phyllis A. Roth, *Bram Stoker* (Boston: Twayne, 1982), p. 37.
11 Fred Botting, *Gothic* (London: Routledge, 1995), p. 1.
12 Maunder, *Bram Stoker*, p. 110.
13 Ibid., p. 111.
14 Hopkins, *Bram Stoker*, p. 3.
15 Roth, *Bram Stoker*, p. 103.
16 Ibid., p. 106.
17 Glover, *Vampires, Mummies, and Liberals*, p. 105; Hopkins, *Bram Stoker*, p. 95.
18 Paul Murray, *From the Shadow of Dracula* (London: Jonathan Cape, 2004), pp. 60–1.
19 Ibid., p. 222.
20 Ibid., p. 180.
21 Ibid., p. 222.
22 Hopkins, *Bram Stoker*, p. 6.
23 Murray and Belford comment on the sea in Stoker's fiction, Belford tracing his
    fascination to childhood when he listened to his mother's stories in Barbara
    Belford, *Bram Stoker: A Biography of the Author of Dracula* (New York: Alfred A. Knopf,
    1996):

    Here was the genesis of his fascination with storms, shipwrecks, and sea rescues, with
    pirate coves, buried treasure, and the unknown. And always the sea, particularly the
    angry sea. In his imagination Stoker envisioned mist-clouded sails protecting cargoes
    of gold and silver, jewels and coins. He conjured up scenes of vast caves filled with
    whiskey brought in by the smugglers who stealthily oared in and out of the hidden
    coves around Clontarf. (p. 15)

    Murray notes that the sea figures as a backdrop for much of what Stoker wrote
    and observes that Stoker's contemporaries noted its pervasiveness in his writing:

    The impact of the sea beside which he had grown up is also evident in Stoker's
    writing. The anonymous author of a profile of Stoker in the *Literary World* in
    1905 divided his fiction into two categories, the supernatural and the marine
    with *The Watter's Mou'* (1895), *The Mystery of the Sea* and *The Man* specimens of
    the latter, 'for they all possess a paramount attraction in their sea-scapes and sea-
    scenes'. (Murray, *From the Shadow of Dracula*, p. 28)

Notes

24 Hopkins, *Bram Stoker*, p. 123.

25 Edmund Burke, *A Philosophical Enquiry into the Origin of our Ideas of the Sublime and Beautiful*, ed. Adam Phillips (London: Oxford University Press, 1998), p. 53.

26 Angela Wright, *Gothic Fiction: A Reader's Guide to Essential Criticism* (New York: Palgrave Macmillan, 2007), p. 36.

27 Ibid., p. 37.

28 Chris Baldick and Robert Mighall, 'Gothic Criticism', in D. Punter (ed.), *A Companion to the Gothic* (Malden, MA: Blackwell Publishers, 2000), pp. 209–28, p. 221.

29 Murray, *From the Shadow of Dracula*, p. 191.

30 Clive Leatherdale argues that Stoker lacked the ability to create more than one great book and that *Dracula*, which 'came first was sure to grab the plaudits, for successive works within the same genre were bound to be derivative, faded imitations of the master template' (*Dracula: The Novel and the* Legend (Wellingborough: Aquarian, 1985), p. 15.

31 Dalby and Hughes (eds), *Bram Stoker: A Bibliography*, p. 65; Daniel Farson, *The Man Who Wrote Dracula: A Biography of Bram Stoker* (London: Michael Joseph, 1975), p. 205.

32 Maunder, *Bram Stoker*, p. 57.

33 Roth, *Bram Stoker*, p. 66.

34 Belford, *Bram Stoker*, p. 297.

35 Murray, *From the Shadow of Dracula*, pp. 226–7.

36 Ibid., p. 227.

37 Maunder, *Bram Stoker*, p. 29.

38 An Egyptian army officer who promoted the overthrow of European colonial powers in 1879, Arabi was exiled to the British colony of Ceylon in 1882. Other references to time include that Ross was made a Queen's Counsel 'in the last year of the Queen's reign' (p. 157) or 1900. The only mention of an exact date is 3 November 1884 (p. 143), the date of Margaret's birth. Nonetheless, astute readers can place *Jewel* into a particular historical context and understand the events and people that might elicit fear in its characters.

39 Murray, *From the Shadow of Dracula*, p. 226.

40 Glover, *Vampires, Mummies, and Liberals*, p. 15.

41 The Desert Island Library edition is one of the few editions to include both endings as well as 'Chapter 16: Powers – Old and New', which is omitted in the shorter 1912 edition.

42 William Hughes, *Beyond Dracula: Bram Stoker's Fiction and its Cultural Context* (New York: St Martin's Press, 2000), p. 36.

43 Glover, *Vampires, Mummies, and Liberals*, p. 173, n. 58; Leatherdale observes that, as well as Queen Tera, one cat also survives (either Margaret's pet Silvio or Tera's familiar, the mummy cat). 'Stoker invites readers to guess which' (*Dracula*, p. 255, n. 21).

44 Roth, *Bram Stoker*, p. 66.

45 Maunder, *Bram Stoker*, pp. 29–30.

Notes

46 William Hughes mentions two other possibilities in *Beyond Dracula*, noting that "'Tera" is the inversion of the last four letters of Margaret's Christian name, though phonetically it is a tempting pointer also to *terror*' (p. 38).

47 Robert Mighall, *A Geography of Victorian Gothic Fiction: Mapping History's Nightmares* (New York: Oxford University Press, 1999), p. 66.

48 Burke, *A Philosophical Enquiry*, p. 78.

49 Mighall, *A Geography of Victorian Gothic Fiction*, p. 68.

50 Avril Horner and Sue Zlosnik, 'Comic Gothic', in David Punter (ed.), *A Companion to the Gothic* (Malden, MA: Blackwell Publishers, 2000), pp. 242–54, p. 243.

51 Ibid., p. 243.

52 Roth, *Bram Stoker*, p. 109.

53 Hopkins, *Bram Stoker*, p. 21.

54 Maunder, *Bram Stoker*, p. 29.

4 Gothic-tinged Romances: *The Man*, *Lady Athlyne* and *The Lady of the Shroud*

1 Bram Stoker, *The Man* (London: Heinemann, 1905). Bram Stoker, *Lady Athlyne* (Southend-on-Sea, Essex: Desert Island Books, 2007). All references will be to these editions and will be included in the text.

2 Bram Stoker, *The Lady of the Shroud* (Westcliff-on-Sea, Essex: Desert Island Books, 2001). References to this edition will be included in the text.

3 David Glover, *Vampires, Mummies, and Liberals: Bram Stoker and the Politics of Popular Fiction* (Durham, NC: Duke University Press, 1996), p. 52.

4 Krishan Kumar, *Utopia and Anti-Utopia in Modern Times* (Oxford: Basil Blackwell, 1987), p. 65.

5 Glover, *Vampires, Mummies, and Liberals*, p. 53.

6 Harry Ludlam, *A Biography of Dracula: The Life Story of Bram Stoker* (London: Foulsham, 1962), p. 146.

7 Phyllis A. Roth, *Bram Stoker* (Boston: Twayne, 1982), p. 38.

8 Richard Dalby and William Hughes, *Bram Stoker: A Bibliography* (Southend-on-Sea, Essex: Desert Island Books, 2004), p. 21 .

9 Andrew Maunder, *Bram Stoker* (Tavistock: Northcote House Publishers Ltd, 2006), p. 123.

10 Roth, *Bram Stoker*, p. 49.

11 Maunder, *Bram Stoker*, p. 121.

12 William Hughes, *Beyond Dracula: Bram Stoker's Fiction and Its Cultural Context* (New York: St Martin's Press, 2000), p. 67.

13 Glover discusses the impact of the Boer War on *The Man* and *Athlyne* in *Vampires, Mummies, and Liberals*, noting that 'the conflict exacerbates . . . a crisis of gender that threatens the integrity of the nation' (p. 108). He also demonstrates that the two novels 'take the national trauma of the Boer War as their point of departure, organizing their narratives of degeneration and regeneration around an exalted heterosexuality' (p. 20).

14 Maunder, *Bram Stoker*, p. 74.

173

[15] Roth, *Bram Stoker*, p. 48.

[16] Maunder, *Bram Stoker*, p. 119.

[17] Ibid., p. 140.

[18] Roth, *Bram Stoker*, p. 23.

[19] I have changed my mind on this question myself. Stoker's monstrous women in the horror tales (especially *Dracula, Jewel* and *Lair*) are so memorable and so horrifying that it is easy to assume that he is misogynistic or at least apprehensive about strong and assertive women. Having read Stoker's works, I believe his attitude to women is more complex and interesting and that his works should be considered on a case-by-case basis.

[20] Glover, *Vampires, Mummies, and Liberals*, p. 106. Stoker names a woman professor after Egerton in *The Man* (London: Heinemann, 1905): 'When Stephen was about sixteen she went for a short visit to Oxford. She stayed at Somerville with Mrs Egerton, an old friend of her mother's, who was a professor at the college' (p. 77). Indeed, Stephen learns a great deal from Egerton. While she decides not to join the college when she remembers that her father would be alone, she returns regularly to the University Mission House in the East End of London, where she learns about providing for the less fortunate, experiences that make her a better landlord and magistrate.

[21] Ludlam, *A Biography of Dracula*, p. 156.

[22] Paul Murray, *From the Shadow of Dracula* (London: Jonathan Cape, 2004).

[23] Ludlam, *A Biography of Dracula*, p. 158; Maunder, *Bram Stoker*, p. 87.

[24] Roth, *Bram Stoker*, p. 75.

[25] Ludlam, *A Biography of Dracula*, p. 159–60.

[26] Maunder, *Bram Stoker*, p. 85–6.

[27] Paul Murray, *From the Shadow of Dracula* (London: Jonathan Cape, 2004), p. 159.

[28] Jimmie E. Cain, Jr, *Bram Stoker and Russophobia: Evidence of the British Fear of Russia in Dracula and The Lady of the Shroud* (Jefferson, NC: McFarland & Company, 2006); Victor Sage, 'Exchanging fantasies: sex and the Serbian crisis in *The Lady of the Shroud*', in William Hughes and Andrew Smith (eds), *Bram Stoker: History, Psychoanalysis and the Gothic* (London: Macmillan, 1998), pp. 116–33.

[29] Murray, *From the Shadow of Dracula*, p. 261.

[30] Hughes, *Beyond Dracula*, p. 24; Cain, *Bram Stoker and Russophobia*, p. 1.

[31] Sage, 'Exchanging fantasies', p. 116.

[32] Glover, *Vampires, Mummies, and Liberals*, p. 8.

[33] Claire Simmons, 'Fables of continuity: Bram Stoker and medievalism', in Hughes and Smith (eds), *Bram Stoker*, pp. 29–46, p. 35.

[34] Hughes, *Beyond Dracula*, pp. 106–7.

[35] Ibid., p. 85, n. 32.

[36] Roth, *Bram Stoker*, p. 79.

5 Stoker's Return to the Gothic in *Famous Impostors* and *The Lair of the White Worm*

[1] There is no place in this study to discuss whether Stoker suffered from syphilis, as Daniel Farson argues in *The Man Who Wrote Dracula: A Biography of Bram Stoker*

(London: Michael Joseph, 1975), or whether Bright's disease and a series of strokes caused the problems Stoker experienced in the final decade of his life. Practically all of Stoker's biographers have an opinion on the topic, however.

2   Paul Murray, *From the Shadow of Dracula* (London: Jonathan Cape, 2004), p. 249.

3   Bram Stoker, *Famous Impostors* (printed in the United States, 1910), p. 32. Future references to this edition will be included in the text.

4   Bram Stoker, *The Lair of the White Worm* (London: William Rider and Son, 1911). References to this edition will be included in the text.

5   Barbara Belford, *Bram Stoker: A Biography of the Author of Dracula* (New York: Alfred A. Knopf, 1996), pp. 317–18.

6   Phyllis A. Roth, *Bram Stoker* (Boston: Twayne, 1982); Lisa Hopkins, *Bram Stoker: A Literary Life* (New York: Palgrave Macmillan, 2007).

7   Roth, *Bram Stoker*, p. 131.

8   Hopkins, *Bram Stoker*, p. 1.

9   Murray, *From the Shadow of Dracula*, p. 256.

10   Ibid., p. 255.

11   Murray, *From the Shadow of Dracula*, p. 223.

12   Roth, *Bram Stoker*, p. 80.

13   Murray, *From the Shadow of Dracula*, p. 262.

14   William Hughes, *Beyond Dracula: Bram Stoker's Fiction and its Cultural Context* (New York: St Martin's Press, 2000), p. 26.

15   Farson, *The Man Who Wrote Dracula*, p. 217.

16   Harry Ludlam, *A Biography of Dracula: The Life Story of Bram Stoker* (London: Foulsham, 1962), p. 165.

17   Bram Stoker, *Dracula's Guest and Other Weird Stories with The Lair of the White Worm*, ed. Kate Hebblethwaite (London: Penguin, 2006), p. xiii.

18   David Glover, *Vampires, Mummies, and Liberals: Bram Stoker and the Politics of Popular Fiction* (Durham, NC: Duke University Press, 1996), p. 6.

19   Andrew Maunder, *Bram Stoker* (Tavistock: Northcote House Publishers Ltd, 2006), pp. 72–3.

20   Ibid., p. 92.

21   David Punter, 'Echoes in the animal house: *The Lair of the White Worm*', in William Hughes and Andrew Smith (eds), *Bram Stoker: History, Psychoanalysis and the Gothic* (New York: St Martin's Press, 1998), pp. 173–87; David Seed, 'Eruptions of the primitive into the present: *The Jewel of Seven Stars* and *The Lair of the White Worm*', in Hughes and Smith (eds), *Bram Stoker*, pp. 188–204.

22   Punter, 'Echoes in the animal house', p. 177.

23   Ibid., p. 184.

24   Seed, 'Eruptions of the primitive into the present', p. 188.

25   Ibid., p. 200. Seed is quoting from *The Lair of the White Worm*, in *Dracula and The Lair of the White Worm: A Bram Stoker Omnibus Edition* (London: W. Foulsham & Co., 1986). My references to the novel are to the first edition: Bram Stoker, *The Lair of the White Worm* (London: William Rider and Son, 1911).

26   Murray, *From the Shadow of Dracula*, p. 263.

27   Hopkins, *Bram Stoker*, p. 134.

Notes

28   Seed, 'Eruptions of the primitive into the present', p. 197.
29   Punter, 'Echoes in the animal house', p. 177.
30   Seed, 'Eruptions of the primitive into the present', p. 196.
31   Punter, 'Echoes in the animal house', p. 183.
32   Glover, *Vampires, Mummies, and Liberals*, p. 98.
33   Ibid., p. 43.
34   Maunder, *Bram Stoker*, p. 97.
35   Glover, *Vampires, Mummies, and Liberals*, p. 106.
36   Maunder, *Bram Stoker*, p. 96.
37   Ibid., p. 99.
38   Roth, *Bram Stoker*, pp. 81, 85.
39   Robert A. Mighall, *A Geography of Victorian Gothic Fiction: Mapping History's Nightmares* (New York: Oxford University Press, 1999), p. 68.

Bibliography

ဆာလ

Aguirre, Manuel, 'Narrative structure, liminality, self-similarity: the case of gothic fiction', in Clive Bloom (ed.), *Gothic Horror: A Guide for Students and Readers*, 2nd edn (London: Palgrave, Macmillan, 2007), pp. 226–47.

Arata, Stephen, 'The Occidental tourist: *Dracula* and the anxiety of reverse colonization', *Victorian Studies*, 33 (1990), 621–45.

Auerbach, Nina, *Our Vampires, Ourselves* (Chicago: University of Chicago Press, 1995).

Backus, Margot Gayle, *The Gothic Family Romance: Heterosexuality, Child Sacrifice, and the Anglo-Irish Colonial Order* (Durham, NC: Duke University Press, 1999).

Baldick, Chris and Robert Mighall, 'Gothic criticism', in David Punter (ed.), *A Companion to the Gothic* (Malden, MA: Blackwell Publishers, 2000), pp. 209–28.

Belford, Barbara, *Bram Stoker: A Biography of the Author of Dracula* (New York: Alfred A. Knopf, 1996).

Bloom, Clive, 'Introduction: death's own backyard', in *idem* (ed.), *Gothic Horror: A Guide for Students and Readers*, 2nd edn (New York: Palgrave Macmillan, 2007), pp. 1–24, p. 1.

—— (ed.), *Gothic Horror: A Guide for Students and Readers*, 2nd edn (New York: Palgrave Macmillan, 2007).

Botting, Fred, *Gothic* (London: Routledge, 1995).

Brantlinger, Patrick, *Rule of Darkness: British Literature and Imperialism, 1830–1914* (Ithaca, NY: Cornell University Press, 1988).

——, 'Imperial Gothic', in Anna Powell and Andrew Smith (eds), *Teaching the Gothic* (New York: Palgrave Macmillan, 2006), pp. 153–67.

Brennan, Matthew C., 'Knowledge and saving souls: the role of the "New Woman" in Stoker's *Dracula* and Murnau's *Nosferatu*', *Studies in the Humanities*, 19 (1992), 1–10.

Brewster, Scott, 'Seeing things: Gothic and the madness of interpretation', in David Punter (ed.), *A Companion to the Gothic* (Malden, MA: Blackwell Publishers, 2000), pp. 281–92 .

Burke, Edmund, *A Philosophical Enquiry into the Origin of our Ideas of the Sublime and Beautiful*, ed. Adam Phillips (Oxford: Oxford University Press, 1998).

Byron, Glennis, 'Gothic in the 1890s', in David Punter (ed.), *A Companion to the Gothic* (Malden, MA: Blackwell Publishers, 2000), pp. 132–42.

Cain, Jimmie E., Jr, *Bram Stoker and Russophobia: Evidence of the British Fear of Russia in Dracula and The Lady of the Shroud* (Jefferson, NC: McFarland, 2006).

Case, Alison, 'Tasting the original apple: gender and the struggle for narrative authority in *Dracula*', *Narrative*, 1 (October 1993), 223–43.

Cosgrove, Brian (ed.), *Literature and the Supernatural* (Dublin: Columba Press, 1995).

Cribb, Susan M., '"If I had to write with a pen": readership and Bram Stoker's diary narrative', *Journal of the Fantastic in the Arts*, 10 (1997), 133–41.

Cunningham, Gail, *The New Woman and the Victorian Novel* (New York: Barnes and Noble, 1978).

Dalby, Richard and William Hughes (eds), *Bram Stoker: A Bibliography* (Southend-on-Sea, Essex: Desert Island Books, 2004).

Daly, Nicholas, 'Incorporated bodies: *Dracula* and the rise of professionalism', *Texas Studies in Literature and Language*, 39 (summer 1997), 181–203.

Davison, Carol Margaret, 'The ghost of genres past: theorizing the Gothic in the Victorian novel', in Karen Sayer and Rosemary Mitchell (eds), *Victorian Gothic* (Leeds: Leeds Centre for Victorian Studies, 2003).

——, *Anti-Semitism and British Gothic Literature* (New York: Palgrave Macmillan, 2004).

Day, William Patrick, *In the Circles of Fear and Desire: A Study of Gothic Fantasy* (Chicago: University of Chicago Press, 1985).

Deane, Seamus, *Strange Country: Modernity and Nationhood in Irish Writing since 1790* (Oxford: Clarendon Press, 1997).

Demata, Massimiliano, 'Discovering Eastern horrors: Beckford, Maturin and the discourse of travel literature', in Andrew Smith and William Hughes (eds), *Empire and the Gothic: The Politics of Genre* (New York: Palgrave Macmillan, 2003), pp. 13–34.

Demetrakopoulos, Stephanie, 'Feminism, sex role exchanges, and other subliminal fantasies in Bram Stoker's *Dracula*', *Frontiers* (1977), 104–13.

Dryden, Lynda, '"The coming terror": Wells's outcast London and the modern Gothic', in Karen Sayer and Rosemary Mitchell (eds), *Victorian Gothic* (Leeds: Leeds Centre for Victorian Studies, 2003), pp. 41–55.

Duncan, Ian, *Modern Romance and the Transformations of the Novel: The Gothic, Scott, Dickens* (Cambridge: Cambridge University Press, 1992).

Eighteen-Bisang, Robert and Elizabeth Miller (eds), *Bram Stoker's Notes for Dracula: A Facsimile Edition* (Jefferson, NC: McFarland & Co., 2008).

Ellis, Kate Ferguson, 'Can you forgive her? The Gothic heroine and her critics', in David Punter (ed.), *A Companion to the Gothic* (Malden, MA: Blackwell Publishers, 2000), pp. 257–68.

Farson, Daniel, *The Man Who Wrote Dracula: A Biography of Bram Stoker* (London: Michael Joseph, 1975).

Feimer, Joel, 'Bram Stoker's *Dracula*: the challenge of the occult to science, reason and psychiatry', in Michele K. Langford (ed.), *Contours of the Fantastic* (New York: Greenwood, 1994), pp. 165–71.

Fernando, Lloyd, *'New Women' in the Late Victorian Novel* (University Park: Pennsylvania State University Press, 1977).

Frye, Northrop, Sheridan Baker, George Perkins and Barbara M. Perkins (eds), *The Harper Handbook to Literature*, 2nd edn (New York: Longman, 1997).

Glover, David, *Vampires, Mummies, and Liberals: Bram Stoker and the Politics of Popular Fiction* (Durham, NC: Duke University Press, 1996).

Greenway, John L., 'Seward's folly: *Dracula* as a critique of "normal science"', *Stanford Literature Review*, 3 (1986), 213–30.

Griffin, Gail B., '"Your girls that you all love are mine": *Dracula* and the Victorian male sexual imagination', *International Journal of Women's Studies*, 3 (1980), 454–65.

Grixti, Joseph, *Terrors of Uncertainty: The Cultural Contexts of Horror Fiction* (New York: Routledge, 1989).

Haining, Peter and Peter Tremayne, *The Un-Dead: The Legend of Bram Stoker and Dracula* (London: Constable, 1997).

Halberstam, Judith, 'Technologies of monstrosity: Bram Stoker's *Dracula*', *Victorian Studies*, 36 (1993), 333–52.

——— *Skin Shows: Gothic Horror and the Technology of Monsters* (Durham, NC: Duke University Press, 1995).

Bibliography

Harris, Jenna, 'Why Dracula no longer frightens us', *Journal of Dracula Studies*, 3 (2001), 50–2.

Hendershot, Cyndy, 'Vampire and replicant: the one-sex body in a two-sex world', *Science-Fiction Studies*, 22 (1995), 373–98.

Hogle, Jerrold E., 'Theorizing the Gothic', in Anna Powell and Andrew Smith (eds), *Teaching the Gothic* (New York: Palgrave Macmillan, 2006), pp. 29–47.

Hopkins, Lisa, *Bram Stoker: A Literary Life* (New York: Palgrave Macmillan, 2007).

Horner, Avril and Sue Zlosnik, 'Comic Gothic', in David Punter (ed.), *A Companion to the Gothic* (Malden, MA: Blackwell Publishers, 2000), pp. 242–54.

Hughes, William, *Beyond Dracula: Bram Stoker's Fiction and its Cultural Context* (New York: St Martin's Press, 2000).

——, 'A singular invasion: revisiting the postcoloniality of Bram Stoker's *Dracula*', in Andrew Smith and William Hughes (eds), *Empire and the Gothic: The Politics of Genre* (New York: Palgrave Macmillan, 2003), pp. 88–102.

Hughes, William and Andrew Smith (eds), *Bram Stoker: History, Psychoanalysis and the Gothic* (New York: St Martin's Press, 1998).

Jann, Rosemary, 'Saved by science? The mixed messages of Stoker's *Dracula*', *Victorian Newsletter*, 72 (1987).

Kilgour, Maggie, 'The curious case of the Miltonic vampire', in Andrew Smith, Diane Mason and William Hughes (eds), *Fictions of Unease: The Gothic from Otranto to The X-Files* (Bath: Sulis Press, 2002), pp. 58–73.

Kline, Salli J., *The Degeneration of Women: Bram Stoker's Dracula as Allegorical Criticism of the Fin de Siècle* (Rheinbach-Merzbach: CMZ-Verlag, 1992).

Klinger, Leslie S. (ed.), *The New Annotated Dracula* (New York: W.W. Norton, 2008).

Kumar, Krishan, *Utopia and Anti-Utopia in Modern Times* (Oxford: Basil Blackwell, 1987).

Leatherdale, Clive, *Dracula: The Novel and the Legend* (Wellinborough: Aquarian, 1985).

Ledger, Sally, *The New Woman: Fiction and Feminism at the Fin de Siècle* (Manchester: Manchester University Press, 1997).

Ludlam, Harry, *A Biography of Dracula: The Life Story of Bram Stoker* (London: Foulsham, 1962).

Lynch, Patricia A., Joachim Fisher and Brian Coates (eds), *Back to the*

Present, Forward to the Past: Irish Writing and History since 1798 (New York: Rodopi, 2006).

Malchow, H. L., *Gothic Images of Race in Nineteenth-century Britain* (Stanford: Stanford University Press, 1996).

Marigny, Jean, 'Secrecy as strategy in *Dracula*', *Journal of Dracula Studies*, 2 (2000), 3–7.

Maunder, Andrew, *Bram Stoker* (Tavistock: Northcote House Publishers Ltd, 2006).

McNally, Raymond T., *Dracula Was a Woman* (London: Hale, 1984).

——, 'Bram Stoker and Irish Gothic', in James Craig Holte (ed.), *The Fantastic Vampire: Studies in the Children of the Night. Selected Essays from the Eighteenth International Conference on the Fantastic in the Arts* (Westport, CT: Greenwood Press, 1997), pp. 11–22.

——, and Radu Florescu, *In Search of Dracula* (New York: Graphic Society, 1972).

——, *In Search of Dracula: History of Dracula and Vampires* (Boston: Houghton Mifflin, 1994).

Mighall, Robert, *A Geography of Victorian Gothic Fiction: Mapping History's Nightmares* (New York: Oxford University Press, 1999).

Milbank, Alison, '"Powers old and new": Stoker's alliances with Anglo-Irish Gothic', in William Hughes and Andrew Smith (eds), *Bram Stoker: History, Psychoanalysis and the Gothic* (New York: St Martin's Press, 1998), pp. 12–28.

Miller, Elizabeth, 'Shapeshifting Dracula: the Abridged Edition of 1901', in James Craig Holte (ed.), *The Fantastic Vampire: Studies in the Children of the Night* (Westport, CT: Greenwood Press, 1997), pp. 3–10.

—— (ed.), *Bram Stoker's Dracula: A Documentary Volume* (Detroit: Thomson Gale, 2005).

Morash, Chris, 'The time is out of joint (O cursèd spite!): towards a definition of a supernatural narrative', in Bruce Steward (ed.), *That Other World: The Supernatural and the Fantastic in Irish Literature and its Contexts* (Gerrards Cross: Colin Smythe Ltd, 1998).

Mulvey-Roberts, Marie, '*Dracula* and the doctors: bad blood, menstrual taboo and the New Woman', in William Hughes and Andrew Smith (eds), *Bram Stoker: History, Psychoanalysis and the Gothic* (New York: St Martin's Press, 1998).

Murray, Paul, *From the Shadow of Dracula* (London: Jonathan Cape, 2004), pp. 78–95.

Nayden, Lillian, 'Virgin territory and the Iron Virgin: engendering the Empire in Bram Stoker's "The Squaw"', in Claudia Nelson and Ann Sumner Holmes (eds), *Maternal Instincts: Visions of Motherhood and Sexuality in Britain 1875–1925* (London: Macmillan, 1997), pp. 75–98.

Osborne, Charles (ed.), *The Bram Stoker Bedside Companion: 10 Stories by the Author of Dracula* (New York: Taplinger, 1973).

O'Malley, Patrick R., *Catholicism, Sexual Deviance, and Victorian Gothic Culture* (New York: Cambridge University Press, 2006).

Punter, David, *The Literature of Terror: A History of Gothic Fictions from 1765 to the Present Day* (London: Longman, 1980).

——, 'Echoes in the animal house: *The Lair of the White Worm*', in William Hughes and Andrew Smith (eds), *Bram Stoker: History, Psychoanalysis and the Gothic* (New York: St Martin's Press, 1998), pp. 173–87.

—— (ed.), *A Companion to the Gothic* (Malden, MA: Blackwell Publishers, 2000).

Pykett, Lyn, *The 'Improper Feminine': The Women's Sensation Novel and the New Woman Writing* (New York: Routledge, 1992).

Richardson, Maurice, 'The psychoanalysis of ghost stories', *Twentieth Century*, 166 (1959), 419–31.

Riquelme, J. P., 'Toward a history of Gothic and Modernism: dark modernity from Bram Stoker to Samuel Beckett', *Modern Fiction Studies*, 46, 3 (2000), 585–605.

—— (ed.), *Dracula: Complete, Authoritative Text with Biographical, Historical, and Cultural Contexts, Critical History and Essays from Contemporary Critical Perspectives* (Boston: Bedford/St Martin's Press, 2002).

Roberts, Bette B., 'Gothic fiction', in Sally Mitchell (ed.), *Victorian Britain: An Encyclopedia* (New York: Garland, 1988), p. 334.

Roth, Phyllis A., 'Suddenly sexual women in Bram Stoker's *Dracula*', *Literature and Psychology*, 27 (1977), 113–21.

——, *Bram Stoker* (Boston: Twayne, 1982).

Sage, Victor, 'Exchanging fantasies: sex and the Serbian crisis in *The Lady of the Shroud*', in William Hughes and Andrew Smith (eds), *Bram Stoker: History, Psychoanalysis and the Gothic* (New York: St Martin's Press, 1998), pp. 116–33.

Schaffer, Talia, '"A Wilde desire took me": the homoerotic history of *Dracula*', *ELH*, 61 (1994), 381–425.

Seed, David, 'The narrative method of *Dracula*', *Nineteenth Century Fiction*, 40, 1 (1985), 61–5; reprinted in Margaret L. Carter (ed.), *Dracula: The Vampire and the Critics* (Ann Arbor, MI: UMI Research Press, 1988), pp. 195–206.

——, 'Eruptions of the primitive into the present: *The Jewel of Seven Stars* and

The Lair of the White Worm', in William Hughes and Andrew Smith (eds), *Bram Stoker: History, Psychoanalysis and the Gothic* (New York: St Martin's Press, 1998), pp. 188–204.

Senf, Carol A., '*Dracula*: the unseen face in the mirror', *Journal of Narrative Technique*, 9 (1979), 160–70.

——, '*Dracula*: Stoker's response to the New Woman', *Victorian Studies*, 26 (1982), 33–49.

——, *The Critical Response to Bram Stoker* (Westport, CT: Greenwood, 1993), p. 70.

——, *Dracula: Between Tradition and Modernism* (New York: Twayne (1998).

——, *Science and Social Science in Bram Stoker's Fiction* (Westport, CT: Greenwood, 2002).

Simmons, Clare, *Reversing the Conquest: History and Myth in Nineteenth Century British Literature* (Piscataway, NJ: Rutgers University Press, 1990).

——, 'Fables of continuity: Bram Stoker and medievalism', in William Hughes and Andrew Smith (eds), *Bram Stoker: History, Psychoanalysis and the Gothic* (New York: St Martin's Press, 1998), pp. 29–46.

Spencer, Kathleen, 'Purity and danger: Dracula, the urban Gothic, and the late Victorian degeneracy crisis', *ELH*, 59, 1 (1992), 197–225.

Stewart, Garrett, '"Count me in": *Dracula*, hypnotic participation, and the late Victorian Gothic of reading', *Literature Interpretation Theory*, 5 (1994), 1–18.

Stoker, Bram, *A Glimpse of America* (London: Sampson Low, Marston & Co., 1886).

——, *The Man* (London: Heinemann, 1905).

——, *Personal Reminiscences of Henry Irving* (New York: Macmillan, 1906).

——, 'The censorship of fiction', *Nineteenth Century & After*, September 1908, reprinted in Richard Dalby (ed.), *A Glimpse of America and Other Lectures, Interviews and Essays* (Westcliff-on-Sea, Essex: Desert Island Books, 2002), pp. 154–61.

—— *Famous Imposters* (United States: n.p., 1910).

——, *The Watter's Mou'*, in C. Osborne (ed.), *The Bram Stoker Bedside Companion: 10 Stories by the Author of Dracula* (New York: Taplinger, 1973).

——, *Miss Betty* (London: New English Library, 1974).

——, *Under the Sunset* (North Hollywood, CA: Newcastle Company, 1978).

——, 'The Way of Peace', *The Bram Stoker Society Journal*, 1 (1989), 34–41.

——, *The Snake's Pass* (Dingle, Co. Kerry, Ireland: Brandon, 1990).

——, 'The Eros of the Thames: the story of a frustrated advertisement', *The Bram Stoker Society Journal*, 2 (1990), 24–33.

——, *The Jewel of Seven Stars* (Westcliff-on-Sea, Essex: Desert Island Books, 1996).

——, *Best Ghost and Horror Stories*, ed. R. Dalby, S. Dziemianowicz and S.T. Joshi (Mineola, NY: Dover, 1997).

——, *Dracula Unearthed*, ed. Clive Leatherdale (Westcliff-on-Sea, Essex: Desert Island Books. 1998).

——, *The Primrose Path* (Westcliff-on-Sea, Essex: Desert Island Books, 1999).

——, *The Shoulder of Shasta* (Westcliff-on-Sea, Essex: Desert Island Books, 2000).

——, *Snowbound: The Record of a Theatrical Touring Party* [1908] (Westcliff-on-Sea, Essex: Desert Island Books, 2000).

——, *The Lady of the Shroud* (Westcliff-on-Sea, Essex: Desert Islands Books, 2001).

——, *Dracula*, ed. John Paul Riquelme (Boston: Bedford/St Martin's, 2002).

——, *Dracula's Guest and Other Stories* (London: Wordsworth, 2006).

——, *Dracula's Guest and Other Weird Stories with The Lair of the White Worm*, ed. Kate Hebblethwaite (London: Penguin, 2006).

——, *Lady Athlyne* (Southend-on-Sea, Essex: Desert Island Books, 2007).

——, *The Mystery of the Sea* (Kansas City: Valancourt, 2007).

——, *The Fate of Fenella* (Kansas City, MO: Valancourt Books, 2008).

——, *The Judge's House and Other Weird Tales* (Doylestown, PA: Wildside Press, undated).

Underwood, Tim and Chuck Miller (eds), *Kingdom of Fear: The World of Stephen King* (New York: NAL/Plume Trade Paperback, 1986).

——, *Bare Bones: Conversations on Terror with Stephen King* (New York: McGraw-Hill, 1988).

Valente, Joseph, *Dracula's Crypt: Bram Stoker, Irishness, and the Question of Blood* (Chicago: University of Illinois Press, 2002).

Vander Ploeg, Scott, 'Stoker's Dracula: a neo-Gothic experiment', in James Craig Holte (ed.), *The Fantastic Vampire: Studies in the Children of the Night. Selected Essays from the Eighteenth International Conference on the Fantastic in the Arts* (Westport, CT: Greenwood Press, 1997).

Vrettos, Athena, *Somatic Fictions: Imagining Illness in Victorian Culture* (Stanford: Stanford University Press, 1995).

Wall, Geoffrey, '"Different from writing": *Dracula* in 1897', *Literature and History*, 10 (1984), 15–23.

Warren, Louis S., 'Buffalo Bill meets Dracula: William F. Cody, Bram Stoker, and the frontiers of racial decay', *American Historical Review*, 107 (2002), 1124–57.

Weissman, Judith, 'Women and vampires: *Dracula* as a Victorian novel', *Midwest Quarterly*, 18 (1977), 392–405.

Wicke, Jennifer, 'Vampiric typewriting: *Dracula* and its media', *ELH*, 59 (1992).

Wolfreys, Julian, 'Victorian Gothic', in Anna Powell and Andrew Smith (eds), *Teaching the Gothic* (New York: Palgrave Macmillan, 2006), pp. 62–77.

Wright, Angela, *Gothic Fiction: A Reader's Guide to Essential Criticism* (New York: Palgrave Macmillan, 2007).

Index

⚘